Sounds of the South

A Report and Selected Papers from A Conference on the Collecting and Collections of Southern Traditional Music

Held in Chapel Hill, April 6–8, 1989, to celebrate the opening of the Southern Folklife Collection with the John Edwards Memorial Collection in the Manuscripts department of the Academic Affairs Library, University of North Carolina

Sounds of
the South

Duke University Press   Durham and London

*Published by Duke University Press for the Southern Folklife
Collection, the Curriculum in Folklore of the University of North
Carolina at Chapel Hill and the John Edwards Memorial Forum with
funding support from the North Carolina Arts Council and the Kenan
Research Fund*

Copyright © 1991 by the Southern Folklife Collection
*All rights reserved   Printed in the United States of America on
acid-free paper ∞*
*Library of Congress Cataloging-in-Publication Data appears on the
last printed page of this book*

Dedicated to

the memory of

John Edwards

of Australia

Contents

List of Illustrations

Preface

"*Sounds of the South:* A Conference on the Collecting and Collections of Southern Traditional Music" convened on the campus of the University of North Carolina at Chapel Hill from April 6 to April 8, 1989. It brought together more than 300 participants and speakers: notable field collectors and record collectors, academic and public folklorists, performing musicians and record producers, librarians and organizers of folk festivals and tours, and other lovers of traditional music. The sponsorship of the conference was equally ecumenical: a joint venture of the Folklife Section of the North Carolina Arts Council and the UNC Academic Affairs Library and Curriculum in Folklore. Its broad funding support came from both state and federal sources (the Folklife Section of the North Carolina Arts Council and the Folk Arts Program of the National Endowment for the Arts), from a private source (the L. J. Skaggs and Mary C. Skaggs Foundation), and from many University sources (The College of Arts and Sciences, the Office of the Provost, the Grumman Fund of the UNC Division of Extension and Continuing Education, and the Manuscripts Department of the Academic Affairs Library).

The immediate occasion for the gathering was the formal opening of the Southern Folklife Collection in the University Library's Manuscripts Department—a major new repository of Southern vernacular music that has as its crown jewel the internationally known John Edwards Memorial Collection. In a larger sense, the Conference was a salute from the academy to all those who have documented, preserved, fostered, and increased the understanding and appreciation of traditional music in the South. The shared conviction that all of us committed to this music would benefit from an assessment of past achievements, of the present situation, and of future needs gave the intellectual justification for the Conference.

The conference program addressed all three of these areas in the following sessions:

Thursday, April 6

"The John Edwards Memorial Foundation: Its History and Significance"—*Norm Cohen*

"The John Edwards Memorial Collection at the University of North Carolina"—*Daniel W. Patterson* and *Michael T. Casey*

Keynote Address, "Evaluating Our Work and Ourselves"—*Bess Lomax Hawes*

"Turning Inward and Outward: Retrospective and Prospective Considerations in the Recording of Vernacular Music"—*David E. Whisnant*

"Collecting and Recording Traditional Music in the South—A Retrospective Assessment"—Panel Discussion, with *Bess Lomax Hawes, Bill C. Malone, Paul Oliver, Ralph Rinzler,* and *Mike Seeger*

Friday, April 7

"Current Goals and Concerns of Collectors and Archivists"—Panel Discussion, with *Billy Altman, Dave Freeman, Ray Funk, Alice Gerrard, George Holt, Guy Logsdon,* and *Dorothy Sara Lee*

"Reports from Major Repositories"

"The Archive of American Folk Culture in the Library of Congress"—*Alan Jabbour*

"The Country Music Foundation"—*William Ivey*

"The Smithsonian Institution"—*Anthony Seeger*

"Southern Folk Culture in Transition"—*Allen Tullos,* with *Charles Reagan Wilson,* Respondent

"Reports from the Field"

"Cajun Music"—*Barry Ancelet*

"Native American Music"—*Charlotte Heth*

"Appalachian Music"—*Helen Lewis*

"African-American Music"—*Worth Long*

"Hispanic Music"—*Dale Olsen*

"Emerging Genres"—*Jay Orr*

"Summary Remarks"—by *Archie Green*

Saturday, April 8

"Working Session for Archivists"

"Special Presentations"

"Early Disk Recordings from Washington County, Tennessee"—*Tim Stafford*

"Early Films Documenting African-American Gospel Groups"—
Fay Funk
"Singing and Shouting at Moving Star Hall: Christmas Watch-Night,
1967"—*Guy* and *Candie Carawan*
"The Influence of African Traditions upon American Folk Mu-
sic"—*Alan Lomax*
"Outlook for New Releases of Documentary Recordings of Southern
Folk Music and Verbal Lore"—Open Forum, with *Billy Altman,
Dave Freeman, Ken Irwin, William Ivey, Barry Poss,* and *Anthony
Seeger*
"The Chapel Hill/Durham Stringband Revival, a Retrospective"—
with *Tom Carter, Cece Conway, Alan Jabbour, Bertram Levy,
Blanton Owen,* and open discussion

Special features of the conference included tours of the Southern
Folklife Collection; a Concert featuring Appalachian music from
Doug Wallin and Wade and Julia Mainer with Mary Mainer Hatley;
African-American music from Etta Baker, James "Junior" Thomas, Anthony "Spoons" Pough, and Willette Hinton; recently arrived traditions with Montagnard singer Y Ngong Knul and Mexican-American
conjunto music with Esteban Jordan y El Rio Jordan; and performances from the stringband revival, with Alan Jabbour, Tommy
Thompson, and Bertram Levy. "The Chapel Hill Serenade," a combined picnic and picking party and dance closed our events.

Much of the work of such a conference takes place in informal,
private conversational exchange of information and ideas. We have
no record of these exchanges, although they doubtless have their
powerful, continuing legacies. Tape recordings of the public exchanges, however, are preserved in the Southern Folklife Collection
in Chapel Hill. In the hope of sharing the work of the Conference
widely, we offer this publication based upon them. Space permits
the inclusion of only a small number of the Conference papers (in
revised form). But we attempt to share the key issues and insightful
comments from other papers and the panel discussions in an introductory essay.

This publication has received support from a grant from the North
Carolina Arts Council and from the Kenan Research Fund of the University of North Carolina at Chapel Hill. The Conference organizers
are grateful to these agencies. We also once again thank all who made

the Conference itself possible: James F. Govan, University Librarian, and all his dedicated and capable staff (and especially Marcella Grendler, David Moltke-Hansen, Richard Shrader, Walter C. West, and Larry Alford); the North Carolina Arts Council (and in particular the able staff of the Folklife Section: Mary Anne McDonald, Wayne Martin, Sylvia Saavedra, and intern Lesley Williams, and their special consultant Jack Bernhardt); the faculty members of the Curriculum in Folklore (in particular, Trudier Harris, Glenn Hinson, David Whisnant, and Charles G. Zug, III); special graduate-student assistants Sally Council, Will Nash, Jenny Innes, and Laura Middlebrooks, and all other graduate students in the Curriculum in Folklore, who helped in every capacity from program planning to chauffeuring and fund raising. The students are too numerous to list by name, but their individual services are gratefully remembered. We thank also other members of the University community for their support: Provost J. Dennis O'Connor, Dean Gillian T. Cell, Edgar B. Marston of the Extension Division, Beverly B. Patterson, and Debbie Simmons-Cahan. Above all we are grateful to Jillian Steiner Sandrock of the Skaggs Foundation, who helped inspire this conference, to the many speakers and participants who traveled far to join us, and to Archie Green, the guiding spirit of this event.

Michael T. Casey
Sound and Image Librarian
Manuscripts Department
Academic Affairs Library
University of North Carolina at Chapel Hill

George M. Holt
Director, Folklife Section
North Carolina Arts Council

Daniel W. Patterson
Curriculum in Folklore
University of North Carolina at Chapel Hill

Sounds of the South

Introduction

"*Here we are,*" declared Bess Lomax Hawes in her keynote
address, "in a pitifully underpopulated field, little-known,
underfunded, with one of the major human tasks—the support and appreciation of the multiplex cultures that have made our
planet habitable—as our primary focus." She declared her admiration of "the elegance of the work done" on behalf of traditional music
by "folklorists, recordists, entrepreneurs, librarians, concert presenters, archivists, small record company producers, broadcasters, discographers, historians, musicians, filmmakers, anthropologists, bureaucrats." With these remarks the Director of the Folk Arts Program
at the National Endowment for the Arts joined the sponsors of the
Sounds of the South Conference in a salute to the enormous diversity
of those present at the meeting and of all those who have labored to
foster the preservation, understanding, and appreciation of the rich
and influential musical expressions of the American South.

The Conference was considered issues arising from the work already done and to suggest directions for future work. It could not of
course present a definitive history or assessment of the study of this
music, for many women and men who have played key roles have
long since exited the scene, taking their scripts with them. Serious
study of how they performed their work has only recently begun.
Some of those currently most active were engaged in other theaters
at the time of the Conference. And furthermore, panel discussions
and talks from a podium are constrained by the oral format. Their
strength lies not in documented exposition but in the spontaneous
exchange of insights, the telling anecdote, the incisive personal tes-
timony.

For this written report from the Sounds of the South Conference,
the altered format has accordingly required the editor to take a three-
fold strategy of presentation: (1) to ask speakers like Bess Hawes,

Barry Ancelet, Thomas Carter, Michael Casey, Norm Cohen, Allen Tullos, or David Whisnant—who came with more formally prepared talks—to revise, extend, and footnote them for publication, (2) to invite others like Ray Funk, Archie Green, Bill Malone, or Paul Oliver to develop papers on points that emerged in their informal remarks, papers that would give better balance to this volume, and (3) to use this introduction (as far as the limited space allows) to preserve and share important points and eloquent lines from the comments of the other participants.

Reflections on Past Fieldwork and Public Presentation

The premise of the Conference was that, while academic folklorists have had a significant role in the study of Southern folk music (particularly Anglo-American balladry), greater contributions have come from persons outside the university setting, persons more open than academics were to the other ethnic traditions in the South, to other musical forms like the blues or religious song, and to popular music rooted in older folk traditions. These researchers have worked with the zeal of persons "called," and Conference presentations showed that most of them first heard the calling in an early encounter with the music itself.

Some of the participants responded to the call of music of their own native culture. In his essay, country-music historian Bill Malone says that his love of the music he has studied is rooted in his earliest childhood experiences. Barry Ancelet of the University of Southwestern Louisiana recounts his own belated rediscovery—in France, as a college student—of the music of the Cajun world in which he had grown up.

Other speakers from outside the South—and not always from a land an ocean away like blues scholar Paul Oliver—described the music as opening casements upon rich but previously unsuspected worlds. Ralph Rinzler of the Smithsonian Institution told of playing the first Library of Congress "Friends of Music" recordings at the age of seven. "I listened to them as if they had come from the moon," he said; "I had no sense I'd ever see those people, or know them, or hear them live"—nevertheless, he described that music as becoming "the strongest motivating force in my life." A similar turning point came for Dave Freeman, producer of County and Rebel Records, when his family took him on a trip from New York to New Orleans in 1954:

> We drove down the old Route 11 through East Tennessee, Alabama, and Mississippi, and at that time on the radio you could hear all sorts of things. . . . Some of it was live music being played in little stations in Mississippi. Others were bluegrass recordings from East Tennessee—probably old Rich-R-Tone records I've never found yet. . . . I remember a little restaurant in Kingsport, Tennessee, where there were two juke boxes, a red one and a blue one—that's how I remember them. One was strictly popular music, the kind of things I was familiar with from New York. The other was all country— a lot of it was obscure bluegrass recordings, now that I think back on it, on little labels probably from that region.

This was a body of music he had never "had the first exposure to" as a kid in New York City; "it really hit me hard, and struck me right there." Back home, Freeman said, "I started to try to find something out about what I'd heard and where I could get the records." Even Alan Lomax—raised in the region, and in a family already dedicated to the exploration of traditional music—described himself as "converted" by a particular musical experience: listening to black convicts in Texas sing "Go Down, Old Hannah" in 1933 "under shotguns, with the spiritual ease of the greatest artists." For him, "how they joined their voices," how they trailed "in and out of the melody, along with the melody" was "pure, pure black magic" that "blanked out Beethoven and Brahms, and Shakespeare." It made him, he said, "into the person that's pursued folk music since then."

Bill Malone, as session moderator, suggested that a powerful emotional commitment to the music may also pose problems for those who undertake to work with it and with traditional musicians. Paul Oliver freely conceded that European blues enthusiasts like himself first heard the music as exotic, and, being already dissatisfied with their own "homegrown music," took a romantic interest in the alien art. But that "deep subjective involvement" was, he felt, absolutely essential to doing the reseach—for virtually none of the European students of the blues have had grant support: "Something has to drive them. Something has to be the commitment that underlies the work that they have done." And he pointed out that consuming intellectual questions also motivated them. They wanted to understand the texts of the blues they heard, and the culture behind the texts. One challenging puzzle they wanted to solve was the discrepancy between the blues on commercial releases and the blues performances in albums issued by Alan Lomax, Harold Courlander, and Frederic Ramsey from their field recordings. This motivated the American field trips of Oliver and other European students of the blues.

Mike Seeger, talented performing musician from a family with unusual musical gifts and training, maintained that his own attraction to the music was grounded not in romanticism but in responsiveness to music. "I was somehow raised," he said,

with at least one confidence in the world, and that was in my musical perception. . . . And I've never felt for a minute any doubt in that. . . . I have a love for this kind of music, and I just want to have other people interested in it. And so I've made these records of other people whose music I really admire.

Panelists also felt that the charge of romantic bias was too simple an explanation of the decisions often made in work with traditional musicians. Bess Lomax Hawes pointed out that the conditions of field work in the early days placed formidable constraints on the fieldworker's choices:

I recall very vividly the day my father came home with the car—the back end of it—torn out because we had just gotten our first recording machine, and literally it broke the springs out of the Ford. . . . I don't know how much it weighed, but the whole back end had to be rebuilt with two-by-fours to carry the equipment. The records were aluminum, but they were heavy. You couldn't go to the store and buy them, either. They had to be shipped in. So on a recording trip you were terribly careful of what you recorded, and how much of it, and if people started to blather, you just stopped, or—and I'm sorry, there had to be a judgment as to whether that was blather . . . and it had to be made right then—because if you ran out of records, you had to wait maybe two weeks on the road with no money, while you got some more from the factory shipped in. . . . they were recorded under conditions of remarkable scarcity of resources, and every one of them had to be . . . a deliberate decision . . .—because if you recorded that, you couldn't record that other thing. And those judgments were going on all the time, and so the repertoire and the performances, I think, have to be looked at with that perspective. It wasn't complete—there was no hope of it.

Bess Hawes also saw one unintended benefit from these limiting conditions of the early recordings:

I sometimes listen to those old Library of Congress records and think to myself, "My God, those performances there are so *on*, they are so excited, they are so terrific." And I realize that the reason was that the recordists were so tense, and they were saying, "*Do* it! Do it *now*! This has got to be *it*! *One* take!" You know, *one take*. And that's very stimulating to musicians.

In more recent times, the field collector or record producer has had wider choices. Tom Carter raised a question whether in documentation and record releases the focus should be on the star performer or be more broadly representative. Panelists' responses varied. Mike Seeger regarded all the music of a community as important but felt "you only put the special stuff on the records." Paul Oliver disagreed, arguing that outsiders should "look for those that the community respects rather than those that we choose to respect"; this course helps the collector to gain new perspectives. Ralph Rinzler offered a middle course:

I used to try, when I'd do recordings in the field, to come out with survey records that would give that range. So "The Watson Family" albums on Topic and Folkways take people who are very fragile sometimes, who sing fragments—you only have a verse or two sometimes, or a little scrape on the fiddle, or Doc Watson's mother, who was a strident but very elegant singer. And the same with the Cajun stuff that I put together on Rounder—that has a lot of marginal stuff. . . . If you record a range, then you include as broad a range as you as an editor feel shows what the limits of the tradition are.

Malone also questioned the role of romantic bias in festival presentations of a musician like Doc Watson: "What happens to the folk process when the collector or promoter begins to assert his own ideas about what the music should be?" Ralph Rinzler said that in the era of Elvis Presley and Rock and Roll,

Doc never even got started, because what he was playing was an imitation of people who could perhaps play it as well or better. But what he *could* play hadn't been heard, because he wouldn't believe the music of his family would be successful.

Believing "that the industry may have produced good things, but it shouldn't be everything—it shouldn't wipe out everything that came before it—" Rinzler talked with Doc about "the kinds of concessions he might make on a temporary basis to find initial success" and possibly "pressed him in ways that seemed arrogant." But Rinzler said Doc

was very resistent—sharp, keen, and self-possessed, as he is. . . . Doc was never convinced that he had to abandon *any* element of his repertory in order to be a successful performer, and ultimately he was totally correct.

Rinzler insisted, however, that these musical decisions were actually reached through negotiation, and Bess Hawes argued the right of the promoter to negotiate:

I think the assumption is that the only two people in the whole negotiation are the artist and the folklorist. Well, that's not what happens in the real world. You know perfectly well there's millions of people coming . . . into that negotiation. Maybe at the moment we have a job to offer or maybe we have a record to offer, but we have no magical power. I think it's perfectly legitimate for us to argue like equals, back and forth. People argue on any artistic form. . . . I think we have just as much right, as lovers and aficionados, as the record companies do, which tell them all the time, as the TV people do, which show them by example, "You're nowhere, you're not on the tube. . . ." Most of the people I talk to, frankly, are just waiting for people to say to them, as most folklorists do, "The thing that you grew up with is really wonderful!"

Paul Oliver partly discounted the influence of the folklorist. His experience was that the singers themselves have "a dialogue, which is with other musicians," and often have "aspirations which folklorists don't want to see met—that applies particularly in blues, where many blues singers really wish to be big names selling large numbers of records, and out in front, and leaving folk origins far behind them." In another session Alan Lomax paid tribute to "heroes" whose interventions, by contrast, went beyond benefiting a gifted musician to the empowerment of traditional communities: Ralph Rinzler, Guy Carawan and his wife Candie, and Allen Jaffe. Rinzler did fieldwork with Cajun music in Louisiana, brought the musicians to the Newport Folk Festival, presented them properly, and in Lomax's view, "the echoes just simply changed everything in Louisiana. Three years later the legislature brought in French in all the schools in Louisiana where there was a French population in the parish." The music "revived the language, and then the culture and the cooking, and then the morale of the culture revived and lives again today." Carawan— "always, thank God, . . . a politicized folklore-activist"—he credited with being "the person who invented and developed the musical movement of the Integration" by going into African American churches and getting them "to change from singing 'Onward Christian Soldiers' to singing their own stuff, . . . and they won." The third figure, Jaffe, went to New Orleans because he liked jazz, got a job in a clothing store, and met an artist there who said he wanted to keep jazz alive. So Jaffe and his wife rented an old empty hall:

There was no action on Bourbon Street then. It had all died away. There were hardly any parades. And they charged a quarter to come in, and their idea was just to give old musicians a chance to play. That's all. The same musicians could perform every night. They became classical artists. So there was a jazz classical artists' group in the middle of the city. And that example was very much noted on Bourbon Street, so that you can't get in it any more—filled with jazz good, bad, and indifferent, but still booming again, and in every neighborhood of the city, every black neighborhood, there's a young people's band that plays for marches on the weekend. The jazz funeral is just as alive as it ever was.

Assessments of Current Needs in Documentation

For fostering and documenting traditional music current resources are slim. Bill Ivey of the Country Music Foundation could see few institutions offering substantial support for this work: mainly the Library of Congress and the Smithsonian Institution, which "from time to time have efforts of their own that can fund some activity out in the field," the L. J. Skaggs and Mary C. Skaggs Foundation (which has closed down its funding program since the Conference[1]), and the Folk Arts Program of the National Endowment for the Arts, which also fosters state folklife programs that offer limited funding.

Mac Benford, a leading performer from the Highwoods String Band, voiced a complaint of folk-revival musicians, who feel they help keep traditional music alive but are generally denied grant support. Bess Hawes (who described herself as a revivalist "all my life . . . until I got this particular job") responded that a scarcity of resources compels granting agencies to set priorities. The total budget of the National Endowment for the Arts is, she pointed out, less than the amount budgeted for military bands by the United States Army, and the Folk Arts Program gets only two percent of the NEA budget. Given the limitations, Ralph Rinzler too favored giving first priority to the support of "vanishing or endangered cultural species" and cited the particular case of immigrants from Southeast Asia, among whom

you'll find . . . extraordinary musics that are very old . . . in the hands of people who are first-generation or second-generation Americans, presenting a long-term continuity, and those people would be the highest on my list of priorities for inclusion in any kind of program of research, documentation, and presentation.

In a subsequent session of "Reports from the Field" Charlotte Heth, speaking as both an ethnomusicologist and a Cherokee, underscored how essential funds are for work with the threatened musical traditions of Native American groups in the Southeastern states and elsewhere. She described a musical culture very different from that of the revivalist. The Indian musicians are not commercial, are not featured in tourist guides, almost never get television or newspaper coverage, do not read music or use fixed-pitch instruments, rarely complete formal courses of instruction or apprenticeships or buy instruments or costumes in stores, and make little if any money using their very considerable musical skills. Large sections of their repertories are not known to outsiders but are reserved for community events. "They organize and participate in Stomp Dances, Green Corn Ceremonies, special tribal religious and honoring ceremonies, family and clan events, hymn singings, powwows, and medicine rites." Many tribal bonding efforts, moreover, depend on this music and the native language. "In most cases, these important bonds of union in Indian life cannot be carried on if the music has been forgotten and ... if the langugage has been forgotten."

Heth fears that the most esoteric Indian music—such as curing songs, "that are somewhat secret and dependent upon specialists, that are bound to native languages—may not survive this century." Heth also raised a second issue, the need for special sensitivity in undertaking work with such music. Outsiders attempting to document and preserve the music must negotiate around fissures in the Native American communities caused by historical events such as the forced migrations that displaced and merged tribes, Christian proselytizing which split communities into adherents of either church or traditional religion, and interracial marriages that pitted social aims of mixed-bloods against those of full-blood tribal members.

Another panelist, Dale Olsen, described a similar complexity in the little documented musical cultures of recent Caribbean immigrants in Florida: groups that may conserve either African-French, African-Spanish, African-British, Native American-Spanish, or Spanish-derived musical traditions, each with its own spectrum of instrumentation, performance styles, genres, and uses, and all of them embodying distinct communal identities and agenda.

Speaking as an African American who has done both fieldwork and public programing with his own community, Worth Long called for the folklorist to make work in such communities "participatory"—to bring the local people in at the planning phase of projects undertaken in their home communities so that they can to a large extent decide for themselves "what is to be looked for, what is to be looked at, how it is to be handled, and how it is to be distributed, and if it is in fact to be placed under glass, where and when and how that is to take place."

Helen Lewis, Appalachian scholar and activist, described self-documentation as she had seen it develop in the Appalachian region over the past two decades. One form of self-documentation has been carried out by local institutions. At Appalshop, Inc., of Whitesburg, Kentucky, for example, young Appalachians have with increasing sophistication produced films, sound recordings, radio programs, and stage productions exploring the region's cultural identity and the political and social issues its people confront. Lewis also described a second, less formal kind of self-documentation that followed from the availability of light, inexpensive recording and videotape instruments. It used to be difficult, she said, to get permission to tape Old Regular or Primitive Baptists; now "the Elders have camcorders and are recording the whole service, and the baptism, and the footwashing." She told of recently taking some seminary students to a black Pentecostal church meeting in McRoberts, Kentucky:

I was going to ask politely if maybe we could record a little of the music, and the minister said, "Oh, don't worry. I've got a videotape set up over here. We're going to videotape the whole thing. We'll send you a copy." So I got this great copy in the mail, that the minister sent me.

A similar movement began to emerge among Native Americans in the 1970s, Heth reported, when some Indians "realized the possible loss of their cultural heritage" and "began systematically to record their tribal traditions." These were not, for the most part, organized tribal efforts, but "the fervent activities of younger musicians equipped only with audio- or videocassette recorders, a little spare time, and a great deal of patience." More recently tribes have also had help from governmental agencies. All these efforts show "a new trend by Indian people themselves to gather recordings from archives, make recordings of elders, and combine the two in order to piece together and revive or document some particular forgotten dance or ceremony."

These accounts by both Lewis and Heth also open a door upon other issues for those currently trying to work with minority traditions. They point out new ways in which persons from the outside can help. In a community project in Ivanhoe, Virginia, Lewis found people already, for example, using the video recorder, so she brought in a filmmaker to show them better ways of using it:

The first thing the filmmaker said was, "Get yourself a tripod, and hold steady on something for a longer period of time." It helped the community, so that we have more usable material from their own local collecting and recording.

She feels that archivists too should find ways to inform communities about how to save and protect the materials they generate. In a special presentation Tim Stafford, media specialist at East Tennessee State University, told of rescuing and publishing disks of local fiddling recorded privately between 1938 and 1951.[3] Both he and Helen Lewis urged efforts to preserve such self-documentation and to develop a network for local collections so others can know about the materials. On the other hand, an archivist working with materials generated within a community may also need to become aware of sensitivities they involve. Heth cautioned, for example, that Native Americans may be offended if church songs and Stomp Dances are stored together on the same library shelf and that delicate issues of access may arise with materials traditionally restricted to one clan or family.

Archival Issues

In several sessions of the Conference panelists and speakers addressed a broad range of other archival issues—ones raised for them by their experiences as collectors or fans of some branch of traditional music, as record producers or performing musicians looking for material, or as archivists responsible for managing collections. As one who has simultaneously filled several of these roles (he has been a professional librarian at the University of Tulsa, a private collector of cowboy lore, and an author of books about it), Guy Logsdon spoke authoritatively of the formation of academic collections. University libraries, he pointed out, "don't create disciplines, they do not create departments, they don't create colleges. They reflect, and if they don't, then they get in trouble. They service the interests of faculty members." Their archival collections therefore also reflect the research interests of the academic community, but Logsdon pointed out that highly important collections of vernacular material are often the work of people outside this community. He cited as an example the Western Americana collection built by Ramon Adams, a candy maker in Dallas who had not attended college but became a leading authority. Collectors, said Logsdon,

don't necessarily have to have the academic background; they have to have this strange drive and have to be obsessed, possessed, and driven. And most academicians don't have that drive. . . . In short, we owe a great deal to collectors. Without them our libraries would be very thin.

The private collection, however, does not necessarily become a public collection. While arguing that "a collection is no good if it sits in a home only for the benefit of the collector," Logsdon spoke of the vulnerability of the private collector. One of his friends with "the largest and most important personal collection of Western Americana in the world" allows no access to it because thirty years ago a scholar-collector borrowed three items and never returned them.

Collectors of traditional music, however, have a history of generosity with their materials and their knowledge. Dave Freeman pointed to ways in which several notable collectors have protected their rare recordings while at the same time putting them at the service of others. He cited Joe Bussard in Maryland as "a source for almost anything you want in the way of early recordings." Bussard circulates a catalogue of his holdings—"some 20,000 recordings probably"—and "he can find any one of them in about five or ten seconds" and "put it on tape for you in a matter of seconds," and does this for only a nominal fee. Freeman also described the mentoring and encouragement he got from other collectors as he was starting out, naming among his benefactors Eugene Earle, Lloyd Beaver, Frank Mare, and David Crisp and John Edwards of Australia.

Freeman himself—and other notable collectors like Chris Strachwitz, producer of Arhoolie Records and proprietor of Down-Home Music—have undertaken in other ways to share their enthusiasm for the music they collected. When Freeman saw the "first one or two issues of the Origin Jazz label" he was impressed by the work that collectors Pete Whelan and Bernie Klatzko had done in singling out choice material for reissue. "I determined," he said, "there should be the equivalent of that" for Southern stringband recordings. Lloyd Beaver encouraged this aim, so Freeman took "some of the records we had and put them on a long-play album," issuing it as County 501. Two English collectors who in the '60s edited a magazine that featured old-time and early country music, further encouraged Freeman "to go full time into the record business. It was through their efforts," he said, "that I actually did and made music my livelihood" as producer of the County and Rebel labels and owner of County Sales, which distributes these and many other labels devoted to traditional and country music. Ray Funk, another collector who has been active in editing reissues of gospel recordings, paid tribute to Joe Bussard and Chris Strachwitz for sharing their collections in yet another way: through radio programs. He attributed the awakening of his own interest in gospel music to the Strachwitz broadcasts.

All private collectors also have to confront the question of the ultimate disposition of their collections. Guy Logsdon pointed out that collectors may understandably choose to have the materials "auctioned so other collectors can enjoy collecting, and the find." In considering his own collection Dave Freeman, however, spoke of two aspects of the question. The unique recordings, his field tapes—including materials never released in albums—probably would go to an institution, to "whoever will give them the most attention and make them the most easily accessible." In thinking about his 78s, he admitted to having "swayed back and forth." He and other collectors have a choice, he said, "of donating the collection entirely, or selling it to another institution besides one of the major ones, or we have the choice of auctioning it off piecemeal." He felt inclined to auction off the 78s rather than donate them to a repository where a high percentage of them might merely be duplicates. Freeman pointed out the particular appeal of this solution to record collectors concerned about the "lack of new blood in the collecting hobby." The difficulty of finding disks discourages young collectors, who "can't do what we did when we started, canvassing door to door and picking up records at twenty-five, fifty cents apiece, including some gems." He believes it important to encourage collecting, because "the competition and the interaction among the collectors results in a lot more creative collecting and more interesting work being done and projects coming up that otherwise wouldn't."

Collectors, folk-revival performers, and others expressed concerns about archival collections too, based on frustrating experiences with them in the past. Logsdon reported that "all too often value judgments are used by librarians and archivists, and it is amazing the number of materials that go out the back door." Most of the comment focused, however, on the need for greater accessibility of archival holdings. Alice Gerrard—performer, collector, and editor of *The Old-Time Herald*—described a wide-spread fear that "if you deposit your collection, it's going to disappear in this black hole, and nobody's ever going to see it again." Archives may be very slow in cataloguing their acquisitions; and their staffs may know too little about their holdings or about the music itself to give the public good service. In looking for fresh song material to perform, Alice and her friend Hazel Dickens had found it much easier to consult a knowledgeable collector like Dick Spottswood than to scrounge for it in an archival collection. Ray Funk further lamented the delays and high charges often encountered in requesting copies of materials from archives:

In dealing with one particular national archive, the first time I wanted some rare recordings that I couldn't get anywhere else, it cost me $40. The second time it cost me $100. I sent off $100 for a 60-minute tape. This place was on the east coast and didn't seem to know the difference between the time zones. I got a call at 4:30 in the morning to tell me they had made my tape and it's another $57. At that time, I've paid more for a cassette of music than I've ever paid before, and I'm incredibly frustrated. . . . And then they don't want me to copy it. They want the next person who ever wants that in five to ten years to go through and pay another $157. . . . We're in a technological age when, it seems to me, this should not be happening.

Responding to these complaints as a staff member trying to cope with requests at the Archives of Traditional Music at Indiana University, ethnomusicologist Dorothy Sara Lee spoke of a new breed of trained archivists who have been working independently to solve these problems. She reviewed many of the difficulties faced by archives like hers, located in academic institutions. Not understanding "what we do" or "how important it is," the parent institutions may be actively hostile to the allocation of scarce resources to an archive.

Archivists, then, have to devote time and energy to interpreting to their own academic superiors the goals and needs of collectors and musicians. The inadequate resources of the archives must be stretched to cover acquisitions, equipment purchase and maintenance, public service, and cataloguing costs, which can be very high. "It's a much more expensive enterprise," Lee said, "than I think people realize—or are willing to understand." But factors that frustrate the user arise not only from budgetary limitations on the archive but also from its obligation to protect the rights of two constituencies: the traditional performers and the original collector/donors. Archivists, she said, feel the need "to speak for the rights of performers, especially these days, as more and more performers are concerned about copyright."

Lee also suggested ways in which field researchers and donors can help archives increase the effectiveness of their work At the time when they record materials that may ultimately go into an archive, field collectors can inform the people they work with "why the material is being collected, what's going to be done with it, and what possible use will be made of the material in the future." They can help by securing appropriate release forms, by carefully documenting and organizing their own materials (which they know much better than any cataloguer ever can)—and even by donating a small amount of money along with a collection to help the archive cover the cataloguing costs.

Representatives of three major public archives—Bill Ivey of the Country Music Foundation, Anthony Seeger of the Smithsonian Institution, and Alan Jabbour of the American Folklife Center at the Library of Congress—described institutional aims very different from those of academic libraries. Bill Ivey defined the Country Music Foundation as an institution with the mission "to preserve the historical culture beyond the lives of collectors, and beyond the corporate interests of those who might own copyrights or own master tapes." Its collections include artifacts, 130,000 sound recordings, 35,000 photographs, and 7,500 bound volumes. The museum component—the Country Music Hall of Fame—draws between 350,000 and 400,000 people each year and is the primary source of income for the entire Foundation. Ivey described the CMF as "a pop-culture organization" with "a folk arts rudder" and "a staff that includes five people with degrees in Folklore." Ronnie Pugh, the head of reference, handles "at least sixty phone inquiries each week, a thousand mail inquiries—correspondence pieces—each year." Ivey summarized the "personality" of the archive, saying, "it's open, it's aggressive, we want to get the material out, we want to service particularly the artistic community, but also scholars and others interested in Country Music." The success of his organization in satisfying its patrons was amply demonstrated during the conference, in warm tributes from Dave Freeman and others to the knowledge and selfless dedication of staff members like Bob Pinson.

Anthony Seeger described the Smithsonian Collections as consisting of two components: the archive of the Office of Folklife Programs—assembled since 1967 in the course of producing the Festival of American Folklife and still growing rapidly—and the Folkways Records collection. The latter consists of about 2,168 albums that Moses Asch produced over a period of forty years, and of "several thousand tapes, acetate transcription disks, and field recordings (many of them unissued)."

Seeger said that in his former post at the Archives of Traditional Music he had wanted very much to "get the music out to the performers, and out to anybody who wanted to listen to it, researcher or not. But there were laws and restrictions of all kinds that made that very difficult." When he was invited to head the Folkways Records project at the Smithsonian Institution, he knew that this would be a "production-oriented archive" serving to mount festivals and issue recordings, and he thought,

Ah-ha, here's a place where the issues of dissemination can finally come into their own, because I know that we can disseminate this material. We own the copyrights to what turns out to be most of it. And we can use it in ways that are really creative and new. . . .

Although the Folkways materials were still in the "piles-of-boxes-in-a-small-space stage" at the time of the Conference[4] and lacking tax dollars to support projects, Seeger had bold intentions for outreach. The Smithsonian has said that it "would keep all of the titles in Folkways Records available for the foreseeable future." It has a distribution arrangement with Rounder Records for the commercially distributable titles and plans to set up what Seeger believes can become "one of the most efficient and best archival on-demand supply operations" for the less commercially viable titles. Seeger's goal is to create a situation where, "If you want it, we can give it to you. We own the rights to it, artists will be paid royalties on it, and we will try to get it to you quickly and with the entire liner notes of the original record." And he wants "to make everybody in the world know that they're available." In another outreach effort he would like to have the Folkways Collection all in digital form and in a system that would let anyone "walk into a place almost anywhere the size of a phone booth, and get copies of any type of music, with royalties paid and the original artist's rights respected." The vision underlying this goal is of "a national museum" no longer object-oriented, one that includes the music and other performing arts of "all of the people and all of the traditions in this country."

Alan Jabbour described the founding of the Archive of American Folk Song under Robert W. Gordon in 1928 and its halcyon period in the '30s with John and Alan Lomax that "conveyed to all of us the image of an archive not simply as a passive repository but also potentially as an active cultural ingredient." When the American Folklife Center was created in 1976, it began very early to build on this tradition with a series of documentary projects in the field characterized by a new thrust and direction. One step was the development of team undertakings like the Pinelands Folklife Project in southern New Jersey and the Lowell Project in Massachusetts. These took fieldwork "beyond what a single collector can do working alone." The quantity of data assembled in these projects led the AFC over a period of six or eight years to a second innovation. Using computers, the Center began first to shift the recording of the documentation into the daily field assignment, and then to incorporate subject retrieval systems into the daily record keeping. These steps dramatically improved both the quality and the accessibility of the documentation for the projects.

In addition, Jabbour described equally dramatic developments in the outreach efforts of the American Folklife Center. One was the well-known Federal Cylinder Project, which had the goal of preserving early recordings that "were literally dying." The wax emulsions forming the cylinders were separating out and coming to the surface, where molds and other agents attacking them were destroying the recordings. Over half of the cylinders, recorded between 1890 and the 1930s, documented Native American music, lore, and culture— one of the "most precious legacies of American Indian culture that existed anywhere." Realizing that piecemeal efforts would not have the "critical mass" to win support, the Center sought funds to not only to preserve the material but also to catalogue and disseminate it. By now,

All of the cylinders have been transferred onto tape. The cataloguing is half to two-thirds done. And the dissemination is about halfway down the line. We are actually paying visits to the separate tribes, . . . making a ceremonial event of the return of the material, in order to highlight it for its . . . cultural potency. . . .

The Center is undertaking a similar initiative, Jabbour reported, with the fifteen to twenty thousand recordings of the "great disk era of the Archive, the era that began first tentatively with Robert W. Gordon and then grandly and boldly with the Lomaxes." Taping the disks with modern technology is easily achievable, and simple cataloguing already exists for the material, but targeted dissemination is not so readily feasible. The Center expects, however, that dissemination will become possible through a bold new initiative called "American Memory" championed by the new Librarian of Congress, James H. Billington. This American Memory project proposes to "disseminate some of the key special collections of the Library of Congress"— including the disk-era folk-archive recordings—using new technological tools such as laser disks or CD's hooked up to a computer. In such forms the Library of Congress will be able to disseminate "not just portions of the archive to home communities or regions, but the whole archive, lock, stock, and barrel, to other archives around the country."

Prospects for the Publication of Recordings

Archivists foresee extraordinary new technologies that will give the public ready access to their holdings. But record producers and distributors describe ways in which new technologies have combined with economic factors to discourage them from issuing traditional music. This is less the situation with major record labels than with small producers and distributors. Billy Altman, music critic and editor of the new RCA Heritage Series, reported for example that RCA has been "incredibly supportive, . . . wanting me as much as possible to stay creative, since I'm not coming into the ranks as an industry person, or as an entrepreneur, or as a businessman, but as a writer and a music fan"; nevertheless, a major record company has "so many administrative changes on so many different levels over the past six months, six minutes, or whatever, depending on who now owns the company," that its executives often have no idea what recordings their vaults hold. When Altman took RCA a list of possible artists for the Heritage Series, the man he spoke with found most of the names unfamiliar: "'Ernest Stoneman—who's that?' And he's going, 'All these brothers—Delmore Brothers? Monroe Brothers?' And I said, 'Bill Monroe.'—'We have Bill Monroe!'" In an organization so complex, the publicity for two of the releases fell through because "the last college promo rep that RCA had was leaving in December and the new guy that was taking over . . . wouldn't start working there until February." Furthermore, Altman says, your entire production budget can get cut if either Daryl Hall or John Oates goes to the bathroom during a recording session, costing the firm in these few minutes "more money than the company has allotted you to do your entire project." In this context, Altman reported, everybody has advised him, "Do as many as you can as fast as you can, because ultimately they'll pull the plug." And that, he added, "is just record company economics. And the market place."

The best hope for new releases remains, then, with the small specialty companies. But their situation is no longer bright. In Dave Freeman's words,

the high period for small labels—for our particular label, County—getting some of these Southern rural albums out on the market . . . was about 1977–78. At one time we had twenty-six distributors around the world, most of them in this country, but several of them in other countries. At that time, every one of them would take at least a box of twenty-five albums of anything we put out, just on the basis of our reputation—what they felt they could sell. Most reordered. Some took in the hundreds, or a hundred or more. . . . You had a fair base of operation there, if you had a specialized interest album, you could do it without worrying too much that you could break even fairly quickly. That number of distributors is down to about seven or eight now. . . .

In Dave Freeman's assessment, producers will continue to put out a record that they really want to issue

as a labor of love, and even lose money on it, but there are a lot of projects that could be done . . . if we'd just a very small number of extra sales there. And we're not talking huge numbers. It may be the difference of selling 2,000 records instead of 1,500. . . . I feel we can and will do that, some way. It's a small extra little push needed.

Part of the problem, as he and other producers see it, is the triumph of the compact disk. Ken Irwin of Rounder Records and Round-Up Distribution Company reported, "A lot of stores, especially on the West Coast, will not stock an LP or cassette, if the title is not also available in CD. . . . And it is not financially feasible to do CDs on a lot of these records." Barry Poss, owner of Sugar Hill Records, added,

Within the last three weeks, three major retail chains in the United States announced that they will no longer carry vinyl records, LPs. But that means for several of us, we're going to be taking massive returns of these records. What we don't know is, will they replace these records with cassettes or compact disks?

Upheavals like these have put out of business many companies that sold "traditional and roots-oriented music," and the ones that remain, said Irwin, "are used to selling by the tonnage, a term that they frequently refer to, instead of selling the ones and twos and threes that we tend to be happy selling." Eugene Earle pointed out that record dealers who ship overseas, as he does, have their sales further depressed by customs charges.

Ivey urged folklorists considering record releases to develop a clearer sense of the demand or audience or potential distribution. They should ask themselves, he argued,

Who wants this material? How will we get it to them? Is a record, CD, or commercially manufactured cassette the best mechanism for getting it out? Should we put singles in juke boxes? Should we do a few cassettes and get them around the community? Should we do a concert instead?

Other panelists suggested taking creative marketing strategies. They felt the need to get the music itself heard and in other ways to improve publicity for the mail-order distribution of recordings. The folk-revival movement, Freeman felt, had generated audiences in the 1970s for recordings of traditional music, and its decline adversely impacted upon sales. Radio broadcasts are an alternative way of reaching and developing a potential audience, but radio is a medium difficult to exploit. In Billy Altman's assessment commercial radio is not a promising vehicle, because broadcast licenses have changed hands for such high dollars during the last decade that everybody running a radio station has to absolutely fine tune that demographic every second of the day. They cannot afford to experiment or serve the needs of special audiences. They simply cannot afford it.

Although Sugar Hill or County or Down Home Music may sponsor a program on a local FM station or even get some national airplay—especially over folk shows on public radio—the company will not greatly benefit when the local record shops fail to carry the album.

Distributors and producers had varying assessments of other strategies for getting out word about new releases. Michael Schlesinger of Global Village Records reported his experience that coverage in publications like The New York *Times* is effective only if the readers are already interested in the music. For the same reason, specialty publications like Alice Gerrard's *The Old-Time Herald* seemed to Dave Freeman very helpful both in publicizing new releases and in generating a new audience for the music. Pete Kuykendall of *Bluegrass Unlimited* reminded those who issue a recording to take the initiative to send information about it to editors like Gerrard and himself, and Joanne Delaplaine of the *United Mine Workers Journal* urged producers to remember labor publications, whose readership is also a natural constituency for many of the albums. Ken Irwin suggested that small labels concentrate their publicity efforts less on costly direct-mail advertising than on lobbying with active mail-order distributors such as County Sales, Down Home Music, and Round-Up Records for reviews and listings in their newsletters and catalogues. Lastly, Bill Ivey urged small record producers to become members of the National Academy of Recording Arts and Sciences, which needs more persons with expertise in traditional music voting for Grammy Awards; this would help worthy albums win awards and get the attendant publicity.

Issues for the Future

A recurrent issue in the Conference was the ways in which many kinds of changes impact upon the documentation, collecting, and study of Southern traditional music. Some spoke of musical changes. Guy Carawan drew a poignant picture of the dwindling of the glorious "shout" singing in South Carolina sea island praise houses in the years since he and his wife Candie taped the performances issued in the Folkways album *Been in the Storm So Long*. Of four praise houses on an eight-mile stretch of road on Johns Island in the 1960s, only the Moving Star Hall still stands, and a singer reports,

We don't have class meeting in the hall anymore. I miss it. We don't have it now because all these young preachers have everything to the church. What are a few people going to do in a big old church like that? I like to go to the hall because you can have your way. You can feel yourself.

On the other hand, Jay Orr, a staff member at the Country Music Foundation at the time of the Conference and currently a journalist covering regional music, urged that genres presently seen as too popular and too modern to be of interest should get serious attention from scholars, collectors, and archives. He argued his case by drawing direct analogies between a 1960s rhythm-and-blues band that played around Kosciusko, Mississippi, and Freeny's Barn Dance Band, a great old-time stringband active in the same neighborhood forty years earlier. His Aunt Annie had known and enjoyed Carleton Freeny and his band in the '20s; in the mid-sixties her son John

grew his hair long, he decided that he wanted to sing in a band, and he formed a band called The Cavaliers. I remember the first time I saw them was at a school dance, and my father took me to see them, because I was too young to be admitted. But I was very taken with The Cavaliers. I thought this was wonderful music that they were making, and my cousin John later told me he was glad we had left when we did because he was about to do a song called "Walking the Dog" that he thought my father would not have appreciated. This was a song by Rufus Thomas. And The Cavaliers gained a state-wide reputation, and played, I think, because of a lot of the same creative impulses that Freeny's Barn Dance did. They would play occasionally at the Armory in Jackson, and that was a big occasion, but they would also play for school dances, for parties, and the like. They did attract some attention from one fellow with a record label, and they made this record on a little label out of Nashville called Spotlight Records. And on this record they recorded a song that was originally recorded by another rhythm-and-blues artist, Arthur Alexander. The song was called "You Better Move On." And this was the only thing they ever did. John quit playing, and went to med school, and became a dermatologist in Tupelo. But John still plays today; he and his band members get together and play at the request of people they used to play for in Kosciusko. They play most often, I think, at Christmas time. And I feel that there are some significant parallels between what John and The Cavaliers do now—perhaps not musical parallels, but certainly if we're thinking about Southern culture, we would want to know in the future about what

John has done, as well as what Freeny's Barn Dance Boys did. And I dare say that there's not an archive represented here that has a copy of this record.

Orr urged collectors, if not archivists, to find and preserve such "roots rock" recordings. Twenty-five years from now, he said, "it will be great to be able to hear Willie Trice, Tommy Jarrell, and the Red Clay Ramblers on recordings preserved in the Southern Folklife Collection. But somewhere . . . we ought to also be able to hear Doug Clark and The Hot Nuts, David Olney and The X-Rays, The Cherrybombs, Arrogance, Don Dixon, and Mitch Easter."

Bill Ivey spoke of a complex of technological, legal, and corporate changes that affect work with vernacular music. Sound and visual documents, he pointed out, are increasingly linked and need to be collected and preserved together. Because of technological changes the master of a recording may not be a single disk or tape, as it was even a decade or a decade-and-a-half ago: "it may exist in several pieces, in several different communities." Changes in the copyright environment also pose difficult issues for archives and for those wanting to issue recordings. We know something, Ivey says,

about the ownership problems with records. We know that there are rights which have to be secured, both for the music and the individual record, if we're going to re-release something. But for tape, for newly recorded tape, under common-law copyright, if you collect something from an informant, unless otherwise specified, that item carries a shared copyright: collector and informant. How do we account for that contractually. The same thing's true with photographs now. Unless you secure a contract to the contrary, the photographic copyright remains with the photographer.

If publication of photographs and sound recordings is to continue, archives increasingly must have not only possession of their holdings but also legal ownership of them. Furthermore, changes in the corporate environment pose actual dangers to the preservation of our musical heritage. As Sony buys CBS Records or BMG buys RCA Records,

the ownership not only leaves the hands of the company, it leaves the United States. Can that company transfer its assets to its homeland? I suspect it can. Is there any mechanism in place to ensure that, if a company decides it needs warehouse space more than it needs those recordings, . . . they wouldn't soon be destroyed?

Allen Tullos addressed social changes in the South and ways these may impact upon vernacular music: the growing numbers of the poor, giving melancholy promise that communities in the South will continue to need music of their own to articulate their identity and aspirations; the immigration of Hispanics, Koreans, Indochinese, and others who add their own musical traditions to the Southern mix, just as they expand the definition of "Southerner"; and the emergence of distinct and insistently self-aware sub-regions within the large, complex section called the South. To his points Charles R. Wilson of the Center for the Study of Southern Culture added the growing influence of American popular culture upon vernacular music in the South. He attributes this partly to the growth of the Southern middle class and partly to the easy access most of the population has to radio, recordings, and television. Johnny Carson would be hard pressed, he thought, to find the kind of "naive" Southerner he likes to interview: the Southerner who has never flown on a plane, who does not have a telephone, and who does not know who Johnny Carson is.

Overarching Issues in the Study of Southern Music

David Whisnant's paper directs attention to other problems framing the study of Southern music: the defensiveness that has too often clouded Southern studies, the late development of an awareness of the South as a place of many sub-cultures, and the unrecognized ways in which racial and sexual bias, political conservatism, and prominent institutions and cultural networks have shaped the documentation and study of Southern music. His paper sketches in the abstract what the Conference illustrated in individuals—the complexity that has characterized the entire enterprise of the study of Southern traditional music.

The last session of the Conference was in fact a case study of a small and illustratively complicated corner of this enterprise, "The Chapel Hill/Durham Stringband Movement." The centerpiece of the session, Tom Carter's reflective presentation, outlined the genesis of revival stringbands in the region in the 1970's, named some of the young middle-class college students who frailed and thrummed their way through the movement, described their contacts with older traditional performers, probed their motivations, and suggested their relation to social movements of the decade. Space did not permit him to describe the astonishing impact of the experience on the subsequent careers of the participants. While Bert Levy became a physician and Pete Hartman a banker, a significant number of the participants remained in one way or another professionally active with traditional music. Some—like Alan Jabbour, Blanton Owen, or George Holt—became public folklorists. Others became academic folklorists, like Tom Carter and Cece Conway, writing articles and books, editing albums, and producing documentary films. Barry Poss set up Sugar Hill Records, producing albums of the music he loves. Tommy Thompson left the graduate study of philosophy to become a performing musician, songwriter, playwright, and actor, his work in all capacities informed by his knowledge and love of traditional music. A few affected by their years in the movement left the academic world altogether. Malcolm Owen abandoned a doctorate in Romance Languages and with his wife Vickie works a hill-country farm. Bill Hicks, who had worked for Duke University Press, became a stone mason. And they continue to make music.

To this session of the Conference many of the participants had returned, and they offered their own perspectives in the discussion following Carter's paper. Alan Jabbour, the seminal figure in the movement, explained the path by which he came unwittingly to found it. He traced his role to his childhood study of the classical violin, his graduate seminar on British balladry with Holger Nygard at Duke University, and his situation as a young middle-class Southerner with traditional roots in a world "changing and re-evaluating itself culturally and socially" in the aftermath of the success of the integration movement. The central stage for stringband activity, as Jan Davidson pointed out, was the music party, "the great educational institution of the time." Fifteen or so people may have gone out to collect traditional tunes, but "literally hundreds," he said, "drifted through those parties and learned a tremendous amount." Cece Conway told of speeding back to a Hollow Rock jam session one night after a trip to West Virginia, "sliding up the dirt road" to the house: "the light was on and the music was going and the intensity and passion of that—the sense of community—was very special then."

One story told by Alan Jabbour had special import. He had moved to Los Angeles from Durham and was invited to serve as a judge at the Topanga Canyon Fiddlers' Contest:

Well, one young Fellow got up with his fiddle and he said reverently, he says, "This next tune is 'Over the Waterfall.' It's a Henry Reed tune. It's from Henry Reed in West Virginia." This was in fact a tune that I had learned from Henry Reed, that our band had played. It was on the Hollow Rock String Band record. It was also, though, a tune that the people we bumped into at fiddlers' contests and other festivals could have learned from us directly. But it was sort of amazing to find that "Over the Waterfall" had arrived in Los Angeles before I did. So these were the first intimations that something even larger . . . was going on here.

That larger scene was sketched by a number of other participants: by Hilary Dirlam, who had been in the Arm and Hammer String Band in New England, learning French-Canadian and Vermont tunes, before hearing the Fuzzy Mountain String Band recording and coming South; by Art Rosenbaum, Michael Schlesinger, Mac Benford, Richard Blaustein, and others who had been attracted into the folk scene in New York City through Pete Seeger or the New Lost City Ramblers; by Alice Gerrard, Hazel Dickens, Mike Seeger, Pete Kuykendall, and others who had been active in a bluegrass revival in the Baltimore-Washington area.

Bess Hawes reminded the gathering that the revival extended not only across the country but back in time, although it has often taken other forms. "I used to be in a group called The Almanac Singers," she said, with a "tradition of singing which was once extremely widespread," now "fallen victim to the great interest in the stringband." Such groups were "message-political" and activist. "We had something we wanted to sing about, and we wrote songs that expressed that point of view." Her brother Alan extended the genealogy further. Before the Alamanac Singers, he said, "there was the Lomax Potomacs in Washington. It was the stringband that we had in the government workers' union," and it "tore the town down with all kinds of progressive songs."

A central issue pervaded this session and all the earlier ones of the Conference: the relation of those studying and working with Southern traditional music—the academic folklorist, the archivist, the revival musician, the record collector and producer, the public folklorist—to the traditional musician. Cece Conway had spoken of getting to know Tommy Jarrell and learning to appreciate that he was not only a wonderful fiddler but also "a great translator of culture." Tommy, she said, "could explain what was going on with other fiddlers in his community . . . to us, and he could explain us weird people to his community." He could also explain traditional musicians to each other. She told of a time when he and another banjo player from Mount Airy were at a festival at Duke with Willie Trice, the bluesman from Chapel Hill:

the fellow Tommy was with started saying, "Well, what tunes do you play? Do you play 'Soldier's Joy'? Do you play 'Sally Ann'?" And Tommy said, "Fred, be quiet. Don't ask the man if he plays your tunes. Ask him what tunes he plays."

Tommy's "sensitivity to cultural distinctions and to musical taste and repertoire," his understanding of "how to try to learn the aesthetic of the other person," was "very helpful to all of us"—"extremely important in our learning, and part of what we're trying to learn as folklorists."

Archie Green addressed this theme eloquently at the close of the session, challenging a "hidden assumption" in much of the discourse at the Conference—that those who work with folk music, being college graduates and "competent in music, articulate with language," represent "an intellectual tradition," while "the folk" are "real people, inarticulate, learning orally at an existential level a subset of values different from our own." He offered three examples of "hillbilly musicians who were as educated, as articulate, as sensitive" as the conference speakers: Tony Alderman, Buell Kazee, and "Haywire Mac" McClintock. He described Tony Alderman of Galax, the fiddler in the original Hillbillies Band, as "a traditional musician of the first rank," but pointed out that Tony's father was an engineer with Appalachian Power and both his parents fluent in many languages and able to read music; and Tony, he said, "could rank with any ethnomusicologist, any philosophy student, any academic, any place, any time." And "Haywire Mac," who "really opened up stringband music in the West," was equally extraordinary:

"Haywire Mac" travelled. He was in the Boxer Rebellion. He was a member of the Industrial Workers of the World, a group of blue-collar people who educated themselves, who read Hegel, who read Darwin, who soapboxed. . . . Highly articulate, highly sophisticated! And I just feel this very deeply— that at some level we have to stop romanticizing and dichotomizing and continuing polarities that unfortunately add to the "power trip."

Traditional musicians and members of their families were also participants at the Conference—among them Kinny Rorrer, kinsman of Posey Rorrer and himself author of writings on the North Carolina Ramblers; Harper and Wanona Van Hoy, producers of the Fiddler's Grove Festival; Liz Smathers Shaw, singer and instrumentalist and daughter of shape-note leader Quay Smathers; Carolyn and Evelyn Shaw, daughters of fiddler Lauchlin Shaw; and singer Hazel Dickens.

At Archie Green's prompting, Hazel carefully described her experience as a budding public performer. She had moved from Appalachia into Baltimore and spoke of her world as "so narrow at that point that I couldn't look much outside of it, because if I did I would get too scared." She was part of a performing band, but as a woman, having a difficult time. The group played in raunchy bars where she many times "ran in the dressing room and hid when the fights would break out." She "would be chased around the back rooms by fiddle players." She got less from the band's tips than male players got. She "could sing tenor circles around most of them that were in the group" but "her place was to sing Kitty Wells songs." And when a male performer came on the scene, the band hired him on the spot and fired her. It was during this time that she met folk-revival singer Alice Gerrard. At a party

someone just suggested that we sing. We had no idea that we'd be singing together. And . . . I actually pursued that duet . . . because we had more control over what we did. We could pick our own material, and it was a matter of being able to be our own person, to be in contol of our own talent and our own forming of the kind of band that we wanted.

Archie Green asked Hazel Dickens for her assessment of her first encounters with folk-music enthusiasts: "When all those intellectual yuppies at Cornell and Yale left their middle-class comforts and came down to visit you and idealize you, how did you feel?" "I felt weird," was the reply, "and I thought they were weird! . . . I had come up and been working in Baltimore in the factories and waitressing and all that stuff to keep alive. I had really actually never met honest-to-God college people or people that had money. . . . It was my first exposure to anyone of that caliber, because the way I was raised was in a coal-mining area where we did not have the exposure to books. . . . And to meet people like this was terribly frightening." But then she added, "—and also terribly rewarding!"

These words seem a fitting epigraph for the Conference. For if a single experience united the diverse participants, it was that most had heard music that struck them as compelling, music that drew them into dedicated labors they had not expected, music that opened a door into ways of life that could at first seem frightening but ultimately proved "terribly rewarding." John Edwards of Australia had set out on such an adventure but had it untimely cut off. His farsighted legacy continues to help others find their own differing roads into Southern musical terrains—and into knowledge of the South that lies behinds the sounds.

Part One

Personal and Historical Perspectives

Bess Lomax Hawes

Evaluating Our Work
and Ourselves

W*hen I first began* working for the National Endowment for
the Arts, a federal granting agency, I was introduced to a
gentleman described as being in charge of the Endow-
ment's evaluation program. I thought this was an interesting thing to
be doing, but I was pretty busy, and I confess I quite forgot about him
until one day when he appeared in my office inquiring exactly how
I planned to evaluate such activities as might emerge from Folk Arts
grants. Well, this was a real poser. I really didn't have a clue as to how
to evaluate anything, but my new friend informed me that formal
evaluations were being required for all federal activities at that particular time. This was, of course, in the green and leafy and hopeful days
of the Carter administration. It all sort of drifted away, like clouds of
smoke, in later days.

Anyway, at that particular time, it was clear I had to think about
how to evaluate folk activities and events, so I did. And the longer
I thought about the problem, the more complicated it seemed to
become. I finally decided to seek outside help, and I turned to Professor John Szwed of Yale University, who at the time was a member of
the Folk Arts reviewing panel. John Szwed, as many of you know, is
possessed of a remarkable, adult, and subtle mind and enjoys—as
the old folk joke puts it—"defining the indefinable and unscrewing
the inscrutable," and he accepted my commission with interest.

Some weeks later I asked him how he was coming on, and he
told me a most instructive story. Quite a large number, he said, of
Washington bureaucrats were, like me, worrying about just how to
do all this evaluation business, so much so that the principal evaluators from all the agencies were getting together weekly for luncheon
meetings where they could share experiences and problems and

calm their troubled spirits. John finally wangled an invitation to such a luncheon, at which he inquired of the assembled experts if they had determined any single principle of evaluation that they had all agreed upon, one that worked reliably under any and all circumstances.

After due consideration, the answer came: yes. They had indeed determined one immutable and totally reliable principle. Under no circumstances, they told John, could the results of any action be determined before it was necessary to take the next action. To repeat: under no circumstances can the results of any action be determined before it is necessary to undertake the next action.

Well. I had to admit, my entire life's experience had led me to much the same conclusion, though I didn't know how to articulate it in such a crisp and devastating formula. All my life I had felt I was sort of muddling along, doing what came to hand and what seemed relatively productive and useful, never terribly clear as to what might result but generally going on the principle enunciated by my domino-playing sister-in-law, that anything beats a blank.

But I had always thought everybody else was smarter than I was and knew more and was better educated. But if nobody could tell the result of any action in time to correct the next action accordingly, then everybody was working in pretty much the same way—trying out what seemed logical and might work, based on parallel observations and one's own reading of history. In a way, it was really worrying. In a way it was a bit liberating. If no one could guarantee results, then all of us might well pull up our socks and begin to try to improve the current situation by putting our own skills and interests to work.

I did have to admit that the Szwed Principle was not going to offer me much help in how to evaluate future activities. How on earth could one even start to evaluate the results of a Folk Arts project— for example, a simple concert? To begin with, what would be a proper time frame (as I learned to call it) when all this evaluating should happen? Assuming one knew what questions to ask, when should one start to ask them: immediately after? the next morning? a week later? in a month? It was plain that the results of any inquiry would be totally different depending simply upon when the inquiries were made.

And then what should the standards be? To try something simple—how about attendance? That sounds straightforward. We could ask grantees simply to count how many people came. But suppose they came and then wished they hadn't? Suppose lots of people came and the event was so boring that everyone went to sleep? Or went home? Suppose nobody came at all, hardly, but the performers had a wonderful party and thought it was all a great success?

I can tell you about a remarkable occasion when just that happened, and five years later people are still talking about what a seminal event it was and how many significant developments have stemmed directly out of that "disastrous" occasion in later years. The event—a "simple" concert—was essentially conceived of and energized by a single person, an independent researcher and discographer named Douglas Seroff, who had spent many years of self-imposed drudgery discovering and straightening out the complex history of the African-American unaccompanied vocal quartet movement, especially that part of it that had been captured on 78-rpm records.[1] This had been a true labor of love—essentially unpaid, unpublished, and unsolicited. He never received an A from a graduate instructor for that work, or a nickel as far as I know, or even much of a pat on the back, because very few people knew what he was doing. (Of course, many other people have done just this same sort of thing—contributing their expertise out of love, for very little return, but I can't tell everybody's story!)

Douglas Seroff came up with what he thought was a wonderful idea for a concert—a great reunion of all the old-time quartets that had risen up around the city of Birmingham, Alabama, during the 1920s, '30s, and '40s, the heyday of quartet singing. He elicited Folk Arts support at the Endowment; he involved Hank Willett, at that time Folk Arts Coordinator for Alabama and long-time lover of the genre; he tracked down the old-time singers, now scattered from California to Brooklyn; he wrote and edited and published a program containing the best of his historical photographs of the older quartets and biographies of the singers and an over-view history of the movement.[2] He rented a hall where many of the great concerts had occurred in the old days and lined up radio and newspaper publicity, and engaged almost half of a nearby motel, where the fifty-odd singers and their families could be accommodated.

I came down from Washington for the grand occasion. It was in a cavernous hall that could seat perhaps 3,000 people, fronted by an enormous stage with an absolute forest of microphones, maybe twenty of them strung across in a fragile line. And when the performance began, peering around me in the gloom I could see no more than perhaps fifty people, though I later heard there were 200 more scattered through the hall. And at least three of them were from the Endowment. It was hard to know where to look, what to do, what to say. But then the first quartet came striding out on the stage, all duded up in matching pin-striped suits and ruffled white shirts, full of excitement, raring to go. They grabbed four microphones at random and began to sing with obvious and unblemished delight in the power and excitement of their own performance. Other old gentlemen peeked out from the wings, whooping them on, running out to give them high fives and big hugs between songs.

The audience began to cheer up. We clapped and stamped, trying to make up in enthusiasm for our small numbers. And the quartets kept coming, one after another, bounding out like young superstars onto the stage, ripping the mikes off their stands and parading down through the empty aisles as though thousands were cheering them on. As we left the hall at the end, one of the wives who had been sitting near me turned and said, her face glowing with triumph, "Well now, wasn't that just the nicest thing! When are we going to do it again?"

I just couldn't answer her. From every technical point of view, it could hardly have been worse. The sound in the hall was appalling, as the excited singers grabbed microphone after microphone and put them back on the wrong stands; by the end of the evening the cords were literally in knots all over the stage, and after the first few numbers, we never heard a balanced sound again. None of the quartets would leave the stage until exhaustion had set in, so the whole thing dragged on for hours until well past midnight. And—bleakest of all—the local audience had simply not shown up; they had not supported their own. Worth Long and I discussed it in whispers. Had the whole idea been mistimed? Had it been the wrong thing to do, to begin with? Had the execution been at fault? Had some terrible cultural gaffes been made?

Still, as I flew back to Washington, it just didn't feel that wrong. Something about that bizarre event had been an absolutely resounding success. I kept remembering the breakfast the morning after the concert, when I was in the dumps but when about twenty of the singers had sat hours at the table, filling themselves with grits and sausages and falling out with laughter over story after story about their early singing exploits—which little country churches they had sung in, how they had duded themselves up, how they had shined up their shoes and their rattletrap old cars so as to look prosperous and professional, which songs they had sung, what strategies they had used to put down the previous singing groups, what a blast that whole life had been, how much it had meant to them.

Well, as I said, I flew back to Washington, and in the fullness of time, I closed out the grant and took several quiet breaths, hoping that nobody would notice that the ordinary measures of success hadn't been fulfilled, that the project hadn't produced the results that might have been expected. Indeed, that I would have expected. I'm no different from anybody else in this culture: I want lots and lots of big numbers to validate the beauty and importance of what I help present. But in this case, I guess I hoped not too many people would notice—and of all things I hoped people wouldn't think it had been a failure.

But back in Birmingham, Douglas Seroff's thorough and scholarly and fact-filled program booklet began to circulate. Hank Willett made sure that a number of the most forward-looking high school music programs got copies, and he made sure also that local school music teachers knew that there were several African-American *a cappella* quartets of historical significance still working in the Birmingham district. These quartets began to appear at a few school assembly programs, and everywhere they appeared they handed out copies of the program booklet. (There were a lot left over.) Doug and Hank also began to establish a more solid relationship with the Black disc jockeys of Birmingham, a few of whom began to broadcast the older recordings along with some new cuts from Brenda McCallum's record (brought out two years after the concert) of the classic Birmingham quartet singers.[3] The fabled Fairfield Four quartet of Nashville, that had been reunited for the Birmingham event, stayed reunited and began appearing together again regularly.

And then one day Folk Arts heard from the Florida Folklife people that some folks in Jacksonville, Florida (original home of the Five Blind Boys), were interested in having an *a cappella* quartet concert too, and ethnomusicologist Doris Dyen went in to help work on that one. Her devoted and professional work helped to put on a musically exciting concert that was also poorly attended. But then folklorist David Evans' students in Memphis began to talk about a quartet concert there, and it also ultimately came to pass, with Kip Lornell and others involved.

I began asking my southern-based friends about the state of *a cappella* quartet singing in their areas, and they began to report that it was simmering along—that most groups had annual home-comings, that the younger men still went out to sing in the more remote churches, that women's groups were certainly not unheard of and in some areas were becoming downright fashionable, that there are still some active old-time "trainers" who go around and put the final polishing touches to the younger groups—little pieces of news like that, which led me to feel that on the whole this tradition is moving along as one would hope it would—differently in different places, firmly attached to its roots, but out there in the sunshine too. Douglas Seroff put on a highly successful concert in the auditorium at Fisk University last year honoring the Fairfield Four quartet, and negotiated with Ladysmith Black Mambazo to put on a joint *a cappella* concert with the Sterling Jubilees Quartet in Alabama, since it turned out that the two groups like each other's sound.

Well, plainly, this is a story that hasn't ended yet. Very few stories do in our field. They aren't supposed to. We're concerned with continuity, with on-goingness. But I do think there are a few lessons to be drawn from what we've seen happen so far in the African-American *a cappella* quartet-singing tradition, ideas that might help shape some future activities. I will not here try to consider why the local community—black and white—did not support that concert. It seems possible that certain unknown norms in Birmingham for successful African-American event organization were not observed. It is equally possible to observe that the first few times anything at all is tried, especially in a conservative Black community, it may not be widely supported, at least not until the word gets around. What I can outline are a few of the factors that went into the long-range fruitfulness of the concert:

(1) The traditions celebrated had real historical depth and real cultural significance and meaning—the event was intrinsically gorgeous. It was important.

(2) The research into the tradition had been done with great thor-

oughness and scholarly care, resulting—among other things—in the logical selection of Birmingham, Alabama, a major center in the development of quartet singing, as the concert site. (Other centers could have been chosen, of course, but this was one of the important ones. The concert was not staged in Hollywood or Washington, D.C., or other more fashionable venues.)

(3) Again, as the result of intensive research, the right singers had been invited, the right ones in this case being all the groups that had participated in the development of the Birmingham style. Not everyone was still alive or could participate, but all the singers present knew that a serious attempt had been made to include everybody who should have been included. And that made for an atmosphere of joyful relaxation amongst the singers. They were having a reunion—who cared about anything else!

(4) The actual research was presented back to the researched community in an inexpensive, profusely illustrated, interesting, verifiable form. It is impossible to look at that program booklet and not be impressed by the extraordinary story of the development of quartet singing in Birmingham. The availability of solid pains-taking scholarship has the effect of empowerment to the community studied, allowing the development of legitimate pride. It can form a bridge, too, for contact across caste and class lines. But it has to be made available, and that requires major effort.

(5) And then there was a concert. The living singers came together, and they opened their throats and poured their passion and skill and liveliness and humor out over the empty hall, and no one who heard them could ever be convinced that this was a dying art. I am in favor of books, publications of all kinds, musical transcriptions, tapes, records, films, but in spite of all the technological and electronic gadgetry in the world, the primary gestating act of music, I believe, only happens when musicians and listeners assemble.

Referring now back to the Szwed Principle, perhaps our best method of evaluation is to extract from any situation the elementary factors like the foregoing that can be compared with other like events. Then, extracting still further, we may come up with principles like the ones that appear to me to have been key in the Birmingham situation. One: long-term dedication. Steady and consistent effort was applied before, during, and after the event. Two: solid research.

One of the two major people involved knew the quartet history thoroughly; the other was an Alabama man who knew his state equally well.

At the beginning of this paper I put the evaluation problem within a bureaucratic context, and I complained, in a typically self-pitying bureaucratic way, about the nonsensicalness of having to work out evaluation methods. But evaluation is a real problem, and it exists out there in the real world, not just in terms of governmental requirements. Evaluation doesn't just happen on paper. We may never have to fill in an evaluation form, but the hard fact is that we do go on evaluating our own and others' work in this field continually.

And when I say "we" here, I mean everybody—artists, audiences, everyone who has been touched in any way by the particular event. Everyone evaluates—out loud or in silence. An on the basis of those evaluations, the next event will rise or decline, will grow or shrink, will take place or die a-borning. We all need to try to become better evaluators, more cogent critics, broader in range, more precise and more understanding.

One way in which we could improve our evaluations would be to try to remember that cultural events reflect many interests, that these interests may and generally do vary, that one man's success may be another man's tedium or even disaster. We should try to notice these variances and think very specifically about them. Then we could work at breaking down the significant component elements of a cultural event: the nature of the tradition itself, the location of the action, the scholarly research effort, the publication record, the experience of the artists themselves among others.

But I am beginning to think that the most important perspective to maintain in all our analyses is the long-term. The Birmingham concert was one highly visible move in a long series of events, some coming before and some after, all converging around the central tradition of African-American *a cappella* quartet music in all its splendor. It takes more than one concert or recording project or research effort if a tradition is to continue lively and creative. We should try to hang on to a long-range perspective; we should try to look at events in the context of what has gone before and what could come after; we should temper our evaluation of the moment with some understanding that there has been a past and there will be a future.

And what does this mean for us? Here we are, in a pitifully underpopulated field, little-known, underfunded, with one of the major human tasks—the support and appreciation of the multiple cultures that have made our planet habitable—as our primary focus. (You may have thought you were attending a conference called Sounds of the South, but I assure you we could also be attending Sounds of the Southwest or the Northeast, or Sounds of Portland, Oregon, or Sounds of the Nile Basin, or Sounds of Australia, and I assure you the problems discussed would be exactly the same. Only the particulars would be different.)

We spend far too much time in various kinds of quarreling— scrabbling about, I'm afraid for the small amount of money at the bottom of the barrel. We spend far too little time admiring each other for the enormous advances that have been made by our underpaid, overworked coterie. And—most grievous sin of all—we far too seldom combine forces in cross-disciplinary meetings like this, where we can observe the elegance of the work done by the many component parts of our world—whether they are folklorists, recordists, entrepreneurs, librarians, concert presenters, archivists, small record company producers, broadcasters, discographers, historians, musicians, filmmakers, anthropologists, bureaucrats. And if I've left out anybody, I'm sorry. Every one of these roles, these perspectives, is essential. We're not doing something simple.

And every one of these roles must be filled by persons who are not only well-informed and industrious but just a little bit brave too. Let me tell you one final story. Our national capital, you now, wasn't always a democratic capital (small "d" democratic). It was known throughout the South, at least, as a Jim Crow town for a mighty long time. Marian Anderson demonstrated that before the entire nation in the year 1939. But where did the first major indoor concert of indigenous African-American music, presented by African-American traditional musicians and commented upon and introduced by African-American scholars before an integrated audience occur in our national capital? In the Coolidge Auditorium in the Library of Congress in the year 1940.

The Coolidge Auditorium is a small, elegant, totally select concert space where every year the Library of Congress, acting in accordance with the bequest of Mrs. Grace Coolidge, unveils its superb group of Stradivarius stringed instruments in a series of concerts designed to liberate the instruments from their year-long silence and to elevate the spirits of the hard-pressed Washington aristocratic elite. I don't mean to poke fun. My brother Alan and I used to attend these concerts regularly. We would come down from the attic where the Library of Congress powers had consigned us because of the uncouth sounds (like blues and work songs) we listened to regularly, and we would steep ourselves in the flowing harmonies of the entire Beethoven quartet series. It was a real education.

But the Library of Congress was at that time governed by the Librarian, Dr. George Putnam, a small gentleman, as I recall him, quick-moving, decisive, totally aristocratic. He wore pince-nez, if I remember correctly, on a black ribbon around his neck. The Librarian of Congress took Alan Lomax's recommendation and decided to present Josh White and the Golden Gate Quartet and Dr. Sterling Brown and Dr. Alain Locke of Howard University in a formal black-tie-and-tails concert in the Coolidge Auditorium in the year 1940 because, as a librarian, he thought it was both the scholarly and the intellectually appropriate thing to do. And this was at a period when Congress was assailing the Library, calling for budget cuts because of the uncouth activities of the folklorists in that Library, who had been seeking out and recording the views of criminals like Leadbelly and bums like Woody Guthrie.

Librarians can be bold; they can be brave. They often have been and they will continue to be. Archivists can be bold and brave. Record company executives can be brave. Musicians can be brave. Bureaucrats can be brave. Let us try to use our time together at this Conference well, to put aside our personal grievances and our personal prejudices. Let us try to examine together bravely and boldly and dispassionately the complexity of the tasks that face us and see if together we cannot conceive new ways of appropriately dividing up our responsibilities so that each part of our discipline may work with the others, so that each one of us may perform the tasks for which he or she is best suited. Let us try to be as bold and creative and constructive as our intellectual forebears and as the artists we try to serve.

Bill C. Malone

Country Music and the Academy

A Thirty-Year Professional Odyssey

*M*any of us have spent a lifetime collecting, documenting, and evaluating the varying strains of traditional American music. Our role has not been simply repertorial; in a multitude of ways, both overt and subtle, we have done much to define and even to mold, the music that we study. Like the recording director or festival promoter who influences the repertories of performers, the songbook or record-jacket illustrator who links the music to certain visual images, or the radio barn-dance entrepreneur who determines the stage dress and names of his entertainers, scholars and writers of all stripes have participated in shaping public response to America's grassroots musical forms. Only rarely, however, have we paused to admit or evaluate the motives and perceptions that have influenced our work. The performers and their music should not be the sole objects of our concern. We need to bring into our purview the full range of people who have collected, promoted, advertised, disseminated, interpreted, and written about traditional and country music.

As a modest contribution to this task of self-evaluation, I will discuss my own personal odyssey as a scholar of country and Southern music—the process by which I became involved, the limitations under which I have labored, and also my strengths, intellectual growth, and efforts to transcend those early limitations. Perhaps this undertaking will illuminate some of the problems which have accompanied the evolving country music scholarship, and will provoke questions concerning the roles played by non-performers in the making of American folk music.

Intellectual immersion in a subject to which one has an emotional attachment is obviously a perilous enterprise. I have been acutely aware of the pitfalls of such an undertaking, for it has been my fate to be a student of my own culture. The academic phase of my research did not commence until about 1961, near the end of my Ph.D. program in history at the University of Texas in Austin, when I embarked upon a dissertation on commercial country music. Unconsciously, though, my education had begun virtually at birth. When I began my dissertation research, I carried into the project nothing more than the passionate enthusiasm of a lifetime fan of country music, an amateur's knowledge of the subject gleaned from song magazines, gossip, and untold hours of radio listening, a repertory of perhaps a thousand songs which I could sing passably well, and a whole welter of presumptions absorbed since childhood from both home experiences and popular culture.

I had completed a program of coursework in history, with a concentration on the South, but I had no training in folklore, anthropology, sociology, ethnomusicology, or music theory, or in any other discipline which one might presume would be indispensable for a proper understanding of the topic I had chosen. I began my investigation under the supervision of a professor, Joe B. Frantz, whose specialty was business history and who knew less about the subject of country music than I did. He nevertheless had a receptivity to unorthodox subjects that was then unusual. During this same period he was supervising a dissertation on opera in the West. His initial suggestion was that I should do a history of the music publishing business in Nashville, but he permitted an expansion of the subject soon after the project got underway. There were as yet no repositories of country music material, and no journals devoted to the subject. Except for D. K. Wilgus's master's thesis at Ohio State,[1] which dealt with American folksongs on commercial records, almost no academic work ever touched upon the subject of country music. Nor was country music the subject of any books except for a few fan-oriented items such as Mrs. Jimmie Rodgers' romanticized biography of her famous husband, and George D. Hay's paperback reminiscence of the Grand Ole Opry.[2]

I did carry with me the cultural baggage of my childhood years— a panorama of impressions that has ever since shaped my view of country music. Life on a cotton tenant farm in East Texas, at the end of the 1930s, was almost defined by deprivation and scarcity. But music was a constant positive in our lives. Mama was the first singer I ever heard. I can still hear her clear alto voice raised in harmony at the old Tin Top Pentecostal Church, but my most vivid recollections are of those private moments at home when, nursing a disappointment or slight, she sang "Take Your Burden to the Lord and Leave It There." Although I was much too young to understand or empathize with her emotion, as an impressionable young boy I was struck by the powerful intensity conveyed as she rebelled, through song, against the isolation and confinement of her life.

Although gospel songs were most common in our household, my mother also sang the old-fashioned sentimental songs like "The East Bound Train," "Two Little Orphans," and "Little Rosewood Casket," items which I have since heard described as Parlor Songs. Ours was largely an oral tradition, but it was reinforced by a variety of commercially distributed written materials: paperback gospel hymnals, songs copied in school tablets, clippings from magazines or newspapers which were pasted in old grammar books. I cannot now say with assurance where my mother learned those old pop songs, for that is what they were. She learned some of them as a young girl, but the radio hillbillies, to whom we were introduced at the end of the thirties, also included these same songs in their repertories.

Radio, that wondrous link to the outside world, first came into our lives in 1939, when Daddy bought a little Philco battery set. Many of the songs we heard were old favorites, but they were joined by a growing number of new songs and styles, as well as by a new means of preservation and documentation—the song magazines and the picture-songbooks hawked by the performers (and of course by the phonograph records, which actually came into our house considerably later than did the radio broadcasts). The radio also introduced into our household a new group of participants, enlarging our musical world, because once in our home, they became actively part of our lives. These performers carried monikers like Tex, Slim, Hank, Zeke, and Lula Belle. The shows that reached us from Dallas, Fort Worth, Shreveport, Tulsa, the Mexican border, Chicago, and Nashville created a world of intimacy and fantasy, much like that of the soap operas, where music provided escape, diversion, and emotional release. It was a world of old cabin homes, lone prairies, isolated mountain coves, east-bound freight trains, little country churches, and, of course, that promised home in Heaven. It was populated by cowboys, mountaineers, rambling men, hoboes, railroaders, dying orphans, and Sainted Mothers. Even though the Carter Family came to us each night amidst the tawdry commercial advertising of XERF, for the brief fifteen minutes of their program we were transported to those "green fields of Virginia far away." And when Gene Autry sang "Empty Cot in the Bunkhouse," his lonesome lament about the old cowboy who gave his life to save a young calf from the icy blasts of winter, I easily imagined myself chilled by the norther's winds far out on the Texas plains.

In addition, the musicians also played dual roles. They were fantasy figures, but, in a sense, they were also part of our extended family, almost like brothers and sisters. While we elevated them and made them our heroes, we also identified with them and imagined that we could do what they were doing. Country music was still relatively new as an industry in 1939, but Bradley Kincaid and Jimmie Rodgers had already demonstrated in the early thirties, as Gene Autry and Bob Wills did at the end of the decade, that one could make a comfortable living from performing. The music had become, so it seemed, an economic outlet for working-class boys and girls, an exotic escape from the cotton fields, the coal mines, the textile mills, and the diners and beauty shops. Armed with a Sears-Roebuck guitar, a few chords, and a little luck, we too might have our transcriptions played on XEG, and we too might become part of what we perceived as an exciting and glamorous life. All of this music, then, whether in the form inherited from my mother, or in the styles learned from the radio hillbillies or Hollywood Cowboys, converged and became enmeshed in my total musical and cultural world. I forever carried with me the conviction that music was a major sustaining force in the lives of people like my own. Regardless of the forms that country music might one day assume, or of the far-flung audiences that it might eventually win, country music, for me, would always be bound up with my boyhood experiences on that little cotton farm in the late 1930s.

Although I was not then aware of it, the years from 1954 to 1960 at the University of Texas and in Austin provided a nurturing context for my doctoral dissertation on commercial country music. The music I loved, and which to me constituted the bedrock core of country music—that of Hank Williams, Sr., and his contemporaries—had been battered and almost driven from the radio and jukebox by rock-and-roll, or by country-pop, the so-called Nashville "compromise" which was designed to win a new audience by smoothing out country music's rough and rural edges. To put it mildly, I was no friend of either rock-and-roll or country-pop, and was not then prepared to see either as an extension of country music, nor did I then recognize rockabilly music as still another expression of the working-class South. When a package of RCA country entertainers appeared in Austin sometime in 1956, I went to see Hank Snow, not the headliner Elvis Presley, who offended me not only with his unorthodox performing style, but also with what I perceived to be his threat to traditional country music. By early 1961, when my formal research began, the country-music industry had gained renewed commercial vigor and was experiencing one of its periodic revivals. I welcomed any sign of revitalization, and thought that I heard it in bluegrass and in the styles of performers like George Jones and Buck Owens.

The most obvious example of traditional resurgence in those years, of course, was the music of the Urban Folk Revival. Like most of my "hillbilly" friends—graduate-school buddies who liked the same kind of country music I did and who either sang it or listened to it—I delighted in pointing out the phoniness and inauthenticity of the music and in laughing at the earnestness of its young middle-class converts, people who grew up with neither the music nor purple-hull peas and white gravy, and who knew nothing of Sears catalogues in the little brown shack out back. In retrospect, I realize that we were as phony as they, but that our "phoniness" was of a different stripe. Whatever my reservations, I got caught up in the revival too, as did the country-music business as a whole, and I welcomed the refreshing reorientation that some of the revival musicians emphasized. Led by Mike Seeger and the New Lost City Ramblers, a few of the revivalists began resurrecting hillbilly songs from the 1920s and 1930s, which they reproduced with a literal stylistic faithfulness. Although it was easy to mock the rural pretensions of this trio of city boys, I nevertheless bought their albums and valuable songbook[3] and learned the songs which they revived. My singing buddies and I generally stayed clear of the campus folk-song club and instead spent most of our time at a hillbilly bar on the north side of Austin called Threadgill's. Housed in a one-time filling station, Threadgill's was a typical hillbilly joint run by a genial proprietor, Kenneth Threadgill, who sang and yodeled Jimmie Rodgers' songs. The bar was almost a microcosm of the changes then occurring in popular music, and Threadgill's musical scene was a portent of the kind of cultural fusion that developed in Austin later in the 1970s. Transformed by a few graduate students like myself, who were looking for old-time music, both the atmosphere and musical ambience of the bar were altered even further when spillovers from the campus folk-music club began arriving with their songs and instruments. Tolerance of unorthodox musical expressions or cultural styles was not my strong suit back in those days, and so I was not particularly impressed when a student wearing a sheepskin coat and tattered jeans joined us one night with her autoharp and a little group of companions known as the Waller Creek Boys. Of course, neither Janis Joplin nor the rest of us realized the full musical or cultural import of what we were witnessing, and none of us could have known the directions that she and American popular music would travel just a few short years later. (The worst confession I should make is that on the first night she came in with her group she looked across the room at where I was sitting with my guitar, and she said, "He doesn't want us here." Her perception was probably correct. Although I soon came to admire Janis's spirited renditions of Carter Family and Rose Maddox tunes, my initial reaction must have been, "Well, here come the beatniks and their fake folk music.")

The Folk Revival was accompanied by at least a slight stirring of interest in old-time country music by a few folklorists. My own introduction to these scholars came through the work of Alan Lomax, who had made at least stray references to hillbillies in his published folksong collections. His most explicit statement linking traditional music to modern commercial forms was his famous 1959 *Esquire* article "Bluegrass Background: Folk Music with Overdrive."[4] About two years later I began to learn about the interests of men like D. K. Wilgus, John Greenway, Ed Kahn, and that indefatigable champion of vernacular music, Archie Green. The whole field of folklore scholarship became acquainted with these men in 1965, when the *Journal of American Folklore* published a series of articles by them in its "Hillbilly Issue."[5] These folklorists generally demonstrated interest only in the commercial music of the pre-1941 era, and their research was concentrated on the persistence of tradition in such music. Furthermore, like their more literary predecessors in folklore scholarship, the hillbilly folklorists were preoccupied with the Appalachians as the seedbed and preserve of white American folk music. My introduction to the hillbilly folklorists came almost simultaneously with my discovery, in the Austin Public Library, of that remarkable body of recordings, the Folkways *Anthology of American Folk Music.*[6] Much of the material there, which had come from Harry Smith's private collection of old 78-rpm recordings, was new to me. But I also found selections by such old friends as Uncle Dave Macon and the Carter Family, a revelation which reinforced my belief that commercial country music and folk music were inextricably linked. I later learned that a rather extensive number of folk-music fans were making a similar discovery. These sources directly affected my scholarship, and the perceptions which lay behind it. I leaned heavily upon the hillbilly folklorists because theirs was about the only available academic material that ever touched upon country music. I spent an inordinate amount of time trying to establish country music's folk roots, and, like the folklorists, I was perhaps too concerned with "mountain" origins. My fascination with the Southern mountains long preceded my introduction to either folklore or country music scholarship. The novels of John Fox, Jr., the movie "Sergeant York," a multitude of songs like "The Trail of the Lonesome Pine," "Blue Ridge Mountain Blues," and "Carry Me Back to the Mountains," and musicians with names like the Smoky Mountain Boys and the Clinch Mountain Clan, all conspired to invest the Southern Appalachians with the misty haze of romance and to reinforce in my mind the archetypical image of mountain hollows populated by a peculiarly musical people.

When my research began, the central question I faced was how to properly document and evaluate a topic as massive as the history of country music, and one about which so little had been written. The proper answer, of course, was that one should not undertake such a project, but no one gave me such advice. I looked at anything I could find—scholarly journals and books, folk-song collections, hillbilly picture-songbooks, popular magazines, song magazines like *Country Song Roundup*, Sears and Montgomery Ward catalogues, record-industry catalogues and brochures, record-liner notes, newspapers, and radio and entertainment-industry publications. For instance, I may have been the first person to do extensive research in *Billboard* magazine from 1928 to 1964. My interviews were done in a rather scatter-gun fashion, first in Nashville with the help of Jo Walker, the executive secretary of the fledgling Country Music Association, and later with anyone I could contact among industry people and both active and inactive musicians and their offspring. Having neither a car nor a tape recorder during those first few years of research, my "interviews" were often nothing more than a set of hastily scribbled notes written on the performer's touring bus or backstage during intermission.

Probably the greatest boon to my early investigations, and an incalculable resource for all students of country music, was the exhaustively documented research done by the network of record collectors in the United States and around the world. I learned about some of them through their advertisements in the song magazines and record catalogues, and about others in conversations with Archie Green and Ed Kahn. Through the efforts of these collectors I was introduced to the wondrous science of discography and to the auction lists, mimeographed newsletters, and printed magazines, such as *Disc Collector*, *Country Directory*, *Record Research*, and *Country and Western Spotlight*, where their quiet and diligent research had been appearing for years. The greatest revelation of all, perhaps, was that the collection of American grassroots music was a world-wide enterprise and that an Australian, John Edwards, was one of the great collectors of American hillbilly music. My naivete and newness to the field of discography were undoubtedly irritating to some of the collectors, and a few of them only reluctantly provided assistance. I will therefore always have a special place in my heart for Bob Pinson, who sought me out and unselfishly provided assistance when I was floundering about. (Bob is now employed by the Country Music Foundation, but at that time his private collection was one of the largest in existence.) Although some of the collectors exhibited interest only in the music of the pre-1941 period, or what John Edwards called "the Golden Age of Hillbilly Music," many of these specialists tended to be catholic in their approach to country music. The fascination with Western Swing, for example, which many of them demonstrated, brought some balance to a field too often dominated by an emphasis on the Southeast or by an Appalachian fixation. (The Western Swing advocates, however, sometimes ride their hobby horse too far, and they similarly have to be reminded of country music's diversity.)

As I looked around for academic companionship in the early 1960s, I therefore found some support among folklorists and popular culturists and, of course, among collectors, fans, and ardent "amateurs." I found, though, that even among some of these devotees "commercial" music was suspect. History, my own academic discipline, had usually ignored music, or had dealt only with its High-Art manifestations. In Southern history, and in Southern-oriented scholarship generally, one found little recognition of the role played by music in the lives of plain white people. It is beyond the scope of this paper to explore the reasons for the differing responses made by intellectuals to black and white musical styles, but the interest accorded to white folk music had been minimal compared to that given to black music. At best, one found the tendency to take seriously only the most quaint, antiquated, or romantic forms of white folk music. For example, historian Tom Clark provided wonderful vignettes of nineteenth-century fiddlers in *The Rampaging Frontier*, but in referring to the "hillbilly rabble on the radio" in another book on the Kentucky River,[7] he implied that folk musicians lost their credibility or authenticity when they tried to make money from their talents. Indeed, his larger implication was that they were no longer folk at all. The famous Agrarians of the early 1930s made some comments about the "frolic" music of an older rural South, but said nothing about the rural music that surrounded them in their own time, or that which could be heard from the stage of the Grand Ole Opry in the same city where many of them pursued their scholarship. One suspects that country music was a bit too crass and commercial to fit the static image of folk art that the Agrarians envisioned. In their famous manifesto *I'll Take My Stand*, Andrew Lytle was the only Agrarian who devoted any attention to the culture of the plain folk, and his discussion was highly romanticized. He lists, for example, a number of fiddle tunes and then says, "With a list of such dances as a skeleton, some future scholar could reconstruct with a common historical accuracy the culture of this people."[8] By 1930, when his essay was published, the "folk" of course had already gone far beyond the skeleton of fiddle tunes to which he referred, and despite his advice that they should "throw out the radio," people everywhere had incorporated that remarkable communications device into their everyday culture.

Ignoring, or at best romanticizing, folk music, in both its traditional and commercialized forms, was part of a more general neglect—among scholars of all stripes—of plain folk culture. Since the 1920s a rash of monographs and statistical studies had been appearing, many of them produced by Howard Odum and his students at the University of North Carolina, or inspired by the New Deal's rediscovery of the folk. However, except for Frank Owsley's *Plain Folk of the Old South*[9], a work also marred by a tendency to romanticize its subjects, no general historical survey of the Southern folk was available when my own research got underway.

Why the long scholarly neglect of commercial country music? Long before my academic research began, I perceived that "respectable" people disliked country music because of its associations with disreputable, uneducated social and economic failures—that is, rednecks, holy rollers, and denizens of honky tonks. This perception was reaffirmed once I became part of the world of academic scholarship. Country music did not fit the images that scholars had of folk culture, and, most important, the genre's intense commercialism seemed to set it starkly apart from "real" folk music. Apparently, folk musicians did not travel in sordid surroundings, nor did they traffic in the world of commerce. The "purer" varieties of mountain music, and even bluegrass, won slow and often grudging acceptance from the scholars; Jimmie Rodgers, Hank Williams, and George Jones did not.

Although I shared some of the preconceptions of my colleagues in folklore, and no doubt many of their misconceptions, I also had my own agenda when I first began to write *Country Music, U.S.A.* My first priority, I believed, was simply to tell country music's story; hence my emphasis on narrative at the expense of interpretation. While insisting on the persistence of tradition in country music, arguing that "the folk musician did not cease to be folk merely because he stepped in front of a microphone,"[10] I was just as determined to validate the music's commercial history and to show that folk music and commercial intent were age-old partners. Commercialization, I argued, had been linked to folk music well back into the Middle Ages. The early ballad hawkers, broadside vendors, and tavern fiddlers had been the ancestors of Johnny Cash and Merle Haggard and, indeed, of ASCAP, BMI, and RCA. Commercialization was valuable because it permitted the wide dissemination of grassroots forms, and it was just one additional means by which working-class people found economic alternatives to farming, coal mining, and industrial labor. Most important, it was a fact of American life.

While maintaining that country music was a reflection of societal changes, and of a changing folk—a conservative people whose long history had been marked by migration and incessant economic transformation—I was particularly determined to demonstrate that the music was not simply a mountain-derived form which accompanied the mountaineers' move to the industrial cities. Mountain musicians had certainly made vital contributions to commercial country music. The culture that surrounded them, as well as the music they played, as pointed out earlier, had always exerted a powerful romantic appeal for many Americans. Country music, however, was a remarkably eclectic, "impure" mix that showcased the influence of many styles of music, both commercial and folk, and it was a peculiar blending of urban and rural forms. My own Southwestern origins may have made me acutely conscious of the unique cultural confluence of that region, for one could scarcely listen to the radio during my youthful growing up days without hearing the jazz-inflected dance tunes of bands like the Light Crust Doughboys and Bob Wills' Texas Playboys. These musicians were no less "folk" in origin than those who came from the mountains, and their earliest performing experience came in the fiddle bands and house parties of the rural Southwest. The form of music they created, later described as Western Swing, was an amalgam of city and rural styles allied with the western image.

Country Music, U.S.A., the first published product of my personal and professional odyssey, appeared in 1968. Written by a historian, and perceived by him as history, it nevertheless carried the imprint of the American Folklore Society. The book received generally favorable reviews, and at least a moderately successful commercial reception. It has since remained in print through three different book jackets, three paperback editions, and a thorough revision in 1985. I am aware that a variety of phenomena, both cultural and commercial, contributed to the original publication and continued sales of my book. The burgeoning of the country-music industry, and its aggressive expansion through the leadership of the Country Music Association; the widespread public exposure prompted by the founding of the Nashville Network; the short-lived Urban Cowboy craze; the political conservatism of the last twenty years; Jimmie Carter's presidency and the rediscovery of the South—all have prompted and preserved interest in a music which is presumed to be socially conservative and Southern.

Still, I would like to think that my book has also succeeded on its own merits. I hope that it has contributed in some measure to the acceptance and legitimacy of country music among scholars. It has been particularly gratifying to see the appearance of academic courses on country music. Most of them, however, seem to have been offered in curricula outside of the history profession. What has been the reaction within my own discipline? *Country Music, U.S.A.* was reviewed favorably in most of the historical journals, (although the *Journal of American History* has never reviewed it), and I have given programs or participated in sessions of the Organization of American Historians, the Southern Historical Association, and other organizations. Country music has been the theme of two opening sessions of the Southern Historical Association (in 1977 and 1989). Nevertheless, a reference to the music in a history text or journal article is still rare. Histories of the 1920s invariably refer to jazz; none speaks of Hillbilly. Studies of the cultural ferment and rebellion of the 1960s usually mention Bob Dylan, the Beatles, or Woodstock; none of them makes even a passing reference to Merle Haggard. Textbooks and other studies of Southern history, where one might expect to find discussions of country music, have been surprisingly barren in their treatments of the subject.

It is encouraging to note, however, that a gradual awakening of interest in the Southern plain folk and their culture has been under-way for the past fifteen years or so—much of it influenced and in-formed by the "new social history" and by those who have been concerned with the story of the "inarticulate." The field is still tiny compared to what has been done on Black history, and there is as yet nothing comparable to Lawrence Levine's *Black Culture and Black Consciousness.*[11] One deterrent, of course, has been the relative pau-city of source materials and of repositories to house the material and make it available to scholars. Happily, indispensable information is now available in the Library and Media Center at the Country Music Foundation in Nashville and at the University of North Carolina in the John Edwards Memorial/Southern Folklife Collection, allied with the oral history material in the Southern Historical Collection. Gradually the raw materials for a study of the music and its relationship to the larger culture are becoming available to scholars.

Although little attention has been devoted to the subject of country music in the discipline of history or related fields of scholarship, a few recent works do deserve special mention. Jack Temple Kirby in *Media-Made Dixie*, for instance, argues that country musicians have contributed to the image of a "visceral South."[12] J. Wayne Flynt in *Dixie's Forgotten People* and *Poor but Proud*[13] made a valiant effort to integrate music into the social history of his subjects—arguing rightly that music was a sustaining force and a means of communication—but he seems unable to rid himself of romantic speculation about the music's origins and about its means of dissemination. He emphasizes dulcimers, which were rarely used by the people he discusses, but says very little about fiddles, which were omnipresent among the folk. Grady McWhiney's *Cracker Culture*[14] similarly describes the centrality of music in the lives of the people and is correct in emphasizing continuity between their lives today and their historical past, but is too preoccupied with Celtic themes. When he hears the fiddle, he hears the strains of an ancient bagpipe; somebody else might discern a different influence, including vaudeville or ragtime, that went into the making of the music.

Among the more successful of the recent books have been David Whisnant's *All That Is Native and Fine*[15], Jacquelyn Hall's *Like a Family*[16], and James Gregory's *American Exodus*.[17] Whisnant refuted some of the romantic shibboleths associated with "mountain music" and demonstrated that the dulcimer and many of the songs and dances considered to be the "purest" expressions of Appalachian music were in fact relatively recent imports brought in by cultural missionaries. The Hall and Gregory books, which deal respectively with Piedmont cotton-mill culture and the Okie culture of California, do wonderful jobs of demonstrating the central role that music played in creating an identity for people and in sustaining a form of community during periods of stress and adversity. In Gregory's words, country music was "the language of a sub-culture," an effective instrument used by the Okies, a supposedly inarticulate people, to express their experience to themselves and to the world at large.

In conclusion, I shall not spare my own work a final measure of criticism, and will discuss where I am trying to go next and where all of us in the field of folk and country-music scholarship should be headed. I hope that I have learned and matured over the years, and that my mistakes and false emphases have not misled or lured other people down the wrong roads. The 1985 revision of *Country Music, U.S.A.* was, I think, much better than the original of 1968, but, given the volatile nature of popular culture, the 1985 revision was almost outdated by the time it appeared.

I have always felt that my book was never adequately reviewed. Reviewers, of course, did freely point out both strengths and weaknesses, but almost no one engaged me in the kind of dialogue that would have been useful to me and to the larger world of folk scholarsip. Ardent country-music fans were so pleased to find a serious book on their favorite kind of music that they overlooked mistakes and simplifications, and tended to be displeased only if their heroes were omitted from the story. Critics, however, should not have been so tolerant. While noting errors of fact, they should also have questioned some of the assumptions on which the book was based, or at least should have demanded greater clarification or proof. Is the music Southern in either origin or ultimate meaning?[18] Does it really make sense to discuss both "country" and "western" styles as part of a common entity? Is country music a direct outgrowth of folk music? Or is the music preeminently a product of commercial developments and decisions? And is country music truly a reflection of the society in which it exists? Too often, the answers to such questions have been presented simply and accepted with little challenge, and only rarely have they inspired the kinds of rigorous debate that any field of serious scholarship deserves.

The recognition of country music's diversity has sharpened my awareness of both the South's cultural pluralism,[19] and the interrelatedness of musical forms. This music, like the culture that produced it, is neither socially, ethnically, nor stylistically pure. It is neither Celtic nor Anglo-Saxon. Like Black music—with which it has always had a fruitful interrelationship—it is an eclectic musical product developed on American soil and out of American experiences. While this form of music has often reflected the realities of people's lives, it has just as often appealed to their desire for release, escape, fantasy, and romance. And it has often embodied the confusions and contradictions of the people who have nourished and preserved it. The ongoing dialectic within country music—witnessed both in the industry and among the fans who sustain it—is basically a question of identity and ultimate goal. The music began its commercial existence as a working-class expression, but through almost seventy years of development both it and the people who cherished it have persistently sought entrance into America's cultural mainstream. One finds, therefore, an unending pattern of ambivalence in a music that would be simultaneously working class and middle class, hedonistic and pious, ruggedly individualistic and patriotic, Southern and American. Industry leaders in the recent past have tried to market a musical product that is all things to all people, and have instead disseminated a music that in its attempts to be popular is often lacking in either distinctiveness or substance.

The cultural ambivalence, or what I have described as an on-going dialectic in country music, is merely the most recent manifestation of a similar complex of tensions, conflicts, and paradoxes that have lain at the heart of Southern folk culture throughout 350 years of American history. This conviction has drawn me inexorably toward a thorough study of the relationship between country music and Southern folk culture, an analysis not found or only hinted at in *Country Music, U.S.A.* This project will take the form of a cultural interpretation of the music of the Southern working class, treated thematically and chronologically, from pre-twentieth-century folk roots to the present. The power asserted by myth, symbol, and fantasy in creating the music that I love and study will of course occupy a major portion of my research, as will the efforts exerted by the folk themselves to utilize music for a wide variety of purposes, including survival itself. These emphases, however, will not blind me to the role played by the commercial process. As argued earlier, one of my basic intents always was to demonstrate that country music, as a *commercial* phenomenon, was worth taking seriously, and that this commercialization was part of a process that long predated the settlement of the Southern frontier. My romantic bent, however—the desire to believe that the folk themselves controlled the making and preservation of their music—may have inhibited my ability to recognize the full implications of commercialization.

The most recent phase of commercialization has attracted few serious students of country music or the folk process: that is, the role played by promoters, businessmen, record producers, merchandizers, and studio engineers. Bill Ivey made a similar criticism of my work in his review of the 1985 revision of *Country Music, U.S.A.*[20] His chief complaint was that I still clung the romantic folk emphasis, that I wanted desperately to believe that "the people" really controlled country music, that singers sang what they wanted to sing, that what they sang was what people wanted to hear. Ivey's point was that the process has been so transformed by commercialization that country music is virtually defined by the people who control the studios, by the engineers and sessions directors who produce the records, and by the decision makers who determine which songs will be played on top-forty radio or the eight-in-a-row stations. It is admittedly difficult for someone with a background such as mine, who grew up in a culture where music was a part of daily life, and where it was a part of the emotional fabric of growth and development, to think that the music is controlled by a small group of powerful commercial men in a few music centers around the country. Nevertheless, this is a topic that we all ought to take into account. My historical understanding informs me that something similar to the process which Ivey describes has always been at work in both country music and its folk ancestors.

On the other hand, I also know that regardless of its origins or original intent, music often takes on a life and meaning of its own that may be far different from the designs of those who made and commercially disseminated it. At heart I will always be that little boy of long ago, clinging to the Philco battery radio and thrilling to the sounds of singers like Roy Acuff, the Bailes Brothers, and Gene Autry. I do not know why Autry chose to sing "Empty Cot in the Bunk House," or what sordid merchandising methods may have underlay the marketing of his performance. I only know that the song brought joy into our simple little farmhouse, and that it transported me to a world of enchantment and romance that still sometimes glimmers through the murky haze of commerce that now surrounds the country-music business.

Paul Oliver

Overseas Blues
Europeans and the Blues

Some people say that them overseas blues ain't bad,
(Lord, of course they are . . .)
Some people tell me that them overseas blues ain't bad
(What was the matter with 'em? . . .)
It must not have been them overseas blues I had.
                —Charley Patton, "Down the Dirt Road Blues"
                     (Paramount 12854, June 14, 1929)

To many blues collectors the recordings of Charley Patton epit-
omize the early blues: dark, intensely felt, often brooding
songs performed to a rhythmically complex guitar setting and
sung with a coarse-grained but expressive voice. Other collectors
would hand the palm to Robert Johnson, whose short life had the
stuff of legend, and whose shrill, passionate songs were comple-
mented by slide guitar which was to influence the generation of post-
war Chicago blues singers. The recordings of these and literally hundreds of other singers are easily available on long-play disks, and
many on CD, so anyone coming to the blues today can form opinions
on their respective merits, and build up a personal collection without
difficulty. There are innumerable records to choose from, many
books to read, and much advice on new issues to be obtained from
dealers' catalogues.

I must admit that I had been collecting blues for about ten years
before I even heard a record by Robert Johnson, even longer before
I heard one by Charley Patton. Finding out about the music at all
wasn't easy in England during and after World War II, and yet the
curious thing is that much of the research and writing on blues has
emanated from Europe. How was it that enthusiasts who shared nei-

ther country, color, nor culture with the black Americans who created a unique folk music thousands of miles away from them, were
able to contribute substantially to knowledge and understanding of
the idiom? I cannot pretend to be able to answer that question completely, but in this chapter I hope to show something of how it came
about, and what the extent of the contribution of Europeans has been
to the study of blues.

Before going any further I should emphasize that there is a whole
other subject about which much has been written already—the
adoption by young white musicians and singers in Europe of the
blues styles, and their eventual international success in influencing
the course of popular music. From Ottilie Patterson to the Rolling
Stones, from Alexis Korner to Eric Clapton these associations with
the blues make up a story in itself, but it is not one that I intend
to pursue here. My account is concerned with the less newsworthy
unfolding of blues appreciation and documentation—and that is
complex enough.

It would be wise to start at the beginning—if only there were
some way of deciding what the beginning may have been. For instance, it is known that the pianist Jimmy Yancey performed in England at the turn of the century—but as a dancer, not as a pianist.
The guitarist Lonnie Johnson may have toured around 1919 with the
Southern Syncopated Orchestra—but if he did, did he sing blues?
That orchestra did include the soprano saxophonist Sidney Bechet;
he and the New Orleans trumpet player Tommy Ladnier were playing in Europe, even as far as Russia, soon after. There's no doubt that
Europeans heard the instrumental sounds of blues even if they did
not hear blues vocals. But then, singers like Alberta Hunter, Edith
Wilson, Ethel Waters, Maggie Jones all sang in shows in London and
Paris in the 1920s and '30s. They were exponents of what used to be
termed the "Classic Blues"—show singers with a jazz-blues intona-
tion and expression. Clubs like that run by the expatriate black artiste
Ada "Bricktop" Smith featured black entertainers, and some may well
have sung blues as part of their acts. But the meaning of the term was
by no means defined.

The early history of blues study in Europe, like that in the United
States, is bound up with the appreciation of jazz. Writers on jazz such
as Hugues Panassié in France, Joost van Praag in Holland, Robert Gof-
fin in Belgium, or Spike Hughes in England usually gave some recog-

nition of the importance of blues to the form and color of the music. Even if there were no blues singers visiting Europe, there had been a modest number of blues records issued since 1923, when a Lizzie Miles record was released in England. Other records followed, including some by Bessie Smith which sold well enough to induce English Parlophone to commission John Hammond to record her in 1933, for what was to be her last session. When she died as a result of an automobile accident, a "Bessie Smith Memorial Album" of eight discs was issued in Britain and remained in the catalogue for twenty years. By the later 1930s there were recordings by Meade Lux Lewis and the blues pianists whose popularity generated the "boogie woogie craze"—including the powerful modern blues of the singing bartender, Joe Turner.

Most enthusiasts who began to enjoy blues in its own right came to it through jazz, but my own exposure was somewhat different and probably unique. As a young teenager I was doing summer farm work in Suffolk as part of the "war effort" in 1942, and a U.S. air base was being constructed nearby. Black servicemen were "digging in," and I heard two of them on fatigues singing what were to me the strangest, most moving, and most thrilling songs I had ever heard; from that day on I was hooked on blues. Soon after, a 60-page booklet, *The Background of the Blues* by Iain Laing, the China correspondent of the *Sunday Times*, was published by the Worker's Music Association. "The blues is not the whole of jazz, but the whole of blues is jazz. It has no existence apart from this idiom," he wrote unequivocally.[1] My own experience had already called this into question, but I devoured the booklet (as did thousands of others; the WMA could not reprint it fast enough), which had a long section with quotations and some explanation of their content. During the war years two writers, Max Jones and Albert McCarthy, edited a well-produced magazine, *Jazz Music*, which usually included features on blues records, and snippets about singers. It also included a detailed listing of the "Okeh Race Record Series," laboriously compiled from the label details on records owned by collectors.

In the small but enthusiastic European blues world, records figured prominently, for they provided the only real way of getting to know the music. Fortunately, American servicemen were often willing to exchange them for swing discs, and after the War when many returned to the United States, more blues recordings came into circulation. Collectors like myself set up trading links with U. S. jazz enthusiasts, exchanging our Harry Roy, Ambrose and Jack Hylton records for blues. Not knowing what to collect, I tended to go for curious names at first: records by Peetie Wheatstraw, the Yas Yas Girl, Bumble Bee Slim. I probably overlooked discs by Tommy Johnson or Charley Jordan. Many of the records had unfamiliar words, and puzzling titles like "CWA Blues," "Southern Flood Blues," " The Dirty Dozen," or "The Death of Walter Barnes." Fascinated, I tried to find out everything I could about them, becoming in the process a well-known face at the American Embassy Library. An inveterate book-hound even then, I was soon building up a considerable collection of books and references of my own.

One aspect of European jazz research which embraced blues was discography—the listing of all known facts about records by musicians, bands, and singers. During the wartime Occupation of France the discographer Charles Delaunay had produced his *Hot Discography*, covertly writing it on "onion skin."[2] In Britain, researchers sought duplicate copies of the files held by record companies, and clad these bare bones by gathering details about the records in the possession of just about every jazz collector. A network of information exchange built up, but to hear other collections meant a lot of traveling, for until tape recorders came in and were cheap enough for home use, there was no other way of sharing the sounds. Many collections were already remarkable, and were providing the reference base for informed articles.

In 1946 Max Jones wrote a 35-page essay "On Blues" for Albert McCarthy's *PL Yearbook of Jazz*.[3] As far as I am aware it was the first serious analysis and classification of blues to be published anywhere. Two years later, Derrick Stewart-Baxter started a blues column in *Jazz Journal* which was to run for thirty-five years. My first articles date from 1951 for the same journal; three years later I began a regular series on "Sources of Afro-American Music" for *Music Mirror* and had my own platform from which to proclaim the blues news. This led to several radio broadcasts on such subjects as "Washboard Bands" or "City Blues" and started a relationship with the BBC which still continues today. In France Jacques Demetre had his own column in Delaunay's *Jazz Hot* and I made frequent trips to France (ostensibly educational) to meet with him, the discographer Kurt Mohr, and others.

Paris in the 1950s was made more exciting by the many jazz musicians visiting from the States who were prevented, as the result of an inane Musicians' Union-AFM dispute, from working in Britain. It was possible to talk with Sydney Bechet, Lil Armstrong, Sammy Price, or Mezz Mezzrow about the singers they had accompanied. There was also an expatriate community of black American musicians and writers, and through a friend I met up with Richard Wright, who had a profound influence on my thoughts about the significance of blues. We used to meet at his favorite *rive gauche* haunt, *Le Trianon*. I recall it as somewhat seedy but buzzing with intellectual life in those years of existentialism. This year I returned to find that it is now a tourist trap, all chrome and glass; serious conversation there is out of the question.

In 1951 it was possible to hear the blues in person. Hughes Panassié had been instrumental in bringing guitarist and blues singer Big Bill Broonzy and the pianist Blind John Davis over to France; I chased them halfway across the country. Later that year, in September, Alan Lomax presented Big Bill Broonzy to a limited but ecstatic audience at the Kingsway Hall, London. Josh White and Lonnie Johnson had also visited in 1951 as "variety artists" (a way of getting round the Union ban). They misjudged their audiences and disappointed the blues fans, who felt that in Big Bill they were hearing the real thing. Later, it seemed that Big Bill too had somewhat tailored his approach to suit an audience who favored the old-time blues rather than modern sounds. But Broonzy's powerful holler, his faultless guitar work, and engaging personality won him and the blues many friends. Among them was the Belgian blues writer Yannick Bruynoghe, to whom he dictated part of his autobiography, writing the rest in his own hand. In those days I was a part-time graphic artist and was asked to do a few drawings for *Big Bill Blues*, which was published in London by Cassell.[4] It gave me an opportunity to get to know Big Bill rather better—the young Brother John Sellers too, whose knowledge of the recent blues scene helped to fill out the picture.

Then in 1958 Big Bill Broonzy died of cancer. Many jazz writers had considered him to be the "last of the blues singers," but the British bandleader Chris Barber initiated a policy of bringing over other blues singers, still to play as variety artists, until the Union ban eventually collapsed. Brownie McGhee and Sonny Terry, Muddy Waters and Otis Spann—with Muddy playing electric guitar, to the dismay of some—and by 1960 Roosevelt Sykes, Speckled Red, Little Brother Montgomery, Champion Jack Dupree, Jimmie Rushing, and others had all visited Britain. By this time I was writing regularly for Albert McCarthy's *Jazz Monthly* magazine, and I did extended interviews with many of the visitors for this or other periodicals; some have been reprinted in *Blues Off the Record.*[5] Getting to know the singers personally, inviting them to our home, and talking to them at length helped me to unravel what many singers on record were singing about. I had been working for a number of years on a book on meaning and content in the blues, and completed it in 1958. Richard Wright, who showed it to a rather surprised Martin Luther King, offered to write an introduction which I valued immensely. A printer's strike delayed publication for two years, but *Blues Fell This Morning* was published in London in 1960[6]; a French edition (with the blues translated by Jacques Demetre) was published as *Le Monde du Blues* and with the support of Raymond Queneau was awarded the Prix d'Etrangers. I have recently had the pleasure of revising *Blues Fell This Morning* for a thirtieth anniversary edition.[7]

At this distance in time I wonder at my temerity in writing the book without having been to the States. But the simple fact was that I could not afford to do so. Yannick Bruynogue had visited Chicago in 1957 and wrote about the blues singers he had heard. He was followed by Georges Adins, another Belgian, who even stayed with Sonny Boy Williamson (Rice Miller) in East St. Louis. Then in 1959 Jacques Demetre and Marcel Chauvard made a "Journey to the Land of the Blues" (as they titled their articles based on the trip) to New York, Detroit, and Chicago.[8] As an indirect result of the publication of *Blues Fell This Morning* I was offered a small grant "for leaders and specialists" under the auspices of the U.S. Department of State, which enabled me to make a research trip in the summer of 1960. My wife Val and I sank our meager savings into the trip but had no money to do any recording, apart from a commission from the BBC to do interviews with blues singers, with the assurance that they would all be paid. A young collector and discographer, Robert M. W. Dixon, organized a recording fund to make some limited field recording possible. It is indicative of the support and friendship among blues enthusiasts that so many backed this venture, either with loans for recording or with information and contacts.

This is not the place to give a detailed account of that trip, which has been documented elsewhere. Sufficient to say that it took us to Washington, New York, Detroit, Chicago, St. Louis, Memphis, New Orleans, Shreveport, Dallas, Fort Worth, and Oakland, and to numerous small communities in Mississippi, Arkansas, Louisiana, and Texas. We stayed in Chicago with John Steiner and with Muddy Waters, travelled from Memphis with Chris Strachwitz, who was to start his Arhoolie record label as an outcome of some of the recordings made on the journey, met up with Mack McCormick in Texas, Lindberg O'Brien in St. Louis, and other blues enthusiasts who joined us in our searches. It was a difficult time, and the South in particular was soon to change. So too was the blues, though we were not to realize it for quite a while. In all it was an extraordinary experience and one from which I still draw inspiration.

The 1960s witnessed a considerable expansion in the blues audience, and a couple of enthusiasts in the unlikely setting of Bexhill-on-Sea (known as a geriatric resort), Simon Napier and Mike Leadbitter, decided to start a blues magazine. It was not the first: credit for that goes to the Belgian Serge Tonneau and his *R and B Panorama*, which had, however, a modern blues emphasis. The new magazine which started in 1963, *Blues Unlimited*, was the first English-language publication. There was no shortage of contributors, and it maintained a monthly publication schedule for many years. It was a decade before the first American blues magazine, *Living Blues*, was to appear. By that time there were many European blues magazines. In 1965 Bob Groom started his *Blues World*, also in England, while Neil Slaven and Mike Vernon ran *R and B Monthly* for a couple of years in the mid-1960s. In Europe there were also many blues magazines appearing, such as *Mr Blues* published in Holland, or the Swedish magazine *Jefferson*.

Mike Leadbitter was unquestionably among the most active blues researchers of the 1960s. While still in his twenties he amassed formidable files, particularly on post-war blues singers, and he published a steady stream of articles in his own magazine and in others, as well as many record-sleeve notes and discographies of individual artists. Discography had always been a prominent field of activity for European enthusiasts, who perhaps placed more importance on recorded sound in these years than some of their American counterparts, largely cut off as we were from the live music. It had come a long way from Delaunay's *Hot Discography*. In 1949 Albert McCarthy, Dave

Carey and Ralph Venables commenced the publication of a multi-volume *Jazz Directory* which, in spite of its name, included all known blues and gospel records.[9] Publication continued until 1957 when, after seven volumes, it had reached K-Lo. The publisher ceased to underwrite it, and the project folded. After a hiatus Jørgen Grunnet Jepsen in Denmark took up the burden in part, with another multi-volume work, *Jazz Records 1942–1962*, which had a similarly catholic approach to contents.[10] Still more comprehensive, if never-ending, was Walter Bruyninckx's massive discography *Fifty Years of Recorded Jazz*.[11] The dean of European jazz discographers, Brian Rust, coped with the earlier period in a 2000-page work, *Jazz Records 1897–1942*, printed at first privately and then by Storyville, publishers of a long-standing British jazz periodical.[12] Rust had no particular interest in blues, but he had a policy of including all blues recordings which had jazz musicians on them, and thus produced a useful, if erratic work.

During this period of jazz collation, blues discographers were also energetically compiling their files. Quite the most complete were those kept by Robert M. W. Dixon and the late John Godrich. I offered to introduce Bob Dixon to Brian Rust, whose exacting standards were more than matched by the blues discographers' meticulous files. As a result Rust took on the publication of *Blues and Gospel Records 1902–1942* by Dixon and Godrich, more generally known by the compilers' names or simply as "the blues Bible." Second and third editions followed, published by Storyville, as collectors continued to uncover more material and sent in their data.[13] Dixon and Godrich were unequalled in their thoroughness, adding to the conventional session information on 78-rpm issues detailed notes on anomalies, uncertainties, mistitlings, and other data. They covered all "Race" material, excluding religious choirs and black non-blues entertainers. Unissued titles were also listed, and an important feature was the inclusion of Library of Congress and other pre-1942 field recordings, considerably expanded by John Cowley for the third edition (which extended from 1902 to 1943). Other discographical works on early blues continued to appear, perhaps the most engaging being Max E. Vreede's *Paramount 12000–13000 Series* devoted to one label, with the addition of composer credits and numerous reproductions of advertising ephemera.[14]

While pre-World War II blues and gospel discography was now

very thoroughly documented, there were serious gaps in knowledge of post-War blues. This Mike Leadbitter and Neil Slaven proposed to rectify. Though apparently a simpler task, being concerned with more recent records, it was in some ways more difficult. In addition to items from the larger companies, post-war blues were issued on a multitude of small, independent labels, a large number of them keeping poor files, if any at all. Leadbitter made trips to the United States to seek out information from such companies, as well as to interview blues singers for *Blues Unlimited*. Eventually *Blues Records 1943–1966* was published in 1968.[15] Though it did not match the immaculate work by Dixon and Godrich, it was still of great value. Gospel records—which had proliferated—were not included, and the editors exercized some decisions on what should be included or omitted that dissatisfied some collectors. Cedric Hayes and Bob Laughton have for many years published discographies of the largely unresearched field of gospel music, and their *Gospel Records 1943–1969* is due for publication. In 1987 a much-expanded volume of *Blues Records 1949–1970* covering A-K was published under the names of the original authors.[16] Sadly however, Mike Leadbitter had died in 1974 of tubercular meningitis at the age of thirty-one. It is a curious and tragic sidelight on European blues research that Boom, Leadbitter, Chauvard, Bruynoghe, and Napier all died prematurely.

While all this discographical activity was in progress, much else was happening in the 1960s. It was the period of a succession of extraordinary "rediscoveries" of blues singers, and the discovery of others, to which British researchers like Bruce Bastin, Mike Rowe, and John Broven among several, made important contributions through self-financed field trips. In 1962 the first of the American Folk Blues Festivals toured Europe; they were organized by Horst Lippmann and Fritz Rau, members of the German Jazz Federation. Carefully chosen, presented well, the Folk Blues Festival was a great success which continued annually for the rest of the decade. The roster of blues singers included veterans and young bluesmen alike, and those who attended the series heard John Henry Barbee, Juke Boy Bonner, Eddie Boyd, Clifton Chenier, Willie Dixon, Sugar Pie DeSanto, Sleepy John Estes, Buddy Guy, John Lee Hooker, Lightnin' Hopkins, Shakey Horton, Howling Wolf, Son House, Helen Humes, John Jackson, Skip James, Lonnie Johnson, Curtis Jones, Little Walter, J. B. Lenoir, Fred McDowell, Brownie McGhee, Magic Sam, Memphis

Slim, Little Brother Montgomery, Whistling Alex Moore, Muddy Waters, Matt Murphy, Hammie Nixon, Yank Rachell, Jimmy Reed, Dr. Ross, Otis Rush, Shakey Jake, Otis Spann, Victoria Spivey, Roosevelt Sykes, Eddie Taylor, Hound Dog Taylor, Koko Taylor, Sonny Terry, Joe Turner, Sippie Wallace, Junior Wells, Bukka White, Big Joe Williams, and Sonny Boy Williamson. To the uninitiated this is a list of curious names and no more; to the blues enthusiast the names are legendary. They give the lie to the canard that the Festival organizers were only interested in the old musicians. So popular were the visiting blues singers that a number were reluctant to return to the United States. Champion Jack Dupree settled in England, Eddie Boyd made his home in Sweden, the extrovert Memphis Slim was lionized in Paris, and the retiring Curtis Jones moved from Spain to Morocco.

Lippmann and Rau's festival tours took in Germany, France, Switzerland, Great Britain, Holland, Belgium, Denmark, and Sweden. They made radio and television appearances and brought blues into the living rooms of millions of homes. With such an exposure to live blues, which previously had been denied to all but a small number of researchers who had made trips to the United States, the audience expanded dramatically. Record companies responded. Polydor, and later Philips and CBS, issued the official LPs of the Festivals—which are in the catalogue still. Karl Emil Knudsen in Denmark secured sessions with many of the visiting singers to produce a series of "Portraits in Blues." An ambitious program of releases of modern blues singers was begun by Mike Vernon, whose Blue Horizon label was among the first professionally produced blues series. But there were also numerous minor labels devoted to specialist reissues: Post-War Blues, Highway 51, Down with the Game, Roots, and a number of others whose label names proclaimed their allegiances.

It was a busy decade for me. After returning from a spell teaching architecture in West Africa and doing fieldwork on music on the side, I arranged an exhibition at the American Embassy in London, "The Story of the Blues," in 1964. It consisted of some 500 photographs, maps, and ephemera, many of them printed on a large scale, and displayed throughout its huge first-floor exhibition hall. Seen by many blues singers from the Folk Blues Festival, the poet Langston Hughes, and the entire Alvin Ailey dance company, not to mention many thousands of visitors, it helped to give blues a further boost in Britain, and indirectly through the Embassy, in the United States as

Figure 1: "The Story of the Blues" Exhibition, United States Embassy, London, Summer 1965. Left to right, Bernard Myers (Embassy staff), Sam Lightnin' Hopkins (blues singer from Texas), Doug Dobell (proprietor of Dobell's Jazz Record Shop and 77 Records), Chris Strachwitz (proprietor of Arhoolie Records), and Paul Oliver (exhibition organizer). *(Courtesy of Paul Oliver.)*

well. The following year Cassell published my *Conversation with the Blues*, based on my field-recorded interviews,[17] and a couple of years later I completed *Screening the Blues*,[18] which endeavored to take further the kind of inquiry I had begun with *Blues Fell This Morning.* As the 1960s ended I wrote *The Story of the Blues*,[19] which used the photographs and other material gathered for the exhibition, and began work on *Savannah Syncopators: African Retentions in the*

Blues,[20] developed from questions that had come to me while field recording in West Africa.

This latter book was to be published in a series of "Blues Paperbacks" (though they appeared in hardback too) which I had been invited to edit. There were many writers in Europe who needed an outlet for their fieldwork in the States: Bengt Olsson from Sweden, for instance, who wrote *Memphis Blues and Jug Bands*,[21] or Karl Gert Zur Heide from Germany, who had researched the circle of musicians around Little Brother Montgomery in *Deep South Piano*.[22] I was particularly interested in publishing a remarkable manuscript written in the 1940s by a young Dutchman, Frank Boom, *Laughing to Keep from Crying*. He had died in his twenties, and eventually his family decided not to go ahead with the book. But there were other important studies: Bruce Bastin's *Crying for the Carolines* based on his work in the Piedmont region,[23] Derrick Stewart-Baxter's work on the blues women in *Ma Rainey and the Classic Blues Singers*.[24] Bob Dixon and John Godrich gave the context of *Recording the Blues*,[25] Bob Groom the history of *The Blues Revival*.[26] The series was house-edited by Tony Russell, who pioneered an investigation into the musical "cross-over" with *Blacks, Whites and Blues*.[27] And of course, there were others in the series by American writers.

A dozen books had been planned and eleven issued. After the series was completed, Tony Russell edited a new series for Eddison, of which the first, *Chicago Breakdown* was by Mike Rowe,[28] based on his extensive research in Chicago. Later he took over the editorship of *Blues Unlimited*. The following year, 1974, *Blues Unlimited* published John Broven's research into New Orleans rhythm and blues, *Walking to New Orleans*[29]; a decade later he wrote another book on the music of the Cajun bayous, *South to Louisiana*,[30] arising from his continuing fieldwork. There had been a growing interest in R and B, and a fuller recognition of its place in blues history. A searching study of the growth of R and B and rock and roll had been written in 1970 by Charlie Gillett,[31] who later, in *Making Tracks*, wrote a monograph on the Atlantic record company.[32] Film crews from France and Italy made television films of blues singers in their homes and clubs. Giles Oakley for the BBC made a series of films which were shown on television in 1976 under the general title *The Devil's Music*, also the title of the accompanying history of blues which he wrote.[33]

New blues magazines started up: Chris Smith and Alan Balfour absorbed Bob Groom's *Blues World* into *Blues Link*. Overstretched financially, they replaced it with *Talking Blues*. There were new ones appearing in European countries too, like *Block* in Germany, *Il Blues* in Italy, or *Soul Bag* in France, well-produced, fully illustrated, glossy journals. It was a trend that was reflected in an enhanced but increasingly erratic *Blues Unlimited* and in the 1980s in the new magazines like *Blues and Rhythm*, edited by Tony Burke and published at five-week intervals, and the quarterly *Juke Blues*, with John Broven as one of its editors and Cilla Huggins as another. (Blues writing and appreciation have been largely a male preserve, but a few women, including historian Mary Ellison and the photo-journalist Val Wilmer, have made important contributions.)

During the '70s and '80s a new generation of collectors and enthusiasts for blues had grown up, whose interests understandably enough, were largely in the post-war period. A steady stream of blues artists was still being booked in, and has continued to be right up to the present, playing clubs in London and throughout the United Kingdom. Jim Simpson's Big Bear Productions, operating from Birmingham, has been responsible over nearly twenty years for a great many of these tours, but in France, Germany, Italy, and other European countries the flow of blues singers from the United States has continued unabated. And so have the interviews and the data collection; the desire for "information" has proved to be insatiable, and the blues magazines continue to meet it, each selling a couple of thousand copies an issue to the dedicated. As a result a standard formula for an issue of a blues magazine has emerged: a verbatim interview with a singer; a feature article on a band, musician, or record label; a discography perhaps of a specific musician; letters; obituaries; and a third to a half of the periodical devoted to record reviews. Theoretical articles and features on meaning or social context are rare. The failure of *Blues Link* was probably caused by its attempt to break out of this mold.

Perhaps because they reach an overlapping but largely different readership, some books are more challenging. One of the earliest to face the problems that the blues posed was Richard Middleton's *Pop Music and the Blues* published in 1972,[34] which investigated the significance of the relationship between the two. New ground was broken in 1974 by a young sociologist, Michael Haralambos, who at one stage had been a disk jockey in Detroit. In *Right On: From Blues to Soul in Black America* he tackled the difficult problem of why blues had gone into a rapid decline in popularity with black audiences.[35] Musical analysis was totally lacking, until the publication of A. M. Dauer's *Blues aus 100 Jahren: 43 Beispiele zur Typologie der vokalen Bluesformen* in 1983.[36] *From Blues to Rock: An Analytical History of Pop Music* by David Hatch and Stephen Millward included less musical analysis than might be expected from these authors.[37] A spate of blues documentation in the late 1970s by European authors led to the 1977 publication in Paris of J. C. Arnaudon's *Dictionnaire du Blues*,[38] K. Bogaert's *Blues Lexicon* published in Antwerp in 1979,[39] and the same year G. Herzhaft's *Encyclopédie du Blues* published in Lyons.[40] There were fewer serious historical studies in the '80s, with the notable exception of Bruce Bastin's *Red River Blues*, based on his work while at Chapel Hill and dealing with the Southeastern blues tradition; it won an ASCAP award.[41] For my part, after the activity of the 1960s I felt like turning my attention to writing on vernacular and popular architecture, and did not publish another book in the blues field for fourteen years. During that time I had fears that the emphasis on blues was drawing attention away from other contemporary black traditions and from the problem of the formative years before recording. *Songsters and Saints: Vocal Traditions on Race Records* published in 1984 was the result.[42] I had also written many blues entries for the 1980 edition of *The New Grove Dictionary of Music and Musicians*,[43] and these were expanded, with chapters on jazz and ragtime by Max Harrison and William Bolcom respectively, in *The New Grove Gospel, Blues and Jazz* in 1986.[44] Most recently I edited the *Blackwell Guide to Blues Records*, with chapters by Bastin, Rowe, Cowley, Groom, Broven and Dave Penny from Britain, and by others from the United States.[45]

Blues Records is intended to guide the reader through the vast number of blues records now available, recommending 100 essential records and a basic library overall of some 500. Every few weeks the mail-order companies—like Red Lick in Porthmadog in Wales—list on average some 3000 blues lps, and an increasing number of CDs currently available. A great many of these are European issues. Some are carefully produced with detailed notes, like Guido van Rijn's Agram series, mainly devoted to 1930s singers, issued in Holland. Among the most immaculate is Francis Smith's 20-volume series of piano blues on Magpie; another is the Flyright-Matchbox series of otherwise unissued Library of Congress recordings, compiled by John Cowley. Flyright and Krazy Kat are labels from Bruce Bastin's Interstate company, with a considerable catalogue of albums leased from companies in the United States, many of them previously unissued in any form. More basic in production but invaluable for the collector of pre-war recordings are the issues on Blues Documents, RST, Matchbox, Wolf, Old Tramp, and other labels, all stemming from the former proprietor of Roots records, Johnny Parth. Based in Vienna, Austria, Parth has a virtual obsession to insure that everything on 78 rpm listed in Dixon and Godrich will be available on LP or CD. In Italy Chess masters are officially leased under the Chess name; in England Ace and Charly have formidable catalogues of post-War R and B—and there are many more.

Who buys all these records? Because they are often only available in Europe, quite a lot of American purchasers do, through importing firms such as California's Down Home Music, managed as it happens, by an expatriate Briton, Frank Scott. But the majority of issues are purchased by Europeans for whom understanding the lyrics is one of the prime motivations for learning English! That my own *The Story of the Blues* has been translated into Spanish, German, Finnish—and even Japanese—is some indication of the breadth of the blues audience. Why does the blues appeal to this extent? At one time it was convenient to assume that blues represented a spirit of revolt. That revolutionary European enthusiasts of the 1960s found the blues symbolic of their own feelings may just have applied at the time, but this does not explain the continuing interest in the blues to the present. That in the years of the Civil Rights campaign in the United States European sympathizers heard in the blues the creative voices of an underprivileged minority is undoubtedly true (without, some might justifiably argue, the attendant problems). But it is hardly a sufficient explanation.

An examination of the backgrounds of the enthusiasts might throw some light on the problem, but when I attempted this some years ago the results were totally inconclusive. Among those referred to in this chapter are an accountant and a cartoonist, landed aristocrat and anarchist, systems analyst and pastry cook, antique dealer and civil servant, company director and picture restorer, primary-school teacher and university professor, shipping clerk and sociologist—

and so on. To find anything in common among them *apart* from the blues is to strain the evidence. But there is one thing that is clear: though a few became full-time record producers, virtually every blues enthusiast is an amateur. There are no professionally trained European blues researchers or scholars.[46] Until the 1980s it was not even possible to attend a course in blues in any European university or college. Today there are limited programs of study at Exeter, Keele, Leeds, and Liverpool Universities, while the occasional international conferences on blues and black music organised by Robert Sacré at the University of Liège, Belgium, are setting new standards in blues scholarship.

I'm inclined to the opinion that there is not one reason for our devotion to the blues but a multitude of them, different for each enthusiast, but all of us finding in the universality of the emotional and musical charge of the blues a meaning that is profound yet personal. The European contribution to blues research and understanding has been various and considerable, as I hope I have shown. But perhaps the recognition that it has given to the singers themselves has been the greatest value. "Some people say the overseas blues ain't bad," sang Charley Patton. "Of course they are," Willie Brown commented. Thirty years later Sonny Boy Williamson went as far as Poland, and he thought otherwise as he departed from Denmark:

"Make me feel so good a thousand miles away from my home and folks.
But I'm leavin' I'm leavin' kind peoples, I enjoyed myself everywhere.
        —"On My Way Back Home"
    Storyville SLP 170 (Copenhagen, 1963)

Thomas Carter

Looking for Henry Reed
Confessions of a Revivalist

I arrived in Chapel Hill during the late summer of 1971. I had come south to study folklore at the University of North Carolina, and when Eric Olson, the banjo player for the Fuzzy Mountain String Band, left to take a job at Appalachian State University, I inherited both his house in the Durham County woods and his chair in the band. I stayed in Chapel Hill two years, leaving in the summer of 1973 for Virginia and a year-long field -recording project funded by the National Endowment for the Humanities. A stop at Indiana University's Folklore Institute came next, and now I've been in Utah, my home state, for over a dozen years, working as an architectural historian and playing music in an ersatz cowboy string band whenever I can.

But I have not forgotten my days in Chapel Hill. Who could? For it was an exciting place in those days. Dan Patterson and Terry Zug were just getting the Curriculum in Folklore off the ground at the University, there was lots of music in town, and several hours away were all those great musicians—people like Tommy Jarrell, Fred Cockerham, Kyle Creed, Luther Davis, and William Marshall, to name a few. Not far away either was the intellectual turmoil of the late sixties. The America of my childhood and adolescence had not survived the anti-war experience, and like many of those around me, I felt a sense of new beginnings. And it didn't seem to matter at the time that Jesse Helms won a senate seat in the 1972 election.

Memory of course is not history. Past experience remains diffuse and formless until subjected to critical thought. So when the planners invited me to speak at the *Sounds of the South* conference, and asked me to place the Chapel Hill "scene," as they called it, in some kind of historical perspective, it seemed a good chance to turn some old memories into history, if that is in fact possible. Thus, this essay con-

73

tains a highly personal but considered appraisal of the folk-music revival in Chapel Hill. Such a statement is important simply because what was going on was important. What happened in Chapel Hill during the late 1960s and early 1970s must be viewed as something of a watershed in the history of the folk-music revival. Before it was one thing, and afterwards it was something else. Basically the shift was from the urban North and vocal stylings to the rural South and instrumental music. And the change was dramatic enough that I find myself dividing my own musical career into two parts, what I call *before* and *after* Hollow Rock, so great was the impact of the Hollow Rock String Band on my thinking and development as a musician. But what happened here also makes us ask some very hard questions about what the revival itself was all about. What were we doing with the music? What did it do to us? What can we learn from this experience? These are some of the issues we must address.

The Hollow Rock String Band did not, of course, start the old-time music revival. There was an on-going music scene in the sixties that originated with the New Lost City Ramblers (Fig. 2). The NLCR came through Salt Lake City—I believe it was in 1964—and I remember the concert vividly. They had all those instruments! And it was the Ramblers that initially pushed the revival toward the folk music of the South—toward what we called "old time" music at the time. The NLCR were noted for their instrumental virtuosity, but their approach to the music still focused primarily on vocals. In recreating and interpreting the music found on the early hillbilly records they did very well and influenced a generation of younger musicians, myself included (Fig. 3). We were not always great musicians, but the music and the life-style that went along with it were powerful forces in our lives, nonetheless. And it was this music that I took with me to Rhode Island and college in 1967.

In Providence I found other students who shared my musical background, and it was not long before we had formed a New Lost City Ramblers-type string band in which we played a variety of instruments and sang. I found that my college social life was severely impeded by my being in a group called the Rhode Island Mud Flaps (Fig. 4), but this didn't matter because we had begun to think of the music as if it were our own. We played a few coffee houses patronized by the university crowd, but mostly we played dances, either out at the naval base at Newport or at the grange halls in western Rhode

Figure 2: The Original New Lost City Ramblers: Tom Paley (seated), John Cohen (left) and Mike Seeger (right). *(Courtesy of the Smithsonian Institution.)*

Figure 3: The Hippo Chorale, or Uncle Lumpy's Friends of Calvin Coolidge String Band, Salt Lake City, about 1966. Left to right, Hal Cannon, Tom Carter, and Chris Montague. *(Courtesy of Tom Carter.)*

Figure 4: The Rhode Island Mud Flaps: Skip Gorman, Richard Graham, and Tom Carter (left to right), in front of University Hall, Brown University, Spring 1969. The changes in the band "uniform" are significant. *(Courtesy of Tom Carter.)*

Island or eastern Connecticut. When we played dances the people—rural people mostly, and many at the naval base Southerners—didn't really seem to care that we were college boys. We just went and played and were the house band.

Our musical world, however, was remarkably circumscribed. In the Northeast during the late 1960s the fiddle-tune repertory was very small. There were about fifteen tunes that everyone knew, including pieces like "Mississippi Sawyer," "Soldier's Joy," and "McCloud's Reel," and you could go about anywhere and find fiddlers playing the same fifteen tunes. And then it happened. A friend gave me an album by a North Carolina group called the Hollow Rock String Band (Fig. 5).[1] This would have been the winter of 1968–69. The first cut was "Kitchen Girl," a spirited fiddle tune played in a

Figure 5: The Hollow Rock String Band, ca. 1967. Left to right, Tommy Thompson, Bobbie Thompson, Bertram Levy, Alan Jabbour *(Courtesy of Alan Jabbour.)*

minor key, and it only took two or three measures for us to be hooked. Hollow Rock tunes like "Billy in the Lowground," "Betty Likens," and "Over the Waterfall" became the new standards, and then there were more tunes, from Frank George, French Carpenter, and others, and soon the pool of fiddle tunes everyone had to know had jumped to fifty, then eighty, and now, it's certainly in the hundreds if not thousands. All of a sudden the fiddle-tune repertory was blown wide open—never to recover. In many ways the Hollow Rock String Band began it all, too, both through their own recordings and—and this is important—by pointing the way for others to find their own tunes through the recording of live traditional musicians.

The Hollow Rock String Band repertory came principally from Henry Reed, an old Franklin County, Virginia, fiddler that Alan Jabbour, the Hollow Rock fiddler, recorded in 1965. Alan learned Henry Reed's tunes from the tape recordings and then taught them to the other band members in person (tape recorders not being widely available at the time). The result was a strictly instrumental old-time string-band sound—there was no singing—and a whole set of tunes no one had heard before. Henry Reed's tunes caught on quickly, and so did the idea that there were fine old fiddlers out there to be recorded. Doing fieldwork soon became one of the requisite duties of the revival musician. Fiddlers and want-to-be fiddlers descended on the South in droves searching for the old masters. We know a great deal about instrumental music in the South (and elsewhere as well, for soon revival musicians in New England, the West, and other places began turning their attention toward their own regions) because of the emphasis the revival placed on fieldwork. Initiating the widespread collecting of old-time fiddle music was then one of the main contributions the Hollow Rock Band made to the revival—and it meant that there could always be more new tunes.

Another significant contribution Hollow Rock made lay in the area of string-band style. The New Lost City Ramblers popularized a band sound that was based, first, on a variety of instrumental combinations, and second, on a series of instrumental "breaks" where the fiddle, banjo, mandolin, or guitar would be singled out to play "lead" while being seconded by the other instruments. NLCR-style band members changed instruments often and shared the lead role on different tunes and songs. The Hollow Rock String Band chose a different ensemble approach: each member played only one instrument, and all instruments except the guitar played the melody, or lead. It was a unison sound that had precedent among traditional country musicians and some revival bands—for example, Uncle Willie's Brandy Snifters from Minneapolis, who had several cuts on John Cohen's *Old Time String Band Project* album[2]—but it was, I will argue, the Hollow Rock band that popularized the sound during the early 1970s. Alan Jabbour played the melody on the fiddle, and Bertram Levy and Tommy Thompson followed the fiddle music closely, almost note for note in fact, on their instruments, the mandolin and banjo. Bertram may be credited for elevating the mandolin to an estimable position in old-time string-band music and Tommy Thompson was probably the first revival banjo player to devise a complicated melodic style of drop-thumb noting—a technique that elaborated on and expanded the traditional clawhammer method of limited drop-thumb noting, thereby making the banjo an equal partner to the fiddle and mandolin.

The Hollow Rockers' choice of the unison ensemble sound is intriguing from a cultural point of view. Alan Lomax has suggested that there are definite cultural preferences expressed in musical styles, and polyrhythmic and polyphonic sounds are characteristically African-American, while the unison and monophonic style is indicative of Western European tradition.[3] From this perspective Alan, Bertram, Tommy, and Bobbie were in reinventing an older Anglo-American musical style. And it was not by accident either, as Alan wrote in the liner notes to the first album, "because the style is so closely associated with dancing, it focuses upon the music, not the musicians: there are no 'breaks' showing off the individual instruments, and the melody is repeated with only slight variations. All the instruments but the guitar play the melody, and even the guitar occasionally takes up the melodic line."[4] Jabbour's description stressed function and social integration—the fusion of music and dancers, of performers and audience. There are strong overtones of self-denial and of affirmation of the group—the unison style sacrifices the individual instrument for the good of the whole, for the band sound. And what Alan and the others were laying out, it seems to me, was quite a revolutionary musical asethetic reflecting an essentially egalitarian ideology. Everyone in the band, even "occasionally" the guitar, played the melody, and the logical extension of this approach was the idea that the number of people who might join in at any one time was, at least theoretically, infinite. One fiddler or five, one banjo player or six, one mandolin or two, one guitarist or a dozen—it didn't matter, for the sound would be the same, only louder. The unison format gave the string band an open-ended structure that differed sharply from the one found in bluegrass or even in NLCR-style bands, where different instruments were featured in a prescribed order: there are five instruments in a bluegrass band; in a Charlie Poole-style arrangement there are three; and so forth, according to the rules. Not so with the new Hollow Rock formula; if you could learn the tunes and get in tune, then you could play along, or so we thought.

So the legacy of the Hollow Rock String Band grows, for in popularizing a band sound that was more social than musical, they produced a music and a musical philosophy that was right for the times—and one which has lingering power today. Their brand of old-time music made sense to a generation looking, as Alan Jabbour has mentioned, for roots, for some kind of toe-hold in a rather turbulent world. And it did not matter whose roots they were, particularly, for we were looking for a whole new life-style, one that differed from the one of our parents' generation. We were looking for alternative roots, I think, that suited our needs at the time, and we found them in the music and what the music stood for, and this was rural life. The music was a first step back to the land. The idea of living in the country was a fundamental part of the music's attraction, and many revival musicians eventually moved to farms and small towns. Most of us at one time or another dreamed of living in the country—whatever that meant—and our world was dominated by powerful if dimly understood symbols like *the woodpile*. Heating with wood was part of the old-timey scene, and a person's woodpile (Fig. 6) was not to be taken lightly.

Allen Tullos has spoken about a second factor that helped fuel the Chapel Hill revival, and this is the so-called "reawakening" of Southern consciousness. By the late 1960s and certainly by the 1970s it was suddenly all right to be Southern. The "stigmatism of the South," as David Whisnant aptly puts it, was lifted, and we were allowed to take the South for what it was—a region of the nation. No longer did we need to disguise it in the romantic trappings of old FSA photographs that depicted an exploited and disenfranchised people—folks we could identify with, for we felt, whatever our economic backgrounds, that we also existed outside the political power

Figure 6: Tom Carter, Malcolm Owen, and Armin Barnett (left to right) sitting in front of Tom's woodpile, Meadows of Dan, Virginia, Thanksgiving 1973. *(Courtesy of Tom Carter.)*

arena. But now, we were embracing the life-style of real Southerners, people whose ideas about politics and matters of racial equality did not exactly coincide with our own, but we accepted them for what they were and they us, I guess. This identification with the everyday life and people of the South was so powerful that it was very important to us actually to play in a band with a traditional musician. Many revival musicians played in Ernest East's band, and both Blanton Owen and Andy Cahan toured with Tommy Jarrell (Fig. 7).

One other thing we were looking for was a sense of community. More than anything the music was our attempt to reach out, to find a place for ourselves in the craziness of the nuclear age. I believe that the basically egalitarian style that Alan Jabbour articulated and that Bertram, Tommy, and Bobbie painstakingly worked out, was part of this search for community, for connection. You could feel a sense of fellowship with the people in your band—in my case the Fuzzy Mountain String Band (Fig. 8)—or just with other old-timey musicians, people like Dave and Trina Milefsky, Armin Barnett, Ray Alden, Nowell Creadick, Richard Blaustein—the list is endless. We had the idea that we could attend a fiddler's convention or a party and meet other musicians and immediately feel a sense of acceptance. Once—it would have been in the summer of 1972—I stopped at Art Rosen-

Figure 7: Blanton Owen, Tommy Jarrell, and Mike Seeger (left to right) on their California Tour, Spring 1975. *(Courtesy of Tom Carter.)*

Figure 8: The Fuzzy Mountain String Band Practicing for the Fiddler's Convention at Independence, Virginia, Summer 1973. Left to right, Tom Carter, Sharon Poss, Blanton Owen, Malcolm Owen, and Vickie Owen. *(Photo by Barry Poss.)*

baum's house in Iowa City. He didn't know me, of course, but I had heard of him and it seemed natural to stop to say hello, play a few tunes, and stay the night. And I did. And I had not seen Art again until the "Sounds of the South" Conference. But this sense of belonging to a larger community, a community of old-time musicians, was central to the movement's vitality.

The community in fact may have been largely imaginary. Sure, there were the legendary Friday-night parties at Tommy and Bobbie Thompson's place in Hollow Rock, but even then, I suspect, there were concentric circles of players: the center being reserved for the "best" musicians. And by the time I arrived in Chapel Hill things had changed considerably. Alan and Bertram had moved, and the parties had ended. What was left were a number of local string bands with the Fuzzy Mountain String Band at the center.[5] The Fuzzies were the inheritors of the Hollow Rock mantle and were literally connected with the earlier band by Bobbie Thompson's presence on guitar. Malcolm Owen, Eric Olson, Dick Zaffron, Dave Crowder, and "Claire June" Stokes were the original members. Later came Vickie Owen, Bill Hicks, and Blanton Owen, and then myself and Sharon Poss. There were several other string bands as well, with constantly changing personnel that included among others Barry Poss, Lex Varela, Marilyn Engle, Bill Phillips, Chris Delaney, George Holt, and Wayne and Margaret Martin. All these bands shared a repertory of dance tunes that was always growing and changing as new traditional fiddlers were discovered and recorded.

And what of the folk musicians? What was our relationship to them? It's something we don't often talk about. When the conference planners asked me to speak, they wanted a title, and I thought almost immediately of "Looking for Henry Reed," or better yet, "Still Looking for Henry Reed." Henry Reed (Fig. 9) was the quintessential informant, the ultimate "discovery," as we used to say. In our world tunes did two things. First, if you could play the basic repertory you could gain entrance into the players' circle. Second, if you found good new tunes—usually through fieldwork—then you could influence the musical direction of the circle. Either way, tunes were a source of status and power within the community, and therefore discovering a musician like Henry Reed, a fiddler with a large repertory of melodically interesting tunes, was something we all thought about.

In a certain way, we were all looking for Henry Reed. We needed him and fiddlers like him to establish ourselves within our own social world. The more tunes you had, and especially the more obscure ones you had, the better. Blanton Owen and I spent over a year collecting music on the Blue Ridge, and in a way we were looking for our own Henry Reed. I know this because one day we actually thought we had found him. I had heard of an elderly fellow living down in Franklin County, Virginia, who was supposed to know the old tunes, so Blanton and I went down there together. It was a warm spring day; I think it was in late March. We found his house, and a knock brought us a faint "Come on in." We obliged and immediately found ourselves in a pitch-black room with a temperature of about 100 degrees. The stove was going full blast, and it was very hot in that dark little room. I found a light, and we discovered the old man sitting in the corner, his fiddle by his side. I ran my fingers across the strings—it was in a cross-tuning and was pitched perfectly. I caught Blanton's eye: this was it. We talked excitedly while we set up the tape recorder and urged him to play. He launched in on what must be the world's longest rendition of "Amazing Grace," which was the only tune he remembered, and in the heat Blanton and I both fell asleep. He had to wake us both later, so we could leave. It was an elusive kind of thing, this looking for Henry Reed, but we kept at it, and are still at it perhaps, even today.

So I think that we need to understand our connection with the tradition itself, for this seems very important. We gave the musicians a great deal. We gave them something by constantly showing up, in a sense, renewing their lives and giving them a certain recognition in their own community. But we took a lot too. We took a part of their world and made it our own. There were some revivalists who fully adopted the rural life style, but most of us took only what we needed and that was the music. We took the tunes and turned them into power. In this way the music helped us acquire prestige in our own circles, which remained—despite such trappings as coveralls and woodpiles—very different from the rural culture of the music itself. All this happened rather randomly, and it was hardly malicious. But it was a fundamental fact of the revival and something that we need to make ourselves more aware of as we pursue careers in culture-related studies.

The Chapel Hill revival produced a particular brand of highly personal, academic, and introverted music that could not last. The club was too exclusive, and it took too much effort to belong. And after all, the music was just too good to be kept under wraps for long. One has only to look at a picture of the Fuzzy Mountain String Band in concert (Fig. 10) to recognize the limits of the Chapel Hill style. The pose—heads down and eyes shut—is one of detached reverence. There was a certain smugness in our tune introductions. We would say we learned this particular tune from so and so, and it is a version of a more widely known tune, which has antecedents in the British Isles, and so forth. These little verbal pedigrees helped reaffirm our alliance with the tradition, as if to say, "We went out and learned these pieces from the real guys." Sometimes we had, and sometimes

Figure 9: Henry Reed and Bobbie Thompson at the Fiddler's Convention at Narrows, Virginia, 1968. *(Photo by Katherine B. Olson.)*

Figure 10: The Fuzzy Mountain String Band in Concert at Duke University, Spring 1973. Left to right, Vickie Owen, Tom Carter, Sharon Poss, Bill Hicks, Dave Crowder, and Malcolm Owen. *(Courtesy of Tom Carter.)*

we hadn't, but the audience's perception (which we were unlikely to disabuse them of) was that we were part of a seamless tradition—just folks playing the old-time music the way it had always been done.

The highly scholarly approach to the music introduced by the Hollow Rock String Band and perpetuated by the Fuzzy Mountain String Band could not last. The Fat City String Band, later known as the Highwoods String Band, saw to that. The Highwoods' infectious enthusiasm and disregard for the tradition ("That note got in the way so we got rid of it") helped usher in the next phase of the old-time revival, one that is still alive around the country today. The Highwoods Band reintroduced singing and fell back on the older New Lost City Ramblers repertory (only now the music was available from the original performers whose 78-rpm discs were being reissued in vast quantities), but they remained essentially a fiddle band, preserving many of the Chapel Hill tunes and making them available in more palatable form to a new generation of urban revival musicians. The fieldwork apprenticeship—the connection with the old-time musicians—that had typified the Chapel Hill revival, however, was missing.

It was an exciting time, and it is important for us to think about what went on back then, about what the Chapel Hill "scene" meant for those of us who were there. It is a time, of course, that has come and gone, and maybe that's why so many of us came back for the Conference. In closing I'm drawn to Bess Lomax Hawes's use of the *Szwedian Principle*, the notion that the results of any action cannot be determined before it's time to take the next action. In the early 1970's, we were unable to evaluate what was going on around Chapel Hill: we were either immersed in it or had moved on to other things. It is only now, in retrospect, that we can gain some perspective on the events of those days and place them in a proper historical context. It is time to acknowledge (to put it in the folklorist's terms) our *revivalness*—our association, our identification, with the folk-music revival. Not only will this affirmation help us to distinguish ourselves from the folk (and this is not always as easy as it should be), but it also gives us a powerful new perspective as folklorists on the motives and meanings of our scholarship.

Ray Funk

Research Approaches to Black Gospel Quartets

*I**t all started* with the Golden Gate Quartet. I was in law school at the University of California at Berkeley in the late seventies and was already a long-time fan of blues and jazz, having grown up in Chicago. But while at Berkeley, I came under the influence of the Chris Strachwitz's radio show on KPFA. It expanded my horizons to the whole range of "down home" music. I started to collect many kinds of music from the numerous record stores in the East Bay, and it was the purchase of a couple of old albums by the Golden Gate Quartet that led me to become, first, a collector and, then, a researcher of black gospel and vocal-harmony music. Since that time I have become one of a small group of non-academics and a few academics who devote an enormous amount of spare time to researching black gospel quartets and related traditions. From that initial focus, I have expanded my research to many other gospel performers.

During the whole time I have engaged in this research, I have lived and worked as a trial attorney in Fairbanks, Alaska. The local resources for the research are sparse. This has shaped the ways in which I have been able to do research and the directions I have chosen. In trying to set forth in this article some of the highways and more often byways of this research, I intend to describe the interrelated paths that this research has taken and the many areas yet to be explored. My remarks center on black gospel music and, within that, on the sub-field of male quartets, which has been my primary focus, although in the last few years I have begun to do interviews and gather materials on a range of non-quartet artists. Gospel music is itself but a subset of the wide expanse of black religious music.

While at the "Sounds of the South" conference, in those important

Figure 11: Chicago Gospel Tabernacle Record. *(Courtesy of Ray Funk.)*

between-meeting and late-at-night discussions with other participants, I heard of other fascinating styles of black religious music just
now being explored. Tom Hanchett and Mike Schlesinger, for example, told me about the shout bands (brass bands featuring primarily
trombones) that play in the worship services in the House of Prayer
for All People churches, a denomination started by Daddy Grace. At
the conference, I also met Michael and Debbie Luster, who are working with black sea-shanty singers in eastern North Carolina whose
repertory includes religious material.

Furthermore, all gospel-song performance is also intimately tied
up with that other major form of black religious performance,
preaching. The whole relationship between preaching, testifying,
and singing is one that needs further research. Many gospel performers are preachers or began their careers as singers only to abandon
singing later for preaching or evangelizing. In an appearance by almost any gospel performer, the singing will be mixed in with either
preaching or testifying, which are seen as part of the concert experience.[1] The basic aesthetic is not to entertain but to bring the spirit to

the participants and audience, and therefore the singing, preaching, and testifying are merely different ways to reach the same goal.[2]

Records and Discography

The beginning for me and for most people is the music itself, especially as preserved on those fragile artifacts, the 78-rpm phonograph records. From the 1902 recordings of the Dinwiddie Colored Quartet on Victor[3] to the late fifties there are several thousand gospel-quartet 78s. I started collecting them at a time when they were not as popular among collectors as they are only ten years later. While the value of many rare blues 78s has risen to hundreds and, in some cases, thousands of dollars, the average post-war gospel-quartet 78-rpm disk has also increased dramatically in value in the last ten years, but it was a rise from say $5 to $25. Surprisingly, the majority of non-quartet gospel 78s can often still be bought, even through collectors' auctions, for only a few dollars.

As a collector starting off, I found these much more in my price range and soon caught that deadly fever of loving to listen to the sound of the original 78s and of enjoying the variety of the labels on which they appeared. Since I was getting them through the postal service, I worried whether they would ship successfully to Alaska, where the postal forces are not always gentle and the UPS has only recently arrived. Unlike many places where people collect 78s, in Alaska opportunities to find 78s in junk shops are non-existent.

Much more important than the few 78-rpm records I have actually managed to collect myself has been the trading of the 78s on cassette. Since it was the music, not the artifacts, that I was after, the trading of cassette tapes with a dozen similar collectors let me quickly gain access to this music without prohibitive expense. This enabled me fairly quickly over the last ten years to get a majority of all the gospel records, especially quartet records, made between 1902 and 1960. For a good number of my collector friends, gospel records were not a major focus for collecting—they often preferred jazz or blues records—but they would pick up interesting gospel records as a side line and were often very willing to let me tape their gospel sides. I had no other options in doing this research but to go after the 78s themselves or to trade tapes with other collectors since there were almost no obtainable commercial reissues of this material on album. Only a couple of handfuls of reissue albums are currently available to represent the golden age of quartet singing.

Collecting the early recordings systematically has been made easier by the fact that much of the primary discographic research has been done. All the pre-war gospel records are listed in Dixon and Godrich's *Blues & Gospel Records 1902–1943*,[4] and the post-war follow-up *Gospel Records 1944–1969* by Robert Laughton and Cedric Hayes which is due for publication in England some time in the next year or so.

The question of discography becomes much more complicated in the post-war era because of the multiplication in the number of record companies that issued gospel records. Many small labels published black gospel records about which little or nothing is known. A few releases from such companies have been found, but many more are suspected. One of the earliest post-war gospel labels in Los Angeles, for example, was Greenwood, issued by a record store of the same name in Watts. A few odd copies of its releases have been found, and they are all that is known of the label. The Dallas company Avant appears for a number of years to have issued both 78s and 45s, with a few numbers like Avant 042 and Avant 068 located, but the gaps in the numerical series suggest that there are still dozens of unlocated recordings.

In addition to commercial releases, there are the much sketchier areas of custom recordings, acetates, and transcriptions. Custom items were pressed for sale by the groups themselves. For black quartets, these go back at least as far as the twenties, when the Christian and Missionary Alliance Quintette had records pressed on the Columbia Personal label. In the fifties, custom 78-rpm releases were issued for groups ranging from the Wandering Travelers of Houston, Texas, to the Leading Light Kings of Waukegan, Illinois. By the 45-rpm era the custom releases were so numerous that complete information on them will never be recovered. Beyond these custom items, there are numerous acetates, both from home-recording devices and from studios that would allow singers and groups to make a single record of their singing in a sound booth. The Jackson Gospel Singers of New Orleans, a leading female group of the forties, owned a home recorder; rather than issue a custom pressing of two numbers, they sold acetates of songs recorded at rehearsals, each one a unique take! Regrettably, none of these is known to survive.

Meanwhile, radio stations also produced acetates and transcriptions of live gospel performances. It is amazing—when one learns how many, many hours of live black gospel performances got broadcast on stations across America—to see how little of it survived. For both country and jazz, the hundreds of hours of surviving radio-show performances have greatly enriched our enjoyment of artists from Hank Williams to Duke Ellington. But almost no such recordings remain of gospel singers or quartets. The Library of Congress has an important series of radio shows of choirs like the Wings Over Jordan and the Camp Meeting Choir from Voice of Amnerica broadcasts in the fifties; meanwhile, for important groups like the Trumpeteers, who had a regular daily broadcast in the late forties on the CBS network, no known air checks or transcriptions have survived. The Fairfield Four for years in the forties had a regular broadcast that was transcribed on a number of stations from Baltimore to Salt Lake City, but no copies of any have turned up. The only really large cache of radio-show transcriptions was found in Memphis. Doug Seroff got acetates from Mrs. Theo Wade that her husband had rescued from the trash when Station WDIA was tossing out records. The best of these discs form the basis of *"Bless My Bones": Memphis Gospel Radio—The Fifties* (Rounder 2063). More recently a complete 1949 radio show by the Spirit of Memphis was uncovered in Los Angeles in the files of an advertising agency. The show featured Carnation Milk commercials sung by the group! It was slated for reissue along with some of the Spirit of Memphis's commercial recordings in 1990 from Gospel Jubilee Records in Sweden. But these few finds are exceptions to the rule; almost none of these radio-show broadcasts survive.

Interviewing Singers

My first interest in interviewing quartet singers came after I had attended the Birmingham Quartet Reunion in 1980. On that trip, I had a three-month Greyhound Bus pass to visit various friends across the country. Since most of my friends were working during the day, I had lots of free time. I ended up searching for gospel quartets in each city I visited, on a trip that took me from New Orleans to Atlanta, Charleston, S.C., Greenville, N.C., Richmond, Va., and Washington, D.C. Doug Seroff gave me a list of leads for various cities, and off I went, seeing friends in the evenings and each morning making calls from the public library, as I tried to find singers who had been active in the forties or earlier.

Often these visits were very short. I had one day in Atlanta but managed in that day to get around to see several singers. That single day's research, with the addition of some telephone interviews, was the basis for a reissue album a few years later.[5] While some scholars might be shocked by the shallowness of this research, to my knowledge no one before or since has tried to do any more research on the Atlanta quartet groups. No doubt, much more could be learned by anyone with weeks to study there. There don't appear to be grants for ethnomusicologists to do such historic research, much less for Alaska lawyers trained in criminal law, adoptions, probate, and tort defense, so I'll just have to muddle on.

Since that first trip I have interviewed hundreds of singers in person and on the telephone. If I had my druthers, I would do all the interviews in person, since you can't in a telephone call show the singers photographs or play them tapes of their records or look at what they may have retained from their singing careers. But since I don't travel much, telephone interviews have been a necessity.

It is harder to develop rapport when you call people cold and tell them you are an attorney in Alaska and want to know about their singing careers. Who trusts lawyers anyway? I find that I can get a more willing informant on the second phone call if I have in the meantime sent him a cassette or videotape that he doesn't have of his own performances or, if he didn't record, sent copies of recordings of his favorite groups.

While I also love other forms of music, I always find my gospel interviews exciting because they are often the first time that anyone has shown interest in a singer's career. They were not like doing the seventh interview with Dr. John that month or interviewing someone whose biography had already been written. I've had the thrill of breaking new ground throughout the research I have done.

It is also obvious to me now that one can learn only so much from one or two interviews and that real understanding of the music comes from repeated interviews, where more and more subjects are brought up and rapport improves. I am always astonished, when I go back over an interview transcript, to see leads I didn't follow and matters I didn't cover. I find it useful to see what other researchers get from the same informants with whom I have talked. Other interviewers always seem to uncover new pieces of information. It is always fun to do the interviews—and always no fun to transcribe them. Fellow researcher Doug Seroff is always on my case about the number of taped interviews that I have not transcribed. I feel guilty, and yet feel the need both to do more interviews before other important singers die and to get articles and reissues out. I dream of the luxury of having a secretary to transcribe interviews and at the same time have to keep reminding myself that this research is a hobby.[6] So I keep working to catch up with the many things that I have not accomplished.

Regional Research

While living in Alaska has given me the advantage of less distraction from live musical performances, it has deprived my own research of a particular regional focus, since it is as easy to call and interview a singer in Florida as one in California or New York. In fact, given cheap weekend rates, these telephone calls all cost the same. While my research has primarily focused on the artists who had the good fortune to record, I have greatly benefited from the work of several other researchers in tracing unrecorded regional traditions.

Gospel music has had a community character and focus far more important to it than to other types of popular music. The number of participants from the black community who perform some form of black religious music is enormous, not only church choirs but also an incredible number of semi-professional groups, mass choirs, etc. Quartets have very strong community ties, and it is not uncommon for groups to be fifty or sixty years old, albeit with a changing membership over the years. These groups would regularly appear with others on programs on the weekends. One member of a quartet can not only give names, addresses, and information on his group but quite often a great deal on all the other local groups and their members. Even when groups became full-time professionals, they often did so for only portions of their careers, and many of them slipped back into semi-professional status in the same communities they left.

For that reason, gospel quartets are perhaps best studied on a community basis, and patterns that emerge from one community are often repeated in others.

This field of research began with Doug Seroff's extensive investigation[7] of Birmingham, Alabama. It resulted early in a double-record set issued in 1980 to coincide with the Quartet Reunion Concert in Birmingham. The concert and record set are an important landmark in the research and revival of this music.[8] Since then Seroff has spent years working with the surviving quartets in Jefferson County, Alabama, as well as documenting a great deal more about that area. He has also done a lot of work in Nashville,[9] as well as in those other gospel centers Norfolk, Virginia, and Spartanburg, S.C.

Meanwhile, a number of other researchers have focused on quartet centers like Memphis,[10] New Orleans,[11] New York City,[12] and Richmond and the Tidewater area of Virginia.[13] Similar studies that don't focus on quartets have been done on the gospel community of Los Angeles[14] and Washington, D. C.[15] There is much more work to be done across the country and, dear reader, there may well be a gospel community that needs research in your town. So get going!

Most recently I have been working with historian Thomas Hanchett on groups in Charlotte, North Carolina. As an architectural historian who has done work on the history of the neighborhoods in Charlotte, Tom has been able in our interviews with local informants to understand references to places and flesh out such references to the history and interplay of black and white communities and important locations in Charlotte. Tom has also done a lot of work on country music in Charlotte. His knowledge of local radio stations and radio companies helps research like this. My work with Tom makes me aware of how inadequate researching any tradition is when you don't understand all the other circumstances that play into it.

Photographs

One of the primary items documenting the tradition of black gospel music of professional and semi-professional groups has been the posed studio photo often offered for sale at programs. Few quartets recorded who didn't have some posed shots taken of themselves, and many photos and placards survive for groups that never recorded. For some of the more well-known groups like the Dixie

Hummingbirds, a great number of photos have turned up. For others like the Alphabetical Four no photo has yet been found.

In attempting to write about artists and groups in articles and reissues, it is always an advantage to have as much graphic material as possible. Significant patterns emerge in these photographs. For example, certain stylized forms of posing in early quartet photos (with singers lining up from left to right) identify the lead, tenor, baritone, and bass singers. There were also photos with stylized hand positions, such as arms pointed to heaven. Some photos also were made into placards, with singers' addresses, theme songs, and other useful bits of information. Many singers have not retained photos, but every once in a while a singer will be found who has a treasure trove of them. The most amazing discovery I have made was a singer in San Francisco who had two walls of his garage covered with quartet photos from his career both in New Orleans and in San Francisco. These have been a major help in documenting the quartet history of both communities.

These posed publicity photographs survive in some abundance, but what doesn't exist is the stage shot. The Apollo Theatre had regular gospel appearances, and these were photographed to sell to the performers, but in the form of a central photo surrounded by all the others. So far as I can tell, almost no photos were ever taken at church programs. Only a handful of performance shots, then, have turned up. One hopes there may have been a few photographers in black communities who put real emphasis on gospel artists.

I keep a couple of fat notebooks of xeroxes of quartet photos, and on the rare chances I have to travel I take them to interviews. They help get people to open up. Seeing photos of groups often brings out floods of memories.

Black Newspapers

Given the difficulty and expense of travel and the need to do something other than make phone interviews, I have also undertaken a great deal of investigation through black newspapers. Historically, most black newspapers for the prime period of my research, 1920 to 1960, covered gospel music. Fairbanks doesn't have a large collection of black newspapers, but the interlibrary loan office of the local public library has kindly been getting important newspapers for me on microfilm, a couple of reels at a time, so I can rush over at lunch and go through them. While many libraries throughout the country have microfilms of black newspapers, the task was to find a library that didn't mind loaning them. Generally this meant that they were not heavily used locally. Over the years I have been able to get the Chicago *Defender* from Western Michigan University, the New York *Amsterdam News* from Emory University, the Baltimore *Afro-American* from the University of Washington.

The newspapers reveal all kinds of useful information. Often the papers had both a religion page and an entertainment page that can be scanned for relevant articles and advertisements. These may be helpful in gauging a group's popularity, verifying information in oral histories (especially dates, which singers seem to have a great deal of trouble pinning down), finding and dating photos of a group, or establishing its membership and where it came from. Several times clippings have given me the names of group members, and equipped with that information, I have located the singers. At other times surprising bits of information surface. Advertisements for the Soul Stirrers concerts mentioned, for example, that tickets were available at the Soul Stirrers Barbershop. In the several interviews I had already done with members of the group, no one had mentioned this brief (and unsuccessful) business venture. The newspapers occasionally talk of things that happened; an item from the Cleveland *Call and Post* in 1940 mentioned that singer Carey Bradley from the Kings of Harmony passed out on stage.

My research in this area was preceded by an amazing series of events that began with Dave Evans' mother spotting a 1928 newspaper clipping from Savannah, Georgia, on the Imperial Quintet. She sent a copy of the article to Dave, who passed it on to Doug Seroff, who sent it on to me. Despite the enormous time lag, I called telephone information in Savannah and managed to connect with the widow of the group's manager, who had left the phone number in her husband's name after his death many years before. She put me in touch with a surviving member of the group and loaned me a photo of this early recording group.[16] Being able to follow up on a 1928 newspaper clipping has given me faith that a bit of effort can often be rewarded, no matter how old the trail may be.

Most references to gospel musicians in black newspapers are brief notices of local concerts and advertisements. Rarely do they present any in-depth information, but there have been occasional surprises. In the Cleveland *Call and Post* in the mid-thirties, there was a weekly Quartet News column! A similar series of in-depth articles popped up in the Norfolk *News and Guide* in 1950 but was abandoned after only a few appearances. Are there any others? I keep ordering more microfilm in hopes that there are.

Film and Television Appearances

As I began this research, I focused on recordings, not video. Perhaps because I am so keenly aware of my limited opportunities to see live music, when I got a VCR a few years ago I began to trade with collectors for a wide range of music: jazz, blues, country, bluegrass, rhythm and blues, African pop, and really the whole range of ethnic and traditional music. It was natural, then, that I would also focus on the existing film and television footage of gospel performers.

There are very few pieces other than the feature-film appearances and documentaries on Mahalia Jackson. I'd guess 75 percent of all existing gospel footage is of Mahalia! The Golden Gates and the Jubilaires each appeared in a few films in the forties, but since then few gospel artists have done so. A legendary Italian film called *The World By Night* (1960) documents a tour of night clubs and has a section on a gospel show at the Apollo with the Dixie Hummingbirds, the Swanee Quintet, and the Imperial Gospel Singers. The singers vividly remember making it, and all want to see it again. The Zion Travelers in the fifties made two films called *A Miracle through Song* and *My God of the Mountains*, but we have no specific information about them. It appears that these films were made for the black church market and may be lost.

As I interview singers, I always ask if they ever appeared in any films and thus find out about little-known appearances. The great quartet bass singer Jimmy Jones has a solo in *Wattstax* (1973). The Meditation Singers led by Laura Lee are in a low-budget cop movie called *Detroit 9000* (1973), singing a number written for the movie by Holland-Dozier-Holland of Motown fame. Meanwhile, perhaps the strangest film appearance I have recently uncovered is that of the Ward Singers in *A Time to Sing, A Time to Cry* (1960). This film was one of MGM's vehicles for Hank Williams, Jr. At the beginning of the film, Hank goes into the woods, hears the Ward Singers do one number in an outdoor setting, and talks briefly with Clara. The Ward Singers also appear in documentaries on the Newport and Monterey Jazz Festivals.

If the film appearances are limited, the whole area of gospel television appearances is fairly under-researched. Many quartets have appeared on television, and several even had their own shows. But these early shows do not appear to have survived. One national show that got mentioned in newspaper clippings and brought up in interviews was *TV Gospeltime*. Shot in the period from 1962 to 1964, it resulted in 66 half-hour shows. I got a call from a New York tax attorney concerning the valuation the producer had given to the IRS on donating the rights to a university. In helping him on that, I ended up with an index to the shows and a video of two of them. Once I saw the list, I came to realize the importance of the series. The show presented almost every major gospel group of the time at least once. For many artists who have since died, the series holds the only known filmed appearance—as for example, Edna Gallmon Cooke, June Cheeks, and Ethel Davenport—as well as important appearances by groups like both sets of Blind Boys, the Dixie Hummingbirds, and the Caravans. Since then, a film collector has contacted me because he had access to 16mm distribution prints, and I have been getting video and film copies of most of the shows. They have gotten me interested in artists I had ignored before. The discovery of a source for many of the TV Gospeltimes led me off to learn more about a series of gospel soloists that didn't interest me until I saw some performance footage. These shows really awakened my interest in the Consolers, the Reverend Cleophus Robinson, Ernestine Washington, and Emma Tucker, among others. Meanwhile, this batch of material has sent me off to expand my collection with film clips of Bessie Griffin from a 1962 Dinah Shore television show and video clips of a Monkees TV special that featured the Ward Singers.

With the proliferation of VCRs, the amount of video documentation of gospel music is burgeoning. Besides weekly cable shows like Bobby Jones Gospel, commercial labels like Malaco are now making concert videos to accompany a number of their new releases. I found in North Carolina that local videos of quartet concerts were being hawked at programs along with albums, cassettes, and photos. No doubt the scarcity of documentation typical of the early years of gospel will not be as true for the current period.

Sheet Music and Songbooks

Only recently have I begun to take any interest in the written texts of gospel songs. While a certain number of quartets recorded more traditional pieces from songbooks like *Gospel Pearls*, the gospel song publishers that followed in the wake of Thomas Dorsey in Chicago created a whole body of material. There was a large number of gospel sheet-music publishers from the thirties to the fifties, some of whom may have issued only a half-dozen titles, while a few like Martin and Morris in Chicago are still in business and have issued hundreds, maybe thousands, of sheets as well as a number of songbooks. The Southern Folklife Collection just got a cache of these from a Philadelphia gospel record store, as well as some 78-rpm acetates made in the store's sound booth back in the fifties.

I have become interested in the history of certain songs recorded by many groups and in the whole subject of a group's repertory and its sources. We need a close examination of all recorded and printed versions of songs that were performed and recorded again and again—of certain jubilee biblical narratives like "Jezebel" and "Noah" that had a very strong life, as well as of certain recurring themes like riding the train to heaven or telephoning Jesus.

The sheet music and songbooks also hold other useful items, such as photos of performers and songwriters or references to the song's being transcribed "as sung by" some performer never heard of. These open new avenues of research. The way that songwriters got their material out to performers is another fascinating topic that calls for more research.

Further, sheet music may offer a means of getting at another important area deserving of further research, the interconnections between black and white gospel—particularly quartets. While the Swan Silvertones and Soul Stirrers were singing for black audiences, the Statesmen and Blackwood Brothers were across town singing for white audiences. Occasionally but not often, the groups appeared together. Meanwhile, however, these quartets heard each other on the radio and perhaps searched the same sheet music for new material. Charles Wolfe is hard at work on a book on white gospel quartets that will greatly improve our knowledge. Interestingly, young bluegrass groups like Doyle Lawson and Quicksilver and the Nashville Bluegrass Band have been actively listening to black quartet records for material. The topic of such interaction has not been fully explored.

Archives

No archive in the United States or elsewhere has a major collection of recordings or materials for the research of black gospel music. This is not to say that there aren't archives and research locations with substantial resources for various specialized areas of research, but there is no one location where a scholar can go to do weeks of research on all the commercial recordings. This is not true of other important styles of American vernacular music, which are covered by the Country Music Foundation, the jazz archives at Tulane University and Rutgers University, and the blues archive at the University of Mississippi. The gospel situation may be changing,[17] but the absence of a major institutional collection is another indication of the need for more work in this field, especially in light of the growing acknowledgement of the influence of black gospel music on the entire spectrum of popular music from rock and roll to jazz.

While there may be no one great gospel resource library, many facilities have special materials. First, the Archive of American Folk Culture at the Library of Congress has amazing field recordings of black religious performances dating back to the twenties. Alan Lomax was especially strong in recording black religious music in a wide range of situations from church services to prisons. Many of these fine recordings give an important perspective on singing and song styles. Regrettably, while a great number of the classic field recordings from the Library of Congress have been issued for other genres, the same cannot be said for the black religious recordings, which have had only very limited reissue.

Another source of fascinating material is the historic archives of black colleges and universities across the country. One of the strands of the black gospel quartet tradition was the touring of jubilee groups and quartets on behalf of black schools, from the formation of the

Fisk Jubilee Singers in the 1870s to the beginning of World War II. Doug Seroff's on-going research into the lengthy and complex history of the Fisk University Singers has uncovered at Fisk mountains of material on the singers, including letters, itineraries, financial records, and programs, that are allowing him to reconstruct a very complete picture of this group.

It is conceivable that almost every black school of any size participated in this tradition. In the thirties a number of important groups who performed religious material on the radio—such as the Utica Jubilee Singers, the Charioteers, the Deep River Boys, and the Delta Rhythm Boys—all started as black university groups, while the best-known group on the radio in the early thirties, the Southernaires, was made up of former members of university groups.[18] Mysterious and little-known singers like the Carolinians, who recorded for Bluebird in 1938, turn out to be a college group from Johnson C. Smith University in Charlotte, North Carolina. And this was not the first group from Johnson C. Smith to record. The school was formerly called Biddle University, and the Biddle University Quintet recorded for Pathé in 1920. (The school also proved a key to the identity of another early group, the Biddleville Quintette, though this appears to be a local community group that had no connection or substantial contact with the school and may simply have taken its name from the Biddleville neighborhood around the school. Tom Hanchett had done a walking tour and created markers for the Biddleville neighborhood several years ago without knowing that it had any recording group using the name.)

What exists in the archives of black institutions is still a point of great curiosity to me. I would love to visit Wilberforce, Tuskegee, and Atlanta University, among others, to see what their archives hold on the schools' own singing organizations. My guess is that there is some interesting information on this phenomenon in the archive of every black college in America.

A very important source for research on gospel music is the Smithsonian Institution, largely through the efforts of the Program in Black Americans and its former director, Bernice Johnson Reagon. Besides being the leader and guiding light of the important and wonderful *a cappella* singing group Sweet Honey in the Rock, Ms. Reagon has spearheaded a series of amazing conferences at the Smithsonian focusing on many aspects of black religious performance, from the evo-

Figure 12: The Biddleville Quintette. *(Courtesy of Ray Funk.)*

lution of the spiritual to contemporary gospel song and worship practices. Since the first program on the Roberta Martin Singers, these colloquia have presented a wide range of topics, but have especially emphasized important song writers, including Charles Tindley, Thomas A. Dorsey, Kenneth Morris, Alex Bradford, Lucie E. Campbell, and the Rev. William H. Brewster. All these programs were audiotaped and videotaped; these represent a unique and important body of research materials on black religious music.

Regrettably, because I live in Alaska I have not had the chance to make much use of archival sources, given my limited opportunities to travel outside the state and a wife who wishes for vacations to consist of something other than interviews, gospel programs, and visits to record stores and archives. It is likely that there are other repositories of material relevant to these inquiries. However, my impression is that until recently archives made little effort to build up serious research collections of black gospel material.

The files of record companies are another source for fascinating information and something that should be deposited in archives. I've had some access to the Specialty gospel artist files and, beyond discographic data, have found much illuminating information. For example, in a 1952 letter to Johnny Myles of the Swan Silvertones, Art Rupe gave instructions on how he wanted them to record:

Remember, we are making these records for people who can not see you when they listen to the record. Put all the showmanship you can in your voices. Sing like you have 5,000 people in front of you. Sing like you are in a Battle with the Blind Boys, the Spirits, and the Pilgrim Travelers, and you are following them, and they have done such a good job that they already tore the building down, and it looks like you all can't do much more. Then you all come on and really shout and make everybody happier and the old sisters fall out and REALLY TEAR DOWN THE BUILDING!!! NOW, THAT'S THE WAY YOU MUST SING ON THESE RECORDS!

Articles and Reissues

One of the heartening things in the last few years has been an increased interest in black gospel music and quartets. This has resulted in many classic recordings becoming available again, many older singers deciding to perform again, and the publication of a growing body of research that fleshes out the tradition. Someone interested in this music starts today from a very different point than I did ten years ago.

When Tony Heilbut's ground-breaking survey book *The Gospel Sound*[19] was published in 1971, it seemed he had the whole field to himself. Little more of any detail had been written. The only figure in black gospel to have been the focus of a book-length biography was the Queen, Mahalia Jackson.[20] Now, another general survey has appeared, Viv Broughton's *Black Gospel: An Illustrated History of the Gospel Sound*.[21] For American researchers, the most important part of this book is the chapter on the rise of gospel music in England. The magazine *Rejoice*, issued from the University of Mississippi since 1987, has tried to publish articles on the full range of black and white religious music. Other trade-music publications give more coverage to the contemporary gospel scene, like *Totally Gospel* out of Detroit, and many short-term publications like *National Gospel News* and *Gospelrama* have come and gone. Meanwhile, there is a growing coverage of gospel in British collectors' publications like *Blues & Rhythm*, *Voices from the Shadows*, *Music Traditions*, and *Kiskedee*. On the academic front, a surprising number of theses and dissertations have been written in the past ten years, focusing on aspects of gospel quartets.[22] So far, only one of these has been turned into a book,[23] but some of the others are likely to in the years to come.

As important as the various articles and books has been the growing number of reissue albums and cassettes and, more recently, compact discs that don't just present research but do so in a context that gets some of the wonderful music itself out to the public. While it seems that one can walk into any large record store and buy the great recordings of a Louis Armstrong, a Charlie Parker, a Bessie Smith, or a Muddy Waters, the same cannot be said for black gospel artists, with the exception of Mahalia Jackson and perhaps a few quartets like the Soul Stirrers and Dixie Hummingbirds. The major American labels have shown no interest in recent years in reissuing classic recordings from their vaults, and it has fallen to small collectors' labels—mostly outside the United States—to do this.[24]

Concerts and Live Appearances

The first time I ever heard black gospel quartet singing other than on record was at the 1980 quartet reunion concert in Birmingham.

In the decade since then I have been to a number of concerts and programs at churches and to many appearances at the gospel tent over the years at the New Orleans Jazz Festival, as well as to rehearsals and practice sessions. As exciting as this music is on record, the thrill of hearing it live is really special, and I regret I have been so little able to do this.

In particular, live *a cappella* harmony singing at its best can be incredibly moving. At Doug Seroff's request a famous Nashville quartet, the Fairfield Four with roots in Birmingham, got together for the Birmingham Quartet Reunion after having broken up in the sixties. The Fairfield Four have re-emerged over the past ten years to become regular performers at folk festivals as well as church programs. Their *a cappella* performances really excite audiences used to other forms of gospel. In 1989, they were the first group to receive a National Heritage Fellowship. They have made a self-produced cassette, and it is likely they will continue to perform for many years to come.

Regrettably, not many young people are taking up the calling to sing quartet, with the notable exception of Take Six, whose harmonies owe more to the Hi-Los than to the Swan Silvertones. A local Birmingham quartet, the Birmingham Sunlights, has been taking up the mantle of the older quartets and making regular festival appearances as well as a five-country tour of southern Africa during the fall of 1989. In fact, it is the South African vocal groups led by the very popular Ladysmith Black Mambazo that have pointed new directions in the research of this music.

Expanding Research

Research is its own reward. As I have spent time doing this research I have met a great number of wonderful singers, many who clearly live the life they sing about, becoming friends with singers as well as other researchers and collectors who have been sharing their finds and their interpretations of this wonderful music. Not being an academic, I have none of the time constraints of an impending dissertation deadline or publish-or-perish problems, so I can do this work at my own pace—focusing on groups that interest me for one reason or another and putting off looking into other singers who don't. This has made my research far from systematic, but over the years I have let opportunity lead me down its paths when I get a chance to travel to an area that might have a gospel scene.

As time goes on, the picture of an entire world of performers begins to take focus. As in doing a complex historical puzzle, you have thrilling moments when you suddenly reach a singer you have been trying to find for years or on a reel of microfilm find an advertisement with the only known photo of a favorite group whose surviving members don't even know of the photo's existence.[25] Or you suddenly find a bit of film footage that a singer mentioned to you years ago, and you call and tell the singer a video copy is on the way.

Along with the excitement, there is also sadness that so much of the understanding of this musical tradition is slipping away as the elderly singers die. A good number of the singers I have interviewed in the past decade have died, no doubt with innumerable questions unanswered. Other singers have died with little preserved about their careers, and perhaps with little ever to be known of them. While jazz has been the subject of intense scrutiny of collectors and scholars since at least the forties and the blues since the early sixties, it was only twenty years later that gospel music began to get the same kind of attention. To get a handle on the early decades of the music is difficult.[26] Meanwhile the whole field is alive and well, with many current artists recording in a range of styles from traditional to contemporary.

The field of black gospel music—indeed, the wider field of black religious music—is still very open to research. There are enormous gaps in our knowledge of the variety and complexity of this music. The long history of recording and the wide diversity of performance practices makes this especially true. I urge everyone (whether moved by a personal religious conviction or, like myself, by love of the music as music) to hear more of the music—and to help in the research.[27]

Part Two

Archival Preservation of Southern Music

Norm Cohen

The John Edwards
Memorial Foundation
Its History and Significance

John Edwards

I'm thankful to John Edwards for having the foresight, thirty-one years ago, to write a will that led to so much work to save the "sounds of the South." The pertinent sections of his will read:

> In the event of anything happening to me, I would ask that my following wishes be observed, without change:
>
> (1) My records *not be given*, sold or made available *in anyway* to anyone outside the U.S.A. I ask that Gene Earle be contacted re. the collection and be given full freedom to take over the discs, tapes, dubs, files, photos, and all printed matter relative to my collecting interests. . . . All materials to be used for the furtherance of serious study, recognition, appreciation and preservation of genuine country or hillbilly music especially as regards the artists and discs of the "Golden Age" recording era [i.e., 1924–39].
>
> [signed] J. Edwards, Oct. 1958[1]

The most striking aspect of this is the fact that John was just a few months past twenty-six years old when he wrote it. Clearly, John recognized the importance of his collection. Few twenty-six-year-olds draw up a will specifying the manner of disposition of their possessions. John must have sensed that he was preserving an important aspect of a culture that was 10,000 miles distant. John regarded himself as a record collector, and so we think of him also. In actual fact, he was not primarily a record collector; he was a music collector. It is a distinction that requires stressing only because in the arcane world of record collectors there are many who are little more than

Figure 13: John Edwards at Home, June 1960. *(Courtesy of the UNC Southern Folklife Collection.)*

just artifact collectors. Had John simply been a gatherer of old artifacts, we would never have held a Conference. But it was not the discs
themselves that fascinated him, it was their contents, and the histories
of the people who made them.

How did a youngster in Australia, reared in a middle-class home,
of well educated parents, fall under the spell of old-time hillbilly
music? John's introduction to the music came when he was thirteen
years old and a schoolmate told him that there would be a program
featuring the Carter Family over a country-music radio station in New
South Wales. (Even before World War II country music was one of
America's most important exports. In the 1930s, many country re-

cordings by artists such as the Carter Family, Jimmie Rodgers, the Blue Sky Boys, and Mainer's Mountaineers were being pressed and issued in Australia and New Zealand.) John heard the program and instantly fell in love with the music and determined to learn more about it. As his mother later recalled, the friend who had told John about the program was forbidden to listen to hillbilly music because it interfered with his schoolwork. John's mother proudly remembered that "listening to this particular session and others and starting to collect records . . . made no difference to John's scholastic progress."[2] Learning more about it, to John, meant becoming familiar with the music, learning how to play it, and discovering who the people were who made the music.

On his fourteenth birthday, John's grandmother gave him a guitar and paid for one semester's worth of lessons. He began collecting records at about the same time—around 1946—and at the end of the war he bought a second-hand record player, the best that the austere post-war years allowed. By 1953 he had enough of a collection to prepare his first, hand-printed, catalog of holdings. By May 1958 he could truthfully write to a fellow collector, David Crisp, ". . . I know that my collection—this is a fact—is the best outside the U.S. and ranks *with* the best inside the U.S."[3] By this time he had spent thousands of hours visiting radio stations, antique stores, libraries, and other collectors to gather almost every Australian release of an American hillbilly record. To coax old 78s out of radio stations, he would have his American correspondents send him the latest country releases; he would then take these to the station managers and offer them in trade for their old, obsolete 78s.

As I've said, however, John wasn't only an artifact collector. He wanted to learn about the music and the people who made it. In truth, the most important part of the collection that came to the United States after his death was not the records themselves, but all the correspondence, the discographic and biographical data, the photographs, and ephemeral publications that John had amassed. Probably John uncovered the whereabouts of more old-time hillbilly musicians than any American collector of that time. His methods were simple. He made use of old record catalogs, folios, and other advertising matter for references to cities or counties of origin. He would then write to ask the local postmaster if such and such a musician was known thereabouts. Among the musicians he contacted and established correspondence with were Sara Carter, Gene Autry, Carrie Rodgers (Jimmie's widow), Wilf Carter, Dorsey Dixon, Gordon Tanner, Cliff and Bill Carlisle, Charlie Poole, Jr., Slim Bryant, and Buell Kazee. Years after John died Kazee remembered warmly his correspondence with Edwards, writing,

> Several years ago I received a cordial letter from John Edwards in Australia. To a man who had never sought world recognition, this was a great surprise. He asked me to tell him more about myself, but as we continued corresponding I felt that he knew almost more about me than I had been able to tell him. ... From a few notes which I furnished him, he wrote a splendid biography of me which was published in some of the magazines.
>
> I say all this to show how thorough he was in his work and how devoted to his interest in folk music he was. I later was surprised to learn that he was so young. He had given me the impression of much maturity. I came to feel that when John Edwards gave out a statement about folk music, I could rely on exhaustive research to back up its authenticity.
>
> More than this, however, I found in him a warm and unselfish friendship. ... His humble admiration of my work and the almost lavish praise of my efforts, his warm expressions of appreciation and encouragement and his friendly spirit in general made me feel his totally unselfish nature. Many a time I wished I could take my banjo and go over to his back yard or den and have a good session with him.[4]

Kazee's letter helps to explain Edwards' success in his pursuit of his hobby. First, letters from Australia to retired musicians were almost sure to generate curiosity and a response from the recipient, who couldn't help but be flattered by the inquiry from halfway around the world. It was said that inquiries from closer to home were more likely to be set aside for fear they were coming from some Federal revenue officer.

Edwards's diligence in his research proved him a man of intelligence, industry, and dedication—traits evident when he was still young. When he was fifteen years old, he had been evaluated by the local vocational guidance bureau and was told,

> Your tests reveal a very superior intellectual ability with well balanced theoretical and practical aptitudes. Best ratings are in practical reasoning and visualization of shape and pattern, which are both very superior, while verbal and numerical reasoning are superior.
>
> Provided that you apply yourself seriously to your studies you are capable of obtaining a very creditable pass in the Leaving Certificate, with prospects of obtaining assistance in taking a University degree.[5]

John did not go to a university, however, but took a job with the municipal transit agency after completing school. In the 1950s he and Archie Green struck up a correspondence, and Archie urged him to apply to an American university—the University of California at Berkeley or at Los Angeles—so he could come here to study American folklore. I should note that Australian universities were not interested in anything so common as country music, either American or Australian. Archie asked several friends to establish a Friends of John Edwards Committee to help finance a trip to the United States and help him win a university scholarship. Peter Tamony—a San Francisco lexicographer who later donated one of the most important collections to the John Edwards Memorial Foundation, was the first to volunteer, making a $50 donation to start the ball rolling. John hesitated to make the move, but in the meantime he enrolled at Sydney University for night classes, hoping to obtain a degree in the area of folklore.

Most serious students of American folk music know what happened in the ensuing years. Archie and Gene Earle were visiting together in New York over Christmas in 1960, when Gene received a cablegram from Irene Edwards telling of her son John's death in an automobile accident on Christmas Eve. He was driving home from a party, and just minutes from his house his car was struck by a large truck. He was killed instantly.

Gene circulated Edwards's will among collectors, seeking to find a suitable library for the collection, which arrived in New Jersey that summer. Gene, Archie, D. K. Wilgus, Ed Kahn, and Fred Hoeptner decided to form a non-profit corporation in California—the John Edwards Memorial Foundation—to carry out the intent of Edwards' will. Their problem was to find a congenial host university. Vanderbilt University, the University of Texas, and the University of North Carolina were early candidates. But at the time no Southern university had a commitment to regional vernacular culture that would have made the Edwards collection a logical acquisition. Only three universities then had active folklore programs: the University of Pennsylvania, Indiana University, and the University of California at Los Angeles. D. K. Wilgus had just come to UCLA from Bowling Green, Kentucky, and Wayland Hand, the chair of the Folklore and Mythology Center, was sympathetic to the study of American country music. Fred Hoeptner was an engineer living in Los Angeles, Ed Kahn had completed his undergraduate work at Oberlin College and had just come to UCLA to study Anthropology, and Gene Earle had just accepted a job with Hughes Aircraft in the Los Angeles area; so UCLA seemed the best location.

The John Edwards Memorial Foundation at UCLA

The John Edwards Memorial Foundation was established as a corporation in 1960 but had no address. Only in June of 1964 did it become the corporate occupant of a small office in the Folklore and Mythology Center on the top floor of UCLA's Bunche Hall, a building whose face had the appearance of a burnt waffle. Soon after opening its doors the JEMF received a grant of $5,000 from the Newport Folk Foundation. Part of this money brought Archie Green, then Librarian for the Institute of Labor and Industrial Relations at the University of Illinois, out to UCLA as a consultant. Archie established a filing system and archiving procedures to accommodate the ephemeral materials that comprised the JEMF's unique collection. With the remainder of the grant money the Board of Directors hired a part-time secretary/office manager. In the latter capacity, she directed the JEMF's one research assistant, occasional UCLA student volunteers, and work-study helpers, whom we employed to index the record holdings, the song folios, and the tape recordings.

In 1964 Ed Kahn proposed that we co-edit a newsletter, and the JEMF Board of Directors approved the idea when he presented it. Ed hesitated to make a commitment that would drain too much of our resources and energies, and after a lengthy discussion we decided on a modest mimeographed newsletter format. Unsure of our ability to maintain a regular quarterly schedule, we announced, "The *JEMF Newsletter* will be published several times a year at irregular intervals."[6] Its contents would include our foundation reports; works-in-progress items from collectors and scholars; notes and queries; bibliographic, historical, and discographic data; reprints of material from ephemeral sources; and correspondence.

Missing from this list of proposed subject matter was a promise of original articles. We were not quite ready to move beyond the scope of a simple "newsletter" and into the ranks of fan magazines or academic journals. In the first year most of the pages were taken up with annual reports, JEMF news, reprints of newspaper articles about the

JEMF, abstracts of academic dissertations that dealt with "our" music, lists of the JEMF holdings, and "tapescripts"—abbreviated transcripts of interview tapes in the JEMF archives.

In the *Newsletter*'s second year, Archie Green proposed a series of articles about country-music advertisements, posters, circulars, and other printed announcements, to be called "Country Music Graphics." Ed and I spent the better part of an evening pondering the title and its implications, and finally proposed that it be changed to "Commercial Music Graphics"—in order to allow for an eventual broader range of subject matter. We little realized at the time that we were inaugurating what was to become the JEMF *Newsletter/Quarterly*'s longest-running feature and perhaps its most significant contribution to music scholarship.[7]

In its first few years, the JEMF's financial status teetered precariously on the brink of insolvency. Ed Kahn and Archie Green took advantage of their own friendships with people within the record and country-music industries to solicit contributions to the JEMF, but we continually lacked adequate funds to carry out all the projects we envisioned. In 1965 and 1966 Ed and our then-secretary ran food concession booths at the annual Topanga Canyon Banjo-Fiddle Contests in order to raise a precious few hundred dollars that paid for postage expenses, but we realized in retrospect that hawking hotdogs dissipated manpower far too inefficiently.

Throughout 1966 and 1967 one of the goals uppermost in our minds was the inauguration of a series of record reissues that would span all phases of hillbilly music in a set of carefully planned and meticulously annotated LP albums. We had two goals in mind, apart from the subject matter itself of the albums: (1) establishing a precedent for academic institutions to lease out-of-print recordings from the original owners; and (2) setting high standards for the careful documentation of sound recordings. We proudly announced our plans in the September 1967 issue of the *Newsletter*, outlining the contents of the albums that we envisioned.[8] We recognized that our actions were somewhat premature—we had neither the funds nor the committed personnel nor the agreements with the record companies—yet we felt the urgent need to offer a new approach to the reissue problem: the major companies were issuing very little vintage material, and the few small independent companies working with the material were doing so illegally—i.e., without the authorization of the legal owners of the recordings. We thought that a non-commercial, educational institution might be able to secure the cooperation of the major labels—RCA, Columbia, Decca, Capitol—and break an impasse that collectors and scholars alike deplored. Consequently, we plunged into the waters without life raft or even a clear view of the opposite shore.

While we struggled with the problems of permissions, we opened negotiations with philanthropic sources for financial support for the project. Not until 1975 did we receive a grant from the National Endowment for the Arts to support a record reissue project, by which time we had already issued three albums with moneys raised directly on our own. By this time, other companies had become much more active in producing reissues, both authorized and otherwise, blunting somewhat the urgency of our original commitment. We took a much more modest approach to our own program. With the NEA funds we hired Paul Wells as project manager, and in the next six years we produced six more albums. Although our most elaborate record brochures ended up costing more to produce than the albums themselves, in most cases we eventually recovered all our expenses in album sales. Our first album—JEMF 101: *The Carter Family on Border Radio* had sold nearly 5,000 copies by 1983, the year we transferred rights to Down Home Music; and JEMF 102: *The Sons of the Pioneers* had sold nearly 4,000. I count among the JEMF's efforts some of the best-documented folk-music albums ever issued.

As part of our arrangement with UCLA, our student workers and secretaries were on the UCLA payroll, and supplies, telephone, and printing were all paid out of UCLA accounts. To receive this cooperation, we had to make periodic gifts to UCLA, against which all our expenses would be charged. For a few years we managed to keep within our budgets, but in the late 1960s, as we became more ambitious in our various publication programs, we were continually running into the red. Only the inefficiency of UCLA's financial bureaucracy enabled this to continue for months at at time before coming to the attention of the authorities. As our debt to UCLA mounted, we sought more and more desperate measures. Finally, in 1983, when we owed the University over $20,000, we saw no alternative but to sell the collection.

In the 1960s we always kept such a denouement in the back of our minds as we explored ideas for keeping the Foundation fiscally afloat. At annual Board of Directors Meetings we repeatedly argued over the wisdom of allowing our UCLA ledger sheet to go into the red. Wayland Hand, unable to shed his status as a representative of the University, counseled against running a deficit, and most of the other Directors present sympathized with this fiscally conservative position. Archie Green, however, boldly advocated "deficit spending": we always had the assets of the Foundation as security against any debts. If we hadn't heeded his suggestion, fully half of the JEMF's projects would never have been undertaken.

In 1967 Ken Griffis, a long-time fan of western music, contacted Ed Kahn and asked if he could do anything to help the JEMF. Ultimately, out of Ken's eager desire to help arose the Friends of the JEMF, an organization devoted to raising funds for the Foundation; and without Ken's enthusiastic work organizing benefit concerts and other promotional projects we surely would have had to close our doors long ago. Most importantly, Ken's dedication gave us the luxury of separating the fund-raising chores from the executive responsibilities of running an archival and research facility. In 1973, '74, '76, and '78 Ken engineered a series of successful benefit evenings, the most rewarding of which netted more than $20,000 for the JEMF. This enabled us to pay off the mounting debts to UCLA and put us in the black for the next couple of years. In 1968 Paul Soelberg, one of the managers of the Stoneman Family, approached us with a proposal. We had just run an interview and discography of Ernest V. "Pop" Stoneman, and the family was interested in publishing some sort of booklet with a biography and discography as a tribute to the late pioneer recording artist. We had as yet no established mechanism for publications other than the *Newsletter* and scholarly reprints. This enticement prompted us to establish another on-going publication format: the Special Series, deliberately titled broadly so as to encompass a wide range of potential contributions, but distinct from the Reprints Series in that the Special Series would consist of material that had not already been published elsewhere. *The Recording Career of Ernest V. "Pop" Stoneman* became Special Series 1, to be followed over the years by modest bio-discographies of Uncle Dave Macon, Molly O'Day, and others. Eventually Ken Griffis and Johnny Bond wrote what were to become two of the best-selling—as well as the most ambitious—undertakings in the series: Bond's own autobiography/discography and Griffis's biography/discography of the Sons of the Pioneers.

The contents of the *Newsletter* broadened considerably in the third, and especially the fourth, volumes. Discographies and checklists of discographies appeared frequently. In the tenth issue (June 1968) we published the first original article—apart from Archie Green's Graphics series: a biblio-discography of the "Whitehouse Blues"/"Cannonball Blues"/"McKinley" song complex, contributed by Neil V. Rosenberg.

Early in 1969, surprised subscribers to the *Newsletter* received, instead of the publication to which they were accustomed, a periodical in a heavy wrap-around cover with a quaint pen-and-ink sketch of a primitive recording machine, and a new title, the *JEMF Quarterly*. Inside the front cover, following the identification of the editor, appeared the standard sentence: "Please address all manuscripts and other communications to. . . ." The significance of this instruction is that previously the *Newsletter* asked only for correspondence, not manuscripts. An editorial explained to readers that we felt we had outgrown the format of a house organ, that the old title no longer seemed appropriate, and that we now encouraged readers' contributions in the form of letters, discographies, biographical accounts, song studies, or other forms. Furthermore, we reminded readers that "although the emphasis of the *Newsletter* was hillbilly music, we will welcome contributions in parallel areas of commercially recorded folk music: blues, cajun, folk-rock, etc."[9]

Although this editorial prompted no immediate readers' comments, over the next several years we frequently received angry letters from long-time readers who were cancelling their subscriptions because the *JEMF Quarterly* was moving away from the "golden age" hillbilly music so dear to the heart of John Edwards himself. In the Spring 1971 issue we published for the first time such a letter from a dissatisfied reader—and a very knowledgeable student of hillbilly music at that. In an editorial following the letter we tried to indicate the reasons for our position, but evidently many readers each year failed to see the logic in our arguments and harshly denounced the JEMF and its officers as being disloyal to John Edwards' memory.[10]

Occasionally other matters prompted readers to express their dissatisfaction. I recall three: (1) a critical review of a bluegrass songbook, which earned a scathing denunciation from the book's author; (2) an article on the cowboy ballad "The Strawberry Roan," which included a particularly graphic bawdy version of the song—some readers expressed mortification that we should have published such obscenities in the *JEMF Quarterly*; and (3) an article by an Austin, Texas, bartender who had a bit part in the film *Outlaw Blues*. Once again the complaint resounded that the *JEMF Quarterly* was straying unconscionably from its proper sphere of activity—old-time hillbilly music. But apart from a few such instances, the *JEMF Quarterly* readers generally kept their complaints—if they had any—to themselves, expressing them only implicitly in their declining to renew expired subscriptions at the appropriate time.

By the decade's end, we had four publication ventures underway: the *Quarterly*, the Record Reissue Project, the Reprint Series, and the Special Series. At their inception, each of these constituted a major innovation in the scholarship of vernacular music; readers outside the close circle of JEMF advisers and friends remained unaware of the blood and sweat that accompanied the production of most of those items. And yet, something was going wrong: instead of having a steadily growing cadre of colleagues, students, and associates to assist in each new undertaking, we found that responsibilities came to fall increasingly on the shoulders of two or three individuals and no one else. If Ken Griffis and Archie Green had not volunteered so much time, half of our projects could never have reached fruition.

Ironically, as local participation in the JEMF's operations dwindled, respect and admiration for our accomplishments increased around the world. Each week's mail brought requests from high school or college students—sometimes so vaguely general as to defy response ("Please send me everything you have on country music . . ."). Many letters came from barely literate fans: "Please send me a list of all recordings by Ernest Tubb . . ."; or "I want to get all recordings by Hank Williams; please tell me what you have. . . ." We received requests for evaluating records or entire collections—sometimes on the skimpiest of information. "I have a box of very old rare recordings by Paul Whiteman, Guy Lombardo, and Frank Sinatra. Can you tell me how much they are worth?"

We also dealt with more scholarly appeals from students, writers, or fans. Some asked for material, photographs, or dubs of recordings to be used for serious academic studies or forthcoming commercial publications. Unlike other sound-recording archives, we always maintained a policy of willingness to copy out-of-print recordings with no more paperwork than a signed assurance that the items would not be used for commercial purposes. (I hope our friends at the University of North Carolina can continue a similar policy.) Some scholars and students came to Los Angeles expressly to work with JEMF materials. Invariably, they expressed astonishment at the incongruity between the JEMF's reputation and its crowded quarters. In those years, the JEMF was like the Wizard of Oz, whom Dorothy and her friends bravely traveled to see; yet when they found him, their astonishment at seeing what the Wizard really looked like left them speechless. Ultimately, these visits, letters, and phone calls contributed to numberless projects. Apart from the JEMF's own products, we could display a long list of scholarly and trade publications in folk and country music that acknowledged the JEMF for materials.

When the Folklore and Mythology Center moved from Bunche Hall to larger quarters in the Graduate School of Management building at UCLA, the JEMF was generously given two offices. I felt we had arrived in Paradise. But we had been put in Paradise with a forbidden tree in our midst, and that tree was deficit spending. Although tasting of that fruit enabled much of our work to proceed, it ultimately led to our downfall. Discretion restrains me from identifying the various persons representing the characters in this Biblical allegory. At any rate, our salvation lay in banishment from Paradise. Adam and Eve, as you recall, settled somewhere east of Eden when they started the second phase of their lives. Actually, Chapel Hill is some fifty miles southeast of Eden, North Carolina, but perhaps the analogy is still valid.

When I now look back at copies of old issues of the *Quarterly*, I invariably wince as my attention is riveted by a typo that somehow had eluded the most well-intentioned editorial eye. This annoyance aside, I am pleased by the breadth of material that we did manage to encompass notwithstanding the limitations of staff and funds. Though we alienated some readers by our gradual movement away from country music as our exclusive interest, I feel that we provided the first public forum for serious articles on many aspects of vernacular music. Our first article on blues music in 1970 may not have been ground-breaking, but our first bibliographies on rock music in 1972 and on a folk-revival performer in 1976 became early serious contributions to those fields, and our biography/discography on Polish-American fiddler Karol Stoch opened up new territory in 1977. A former secretary of mine still recalls with anguish having to type—in Polish—that discography.

In retrospect, much of what we accomplished as the JEMF could have been done without the collection that was housed in cramped quarters at UCLA. In practice, our material resources were augmented immensely by the collections of Gene, Ed, Archie, D.K., and Ken, all of whom unstintingly made their own possessions annexes to the holdings of the JEMF. The JEMF was called an "archive and research center," but really, the former was only an excuse, not a prerequisite, for the latter. It was these individuals who made the JEMF's reputation, not its collection. It was their dedication, not its resources, that led to its accomplishments. And while they are all to be acknowledged for their role, I suspect each of them must have felt, at some time, that strange, uneasy mixture of importance and bondage; the nagging worry that if they were to walk away, no one would be left to hold the structure upright.

The JEMF at the University of North Carolina

I like to think that what we are giving UNC is not primarily a collection but three other, less tangible gifts: (1) a name, (2) a reputation, and (3) a mandate. The name is that of an Australian enthusiast who facilitated the first institutional archive in America devoted to commercially recorded and published folk music.

The reputation is that of a resource of considerable scope, accessibility, and achievements. The UNC Southern Folklife Collection will have to deal with two problems that faced the JEMF as an "archive and research center." The first is the paramount problem that faces any library: how to balance security and preservation against accessibility. These days, accesibility is more than being able to touch the folios and play the records; accessibility needs to be genuinely creative. Of course, that includes taking advantage of the new opportunities afforded by electronic data storage and retrieval techniques. Creative accessibility, in our context, also means involving ordinary members of the community, so that the archive becomes an extension of living traditions, not just the graveyard of dead ones. We look for an environment that stimulates research and study and interacts constructively, not patronizingly, with the community around it. If the University errs on the side of overzealous security and preservation, rather than accessibility, it risks alienating the public whose support is essential: An archive of vernacular music without vernacular support is doomed. The second problem is simply how to avoid any one individual, or small handful of persons, from becoming indispensible to the operations of the organization. Paradise is a wonderful place to spend a lifetime, but not if you are the gardener there.

Finally, the mandate we extend is that our successors at the University of North Carolina preserve, explore, and support America's grass-roots music—all of it, not just hillbilly or country music. I don't think John Edwards would have objected.

Daniel W. Patterson

The History of the Southern Folklife Collection

I. The Era of Surprise

*N*orm Cohen* has written of the uncanny foresight, dedication, and judicious and sustained effort that built the John Edwards Memorial Collection—now the star acquisition of the Southern Folklife Collection at the University of North Carolina. It comprises seventy percent of our holdings. An account of the history of the other thirty percent of the Southern Folklife Collection—what we used to call the North Carolina Folk Music Archives—is also a tale of efforts sustained with dedication over a considerable period of time. But it is a story illustrative not so much of foresight as of unforeseen consequences and happy surprises.

When I came to the University of North Carolina as a graduate student in 1953, the only folk-music recordings on campus stood in a small bookcase in the office of Arthur Palmer Hudson of the Department of English. He used them to teach his course "The English Ballad." Hudson himself had grown up in rural Mississippi. He heard ballad singing from childhood. He had assembled a sizeable field collection for his doctoral dissertation, *Folksongs of Mississippi and Their Background*, later published.[1] And he left a beautiful and affectionate account of the traditional culture of the world of his youth.[2] But his record collection was small and, frankly, a hodge-podge—partly because so little was available for purchase when he was building his course, but chiefly because his interest in song was literary rather than musical. So in class he played the Kingston Trio's ripsnorting "Tom Dula" and tuxedoed Richard Dyer-Bennett's effete rendition of "The Golden Vanity." He played John Jacob Niles's dolor-ous wailing of "Black is the Color" and the chaste but throaty performance of "Blow the Wind Southerly" by the English classical contralto Kathleen Ferrier. But he also played Horton Barker's "The Farmer's Curst Wife" and Mrs. Texas Gladden's "Mary Hamilton" and Carrie Grover's "The Lowlands of Holland" and Elmer Barton's "The Bonny Banks of Babreo"—traditional performances that he had on one album from the Flanders Collection at Middlebury College and on three or four from the Library of Congress. When he played these pieces in class, Hudson listened as raptly to the over-artful renditions of Dyer-Bennett as to the classic traditional performances of Horton Barker. But for his students—I was one of them—the effect of this strange mixture of recordings was shocking. It educated us in ways in which that admirable teacher never intended, never suspected. For me, the result was that I began to hunt for and discover the albums that John and Alan Lomax, Ben Botkin, and others had edited from the field collections at the Library of Congress, or that Mike Seeger, John Cohen, Archie Green, Ralph Rinzler, Sandy Paton, and dozens of others were editing for release by Folkways and other small commercial companies. Chance had opened my ear.

Then chance threw another unforeseen opportunity at me—I had been hired into the Department of English, and when Hudson retired in 1968 the chairman asked if I would take over the ballad course. I grabbed for it, widened its title and scope to "British and American Folksong," and to glorify the classes began buying the increasingly available albums of traditional performances. I was buying them from my own pocket, and on an assistant professor's salary that got expensive fast. So I asked for permission to buy recordings from the departmental budget for book purchases. Approval for this request came from long-departed and forgotten persons, the members of a departmental committee and a few library functionaries. Those unreflective decisions actually created the Southern Folklife Collection—although we would be twenty years in discovering the fact—because items purchased from public book funds cannot be kept in a private faculty office. They must be housed and accessible somewhere in the library. For another two decades we were not to have an official home within the library, but, unofficially, friendly librarians in the Collections Development Office gave us occasional financial support, and we got work and storage space at one time or another from the North Carolina Collection, the Music Library, and Undergraduate Library.

Accidents continued to spur our development. Several others were of particular importance. First, when we set up the collection in the Undergraduate Library for classroom and student use, we soon found album notes missing and the disks raked with scratches. We saw that we needed to make a copy of each disk for public listening and turn the originals into a protected collection. And that's how we came to define what we were doing: we were building a collection to serve the future as well as the present.

Another accidental stimulation of our growth came from Professor and Mrs. Hudson. As they grew too infirm to maintain their home, they donated his papers and field tapes to the University. That set us thinking about other collections we knew had been made here. We needed to find them and pull them in—those of Ralph Steele Boggs, Hoyle Bruton, Lamar Stringfield, Jan P. Schinhan, Philip Kennedy, Guy B. Johnson, and others. Boggs, when we contacted him, was delighted to send the recordings he had made here of the Dogwood Folk Festival in the 1940s and of hispanic singers he had later recorded in Tampa. His student Hoyle Bruton, who was the first editor of the *North Carolina Folklore Journal*, had made wire recordings in the North Carolina piedmont in the late '40s. I tracked him down in Pennsylvania—only to have him write that the wires had gotten so tangled in the shoebox where he kept the spools that he had thrown the recordings away. Lamar Stringfield appears to have done field collecting while based in a paper organization called The Folk Music Institute at UNC in the same years, but a half dozen of his pencil transcriptions of folktunes are the only things yet recovered from his work. Jan Schinhan's son, I learned from a student who had taken piano from Schinhan in his latter years, still had Schinhan's acetate and aluminum direct-to-disk field recordings, and he was happy to place them in the library. Philip Kennedy's tape recordings, made in the 1950s, during his graduate years at the University, got flooded while stored in a basement in Charlotte and were thrown out. Guy Johnson regretfully (and mistakenly, I'm happy to say) reported that the wax cylinders he recorded with an Ediphone on St. Helena Island in 1928 had not survived a Chapel Hill summer in his attic.[3] From these and similar experiences, we learned one great lesson: that only when collections get placed in a stable institution do they have much chance of survival. Accidents in storage, the collector's loss of interest, and the indifference, ignorance, or burdens of one's heirs may imperil a collection. So we tried to make sure that from then on, materials we generated in the Curriculum—fieldtapes, outtakes from documentary films, photographs, and manuscripts got out of faculty offices and student apartments and under the roof, at least, of the library.

Other happy surprises continued to help us, as for example, the matriculation of graduate students like Laurel Horton (who came with a master's degree in Library Science), Tom Carter (who arrived extremely knowledgeable about old-time fiddling), or Bruce Bastin (who had already published one book on blues before he reached Chapel Hill). Experts like Tom and Bruce served as advisers for our purchases and greatly extended the range and quality of our holdings. Laurel helped us establish reasonably professional procedures for handling our acquisitions, and she and virtually every graduate student in folklore since the early 1970s gave dedicated service to the collection. We had no other staff.

Year by year the collection was growing, but it was still not impressive enough to command much attention from the University. It took the acquisition of the John Edwards Memorial Collection to do that. And we in the Curriculum cannot even claim the credit of foresight or cunning or determination in its acquisition. We simply invited Archie Green here to give a lecture to our program. Unknown to us, Archie and others on the JEMF Board of Directors were already concerned to find a Southern home for the John Edwards Memorial Collection and greater institutional support for it. He and Norm Cohen began to ask whether this University might be interested in the collection. The Curriculum was, exceedingly. But we did not wish to plunder a sister institution. We roused into action only when it became clear that circumstances required the Foundation to act. Then we found it easy to get University support for the purchase of the John Edwards Memorial Collection. From the days of Howard Odum and Guy Johnson in the 1920s the University has been committed to regional studies. The Departments of History and English are widely known for their specialists in Southern history and literature. The Southern Historical Collection in the Library is a center for research in Southern culture. The Library quickly allocated funds for the purchase of this distinguished Southern collection, and a half-dozen other departments and administrators found resources to help us with other costs incidental to the purchase. The acquisition of the John Edwards Memorial Collection in 1983, suddenly gave our entire folk-music-recording collection weight and significance enough to have a legitimate claim on University resources. But the University did not realize it.

That fact too changed as the result of a happy accident. By university regulation, every department and program must undergo a periodic evaluation. Our turn came in 1983, and we had to nominate a distinguished folklorist to come from outside to evaluate us. We suggested Dr. Archie Green. Looking back at this recommendation from the vantage point of the present, my colleague Terry Zug and I can see that this was the most brilliant decision of our careers. But we were not at that time fully aware of what we had done—which was to turn loose upon the University one of the great lobbyists of our time. Archie looked at us and saw, I fear, less achievement than potential. But being Archie, he immediately set about, with all his force and skill, to try to help us fulfill that potential. Two weeks after his departure our allocation for speakers leapt from $25 a year to $2,000. He had spoken on the subject with the Dean. And we got a promise of another faculty member for the Curriculum. Archie had talked to the Dean about that too. Glenn D. Hinson's appointment in 1989 was the fulfillment of that promise. And also, I believe, as a result of his visit (for Archie had spoken of it to him) the Provost decided that the combined John Edwards Memorial Collection and University of North Carolina Folk Music Archives formed a serious research collection and deserved an official place in the library system.

Looking back at this sequence of happy surprises, we feel gratitude to all those who served as agents and catalysts for them—to the late Arthur Palmer Hudson, who shocked us into a sense of the power of traditional performances; to the bureaucrats whose procedures required that materials bought with library funds must stay within a library; to students who imperiled the first albums and made us want to safeguard them; to elderly colleagues who had lost rare collections and thereby taught us to take care of our own; to other students who brought us expertise; to Archie Green, a patron saint who has never stopped showering us with favors; and to administrators and librarians who were so conscientious that they proved susceptible to Archie's powers of persuasion. In all this, I find confirmation of Emerson's wise judgment on "Experience": that "the individual is always mistaken. It turns out somewhat new and very unlike what he promised himself." But with the collection now established in the library, we were at the end of our era of improvisation and surprise, and the story turns into an account of genuine accomplishments, tested procedures, wider service, and ambitious plans.

Michael T. Casey

The History of the Southern
Folklife Collection
II. Recent Developments

On April 21, 1983, a large truck carrying 929 carefully packed boxes completed its coast-to-coast journey and rolled into Chapel Hill, making its only stop at the loading dock of the University's Undergraduate Library. The John Edwards Memorial Collection (JEMC) had arrived at the University of North Carolina, bringing traditional music of the South back home. I was not present for that day of careful unloading. But I was fortunate to land in Chapel Hill four months later to pursue a graduate degree in Folklore, becoming gradually involved in a network of musicians, collectors, folklorists, fans, and other country-music researchers and enthusiasts bound together in large measure by this wonderful archival collection and the ground-breaking work of the Foundation that built it.

Little had I realized in Kent, Ohio (where I was learning about both string-band music and this far-reaching collection then housed at UCLA) the extent to which I would become involved with the JEMC. I vividly remember my friend Jeff Esworthy, inspired by such stalwarts of the Kent old-time music scene as Kerry Blech, Andy Cohen, and Joe LaRose, playing me a song he had learned called "The Jake Walk Blues" and then excitedly showing me a copy of *The John Edwards Memorial Foundation Quarterly* with an article that described the origin of the song. Such are the ways in which fate and circumstance operate: five months later I was unpacking the John Edwards Memorial Collection in Chapel Hill; five years later I was overseeing its growth and development as the crown jewel of the University Library's Southern Folklife Collection.

Norm Cohen has assessed the JEMC's accomplishments while housed in Los Angeles and Daniel Patterson the development of the folklore archives in Chapel Hill. I offer here a view of the growth and development of these collections (simultaneously addressing issues that I believe are pertinent to other small sound archives) from the perspective of a largely unaware graduate student who happened to arrive on campus at roughly the same time as the JEMC, and who several years later gained the opportunity to staff both collections during their infancy in the University Library system.

I remember fairly well that first week in Chapel Hill—going to introductory meetings with students and faculty, scrambling to arrange classes, and negotiating the town's transportation and parking systems. At least our potential work assignments seemed clearcut: the UNC Folklore Archives (sometimes still called the North Carolina Folk Music Archives) was located in a small basement room in the foreign-languages building (with listening cassettes and a card catalog housed in the Music Library) and was functioning pretty well. In the absence of sufficient shelf space, its LPs and open-reel field tapes were stored in boxes, and the archive's audio equipment (mostly consumer-grade) didn't always work as well as we would have wished. But students assigned to the archives logged field tapes, dubbed LPs onto listening cassettes, and answered the occasional research question. In other words, they were able to listen to music from the collection. The Edwards Collection at that time was a stack of 900-plus unopened boxes pressed against the wall of a locked room in the basement of the Undergraduate Library. Few, if any, of the incoming students realized what was in those boxes. The glamorous work, or so it seemed to us at the time, lay in the Folklore Archives.

I had at least a few ideas of what must be in those boxes because of what I had heard in Ohio. And since I didn't get first crack at choosing a work assignment, I began the long task of unpacking the JEMC, assisting fellow Folklore graduate student Joseph Sobol and Library Science graduate student Lucy Powell. The task was formidable, and further complicated by the fact that we had no real archivist (not to mention a sound archivist) on board. Advice from the Library School and the Music Library, support from Don Shaw of the Media Center, and wise counsel from Dan Patterson, the driving force behind UNC's acquisition of the Edwards Collection and then chair of the Curriculum in Folklore, guided our work and prevented us from making irreversible mistakes. We decided early on not to unpack the sound recordings—thousands of 78s, 45s, and LPs lovingly and meticulously laid by Eugene Earle into sturdy boxes for the move—as we knew that eventually the collection would have to vacate the temporary room generously given over to us by the Undergraduate Library. Besides, we had nothing on which to play these recordings and little understanding of the specialized, professional equipment and archival procedures needed to safely recover their sound in a way that also assured their long-term preservation. For the next five years the recordings remained in Earle's boxes, stored vertically on library shelves, while work in the Collection focused on paper materials. Graduate students unpacked and organized artist files into filing cabinets, sorted periodicals and created a Kardex system to track them, and indexed and filed song folios. Slowly, the riches of the JEMC became apparent.

Six months after we started this work the UNC Folklore Archives joined us in our already cramped room. The language laboratories needed additional space, so for the third time the Archives collection was loaded into Professor Terry Zug's van and taken on the road. With the addition of 4,000 or so recordings and four additional graduate students, life was never dull at the bottom of the Undergraduate Library. We were indeed fortunate that our hosts remained willing to give up a significant amount of space for what turned out to be a five-year period. My tenure with the John Edwards Memorial Collection ended in 1985, or so I thought at the time, when I completed course work at UNC and moved on to other folklore-related projects.

In late 1986 the JEMC and the UNC Folklore Archives were placed in the Manuscripts Department of the Academic Affairs Library, and the entity we know today as the Southern Folklife Collection (SFC) was born. It was a wise move, from the perspective of both the Library and the Collection. The SFC formed a natural complement to the Manuscripts Department's well-known and respected Southern Historical Collection, which contains over ten million manuscripts and has served as a center for research into Southern history and culture for over fifty years. The move into the library system provided the JEMC and UNC Folklore Archives with solid institutional support and professional staffing for the first time in the history of the two collections.

In January 1987 I was selected to fill the first full-time position for the Collection and returned to UNC. With assistance from Tim West, the Manuscripts Department's Technical Services Archivist, I began taking stock of the past history of these materials both at UNC and UCLA, and conducted an initial survey and inventory of collection holdings. This made our overall goal for the coming years clear: to establish a professional sound archive incorporating reference, preservation, access, and collection-development functions at a level worthy of the promise that scholars had seen in the collection's holdings for years. Departmental and Library staff gradually came to share this goal as the potential of the Collection became ever more apparent during the SFC's first two years. That this represented large ambitions was evidenced by the fact that no one on staff at the Manuscripts Department, including myself, had much detailed knowledge of how these functions are carried out in a sound archive. So began a lengthy period of self-education that included visiting other sound archives, compiling the few hard-to-find articles on the subject, talking with sound archivists at meetings and on the phone, and participating in annual meetings of the Association for Recorded Sound Collections, the national organization for institutional sound archives and private collectors.

Some of our goals at the beginning were also much more local and practical. In January 1987 I had two immediate and pressing tasks: first, to figure out how to move over thirty thousand sound recordings and related paper materials from the basement of the Undergraduate Library to the fourth floor of Wilson Library, the newly renovated special collections building at UNC-CH and the future home for the SFC. That was happily accomplished without incident in August 1987. Settling the Collection into its new home naturally forced us to address long-term storage and location issues for the seven formats of audio recordings that we held at the time, as well as for the other types of materials contained in the SFC. So we developed a plan addressing how formats would be shelved and where they would be best located for long-term preservation, maximum safety, and convenience, given the space we had to work with.

My second task involved finding ways to provide staff and researchers access to the recordings in the Collection. Physical access was the first concern. Consultations with other sound archivists and with sound engineers gave me a clearer notion of the differences between professional, semi-professional, and consumer-grade audio equipment, as well as suggestions regarding specific items appropriate to the small studio and listening carrels that we were planning. Fortunately, the University Library helped with a one-time special allocation of funds that, along with a donation from The Record Bar, allowed us to purchase professional-grade audio equipment. Further donations from The Record Bar and from Mr. Ben Jones, a loyal alumnus of the University, enabled us to purchase additional audio and video equipment. The result is a professionally-equipped studio where we restore and transfer original recordings for public service use or for archival preservation, and two listening carrels in the public service area where researchers may listen to cassette copies of SFC holdings. Classes in sound engineering and specialized training at other sound archives prepared me to use this equipment in an archivally appropriate manner, and taught me when to seek outside help for materials or formats that we could not handle.

Soon after addressing technical equipment issues, we settled into more difficult questions of how and when to open the SFC for research use. Much of the Collection needed reorganization to current professional standards, and a good bit of it simply required organizing. For example, many of our sound recordings, for reasons described above, were still in the boxes that Eugene Earle had so carefully packed years earlier in California. Shortly after our move into Wilson Library we finally unpacked the recordings, taking three separate runs of 78s and six card catalogs, and combining them into one of each—a massive juggling act involving 14,000 recordings and over 60,000 cards. We also worked with the JEMC's photographic prints, which had been pulled from vertical files containing manuscripts and placed into acid-free sleeves in file cabinets when the JEMC first arrived. We took several additional steps, assigning call numbers, designing a microcomputer database to index the collection, and rehousing individual items into better-fitting archival-quality sleeves stored in document cases. Some of this organizational work continues to this day. For example, we are currently creating a computer-based shelf list for our collection of instantaneous (acetate) disks, while resleeving and rehousing them according to practices followed in sound archives. This represents the first attention that these materials have received. We are also actively transferring the most valuable of these acetate disk recordings—which represent one of the least stable formats in sound archives—onto preservation master tape. We also had to solve problems of intellectual access before the Collection could open. Again, we were fortunate. The L. J. Skaggs and Mary C. Skaggs Foundation in Oakland, California, awarded a two-year grant enabling us to index one-half of our LP collection and most of our field recordings. This work, combined with the organization of the 78s, database indexing of photographs, and a quick indexing of our 45s, provided enough basic access to SFC holdings to justify opening the Collection. The Southern Folklife Collection officially opened to the public in April 1989, during the Sounds of the South Conference. It was our good fortune to have a distinguished array of guests, some of whom appear in this publication, to help us celebrate our coming of age.

The conference and official opening signaled the beginning of a new phase in the history of this collection, one marked by an increased level of activity on several fronts. The SFC now contains over 40,000 sound recordings, having added some 5,000 in the two years beginning January 1989. We have received major new collections during this time period from folklorists Archie Green, D. K. and Eleanor Wilgus, Artus Moser, and Ralph Steele Boggs; from sociologist Guy B. Johnson and publisher/musician Alice Gerrard; from medicine-show performer "Doc" Tommy Scott and public radio station WUNC-FM; from fieldworker/folklorists Nancy Kalow and Wayne Martin; from festival producer Harper Van Hoy (founder of Fiddler's Grove Festival in Union Grove, North Carolina) and businessman Roumel Wm. Taylor, proprietor of the New Gospel Light Music Store in Philadelphia. Their donations of audio and video recordings, photographs, manuscripts, sheet music, song books, periodicals, and other items document African-American spirituals and gospel music, old-time stringbands and bluegrass pickers, medicine-show performers and traditional tale tellers, ballad singers and North Carolina fiddlers, and blues singers and workers' culture, along with many other Southern traditions. We have received important donations from others too numerous to mention here, for which we are extremely grateful.

This new phase in our history is also marked by a shift from organizational work to addressing more persistent problems of long-term preservation and access. We have just received our first preservation grant, enabling us to restore and transfer important open-reel, acetate disc, and cassette recordings experiencing significant deterioration. From the North Carolina Arts Council we have also received another access grant (the Skaggs Foundation grant gave the first), with which we will produce a monthly radio show airing on WUNC-FM's "Back Porch Music." Both of these represent initial steps towards our long-term commitment of preserving the Collection's resources to the highest professional standards, while making them accessible to as wide an audience as possible.

Eight-and-one-half years have passed since the JEMC arrived on campus, five years since the combined folk music collections gained official standing in the Library system, and four years since these materials moved into permanent quarters, allowing in-depth work to begin on them. From a huge stack of unopened boxes in a temporary room at the bottom of the Undergraduate Library, the Southern Folklife Collection has grown into a fully functioning sound archive, actively working to preserve, develop, and create better access to its holdings. Granted, some areas of the collection are in better shape than others, and we still must face basic organizational work and additional upgrading. But we have made tremendous progress since that April day in 1983 when we welcomed the JEMC to Chapel Hill. Our goal is to fulfill the promise that for years many of you have seen in this collection. We hope that the Southern Folklife Collection, with the John Edwards Memorial Collection as its crown jewel and the work of the Foundation as its model, may help to stimulate and shape the study, performance, and enjoyment of the musical and oral traditions of the American South.

Walter C. West and Michael T. Casey

Who's Got What

A Survey of Southern Traditional Music in Public Repositories

*A*s we planned the Sounds of the South Conference, we scheduled a working session for archivists from institutions in the region that collect recordings of Southern traditional music. We wanted to take advantage of this rare opportunity to learn more about our common problems and opportunities. Since it was clear that the staff here knew little about the holdings of other institutions, and we guessed that this was true for other archivists as well, we conducted a survey to give us a firmer basis for discussions.

In February 1989 we sent a form entitled "Southern Folk Music Recordings: A Survey of Holdings and Collecting Activities" to thirty-three repositories. The twenty-two responses we received from the institutions listed at the end of this report provided the information we present below. Our aim with this survey was to share information that would assist archivists working with Southern traditions in two ways. We hoped, first, that it would help all of us shape our collecting. We thought that the survey might enable us to identify genres, ethnic groups, and geographic areas not adequately represented in public repositories, and/or areas in which we were unnecessarily duplicating one anothers' efforts. Second, we thought that having this information would enable us to refer our users, and even potential donors, more knowledgeably to other institutions. A virtually complete compilation of the data that we gathered was distributed to archivists who attended the Sounds of the South conference.

In a special Conference working session on Saturday morning approximately twenty archivists met to discuss issues of mutual concern. We addressed challenges that collectors and other users had issued to us in earlier sessions to make archival holdings more accessible. Further, the group discussed misconceptions that users often hold about public archives, including the costs of doing business, the requirements of copyright restrictions, and the length of time needed to provide service. But our discussion focussed chiefly on problems with, and especially the implications of, the survey. Now we have a chance to present to a broad audience a brief digest of key information gathered by the survey. We hope that those who use our repositories and those who contribute collections to them will find the information useful as an initial guide to working with us in understanding and documenting the region. The survey "results" reported here must be approached with caution, however. They are not a definitive or precise document, but a general guide to what has been done. Bear in mind, as you look over the tables that follow, that some repositories with extensive holdings in our field, including the Library of Congress, are either weakly represented or not represented at all. A few repositories did not return our survey; others were not able to provide information at the level of detail we requested. The information they had available forced most of those who did respond to use at least some, and often much, guesswork in generating their answers. We did not always agree on definitions of "Southern" or "traditional," and found differences in the way that we defined some of the genres. Further, it is likely that there are additional unlisted repositories with Southern holdings, especially outside the region.

Despite these limitations, the survey provides at least a beginning picture of the genres, groups, and geographic regions represented in public repositories with a primary responsibility for collecting Southern traditional music. It certainly gives us more information than we have had in the past, and we think that the picture painted by the survey is suggestive in many ways. Instead of trying to infer definitive results from this data, it seems more appropriate to draw from it a series of questions for further reflection and discussion.

The survey suggests that holdings lag dangerously in some areas, and this gives rise to a few striking questions:

1. Only one repository reports holding even 100 recordings of Native American music. While the number of recordings documenting Native American music is smaller than for some other traditions, can we document Native American traditions more fully?

2. No collection has even 100 recordings of shape-note performances. Are there further recordings, especially ones generated by
fieldworkers and participants, that we can get to document the shape-
note traditions?

3. Only two repositories report significant holdings of African-
American spirituals, and neither of them has even 1,000 recordings;
the same is true for the six collections reporting holdings of black
gospel recordings. Is this ground covered by archives from which
we do not have survey information—in particular, the Library of Congress and the Center for Popular Music at Middle Tennessee State
University, but also the historically African-American colleges and
universities? If so, is the documentation accessible?

Coverage of traditions within individual states also appears extremely variable. The long-standing interest in the folk music of the
Appalachians may well be reflected in the fact that the best documented states appear to be North Carolina and Kentucky, followed
closely by Tennessee, Virginia, and West Virginia. The traditional music of some Southern states, on the other hand, is not at all widely
held by the repositories in our survey.

1. Only the Country Music Foundation, with its principal strengths
in country music and related genres, reports over 100 recordings
from South Carolina. Does the Library of Congress hold extensive
documentation of South Carolina traditions? Or is South Carolina as
seriously underdocumented as it appears?

2. The Country Music Foundation holds over 10,000 recordings
from Alabama, but only two other institutions report holdings from
this state, and both of them have fewer than 1,000 recordings. Are
there institutions in Alabama with sizeable collections not reported
in the survey? If so, are these collections both accessible and marked
for long-term preservation? Does the Library of Congress have extensive holdings from this state?

3. Only one repository reported significant holdings from Dela-
ware; it held fewer than 1,000 recordings—and was in Tennessee!
Only the Country Music Foundation holds over 100 recordings from
Florida. Traditional music from Maryland and Oklahoma appears seriously underdocumented everywhere. Can we encourage fieldwork
in these states or find already collected material that remains in private hands?

These are just a few of the questions suggested by the survey. Others could be asked, though in some cases (the genres of occupational songs, classic blues, and children's songs, for example) it is clear that few recordings are presently available.

We welcome inquiries about the survey or its findings, and would appreciate corrections, supplementary information, or suggestions. We hope that the questions raised here will encourage discussion about how well public repositories are reaching their shared goal of documenting Southern traditional music—and stimulate renewed efforts to fill in the gaps.

Tabulation of the Findings of a Survey of Archival Collections of Southern Traditional Music

Key: Abbreviations for collections reported in the survey.

AS   Appalachian State University, W. L. Eury Appalachian Collection, Boone, NC
BC   Berea College, Appalachian Center, Berea, KY
CMF   Country Music Foundation, Nashville, TN
DEC   Davis and Elkins College, Augusta Heritage Center, Elkins, WV
ETS   East Tennessee State University, Archives of Appalachia, Johnson City, TN
FC   Ferrum College, Blue Ridge Heritage Archive, Ferrum, VA
GS   Georgia State University, Georgia Folklore Archives, Atlanta, GA
LC   Library of Congress, Archives of Folk Culture, Washington, DC
LSM   Louisiana State Museum, New Orleans Jazz Collections, New Orleans, LA
MH   Mars Hill College, Harris Media Center, Mars Hill, NC
MS   Morehead State University, Camden-Carroll Library, Morehead, KY
OZ   Ozark Folk Center, Mt. View, AR
SI   Smithsonian Institution, Office of Folklife Programs, Washington, DC
TU   Tulane University, William Ransom Hogan Jazz Archive, New Orleans, LA
UA   University of Alabama, W.S. Hoole Special Collections, Tuscaloosa, AL
UK   University of Kentucky, Appalachian Collection, Lexington, KY
UM   University of Mississippi, Blues Archive, University, MS
UNC   University of North Carolina, Southern Folklife Collection, Chapel Hill, NC
USL   University of Southwestern Louisiana, Center for Acadian and Creole Folklore, Lafayette, LA
UT   University of Texas at Austin, ECB Texas History Center, Austin, TX
UV   University of Virginia, Kevin Barry Perdue Archive of Traditional Culture, Charlottesville, VA
WV   West Virginia Univeristy, WV and Regional History collection, Morgantown, WV
WC   Western Carolina University, Mountain Heritage Center, Cullowhee, NC
WK   Western Kentucky University, Department of Special Library Collections, Bowling Green, KY

Holdings by Genre and Subject Category

Category	Number of Recordings		
	100–1,000	1,000–10,000	More than 10,000
Ballads	AS,CMF,MH,OZ,SI,UM,UNC,UT	WV	
Bluegrass	AS,ETS,FC,MH,SI,UM,UNC,UT,WV		CMF
Blues—Classic	LSM,SI,UM,UT		
Blues—Country	UT	SI,UM,UNC	
Blues—Urban	TU,UT,SI	UM	
Cajun	SI,UNC,USL,UT		CMF
Children's Songs	CMF,WV	SI	
Country	SI,OZ	UT	CMF,UNC
Country—Early	AS,BC,UT,OZ	UNC	CMF
Creole	CMF,SI,USL		
Gospel—Black	FC,SI,TU,UM,UNC,UT		
Gospel—White	BC,FC,SI,UNC,UT,WK		CMF
Hispanic	CMF,SI	UT	
Native American		SI	
Norteno	CMF,SI	UT	
Occupational Songs	SI,UNC,UT	CMF	
Old-Time	AS,ETS,FC,SI,WV,OZ,UT,DEC	UNC,BC	CMF
Ragtime	LSM,TU	CMF	
Religious Songs	BC,ETS,LSM,MH,SI,TU,UNC,UT,OZ	UNC	CMF
Rhythm & Blues	MH,TU,UT	UM	
Shape Note Songs			
Spirituals	TU,UT		
Western	UNC,UT		CMF
Western Swing	UNC,UT		CMF
Zydeco	CMF,SI,USL		

Holdings by State

State or Region	Number of Recordings		
	100–1,000	1,000–10,000	More than 10,000
Mountain South	AS,ETS,MH,UK,UM,UT,WC	BC,FC,WV,OZ	CMF,UNC
Piedmont South	FC,UM,UT,OZ	UNC	CMF
Coastal South	FC,SI	CMF,UNC	
Alabama	UA,UNC		CMF
Arkansas	SI	OZ	CMF
Delaware	CMF		
Florida		CMF	
Georgia	UNC	GS	CMF
Kentucky	BC,SI,UK,OZ	UNC,WK	CMF
Louisiana	LSM,SI,TU,UNC,USL,UT		CMF
Maryland	SI	CMF	
Mississippi	SI,UNC	CMF	UM
North Carolina	AS,BC,ETS,FC,MH,OZ	CMF	UNC
Oklahoma	SI		CMF
South Carolina		CMF	
Tennessee	BC,ETS,SI,UT,OZ	UNC	CMF
Texas	SI,UNC	UT	CMF
Virginia	BC,ETS,SI,	CMF,FC,UNC	
West Virginia	BC,UNC	DEC,WV	CMF

Holdings by Repository

Repository	Total Rec's*	Regional Strengths (over 1,000) recordings	
		Genre	State
AS	1,311		
BC	2,500	old-time	
CMF	120,000	bluegrass, cajun, early country, white gospel, old-time, religious songs, western, western swing, honky tonk, occupational songs, ragtime, rockabilly, cowboy	AL,AR,GA, KY,LA,OK, TN,TX,WV, FL,MD,MS, NC,SC,VA
DEC	1,900		WV
ETS	831		
FC	2,800		VA
GS			GA
LC	16,000	unknown	unknown
LSM	50		
MH	2,000–3,000		
MS	60		
OZ	1,250		AR
SI	10,000	American Indian, blues (classic, urban, country), children's songs	
TU	1,000		
UA	600		
UK	550		
UM	30,000	blues (country, urban), rhythm and blues	MS
UNC	32,000	country, blues (country), early country, old-time, religious songs	KY,NC,TN,VA
UT	2,000–3,000	country, Hispanic	TX
UV	1,550		
WV	2,415		WV
WC	135		
WK			KY

*Indicates total number of recordings of Southern folk music as reported in early 1989.

Barry Ancelet

The Center for Acadian and Creole Folklore
An Experiment in Guerrilla Academics

*T*he *joke* around Louisiana these days is: "The good news is that Cajun is hot; the bad news is that Cajun is hot." Journalists have asked me so often lately to tell them what I do that I have been tempted to answer, "What I do is tell journalists about what I used to have time to do before the flood of interest in things Cajun." But fads come and go and when this one is gone, I hope to be still doing what I have done since I wandered into this profession in the mid-1970s.

I became interested in Louisiana French culture while studying in France. I was born and raised near Lafayette, Louisiana, in the heart of Cajun country, speaking Cajun French. But when I began taking French courses in high school, I was led to believe that it was a foreign language. By my junior year in the university, I was convinced that the language we spoke at home had nothing to do with the French language. Never mind the fact that ninety-five percent of the words were the same.

In 1972–73 I spent an academic year in France, at the University of Nice, where I began to understand that the language I had learned at home in Louisiana worked just fine to communicate on a daily conversational basis with the French, though there were some cultural, referential, and syntactic differences. My professors often told me that what I had just said was not said, and my French friends thought my accent and expressions were cute. By the middle of the year I was homesick.

One day while I was walking down the streets of Nice, a poster aroused my curiosity. It read, "Roger Mason chante la musique traditionnelle de la Louisiane française" ("Roger Mason sings the Tradi-

148

tional Music of French Louisiana"). I went that night and learned that Roger Mason was an American Air Force brat who had grown up in France and had somehow discovered and fallen in love with the Cajuns through the folk-revival movement. Now he was an American in Paris playing Cajun music for French audiences. It was American folk music that they could understand.

When I arrived at the theater, I heard him begin playing the "Crowley Two-step," and I told the lady at the ticket counter, "I don't want any change, I don't want any tickets, and I don't want anybody to get in my way." I rushed down to the edge of the stage, where I remained for the rest of the evening. What I heard flowed over me like a warm bath. I began to realize what it was that I was missing. I began to understand what was causing my *ennui*. I was tired of the low-grade daily strain. Though our languages were basically the same (despite what they said), the system was different. And I had not heard anything like the music Roger Mason was playing in months.

I went to speak to him after the performance. I told him I was from Louisiana, and that he'd never understand the world of good that his music had done for me. I didn't understand fully either. He said, "Oh, you're from Louisiana. Well, you must know Dewey Balfa and Nathan Abshire and all the people I learned from." I didn't know any of them. I had been studying French in Louisiana for seven years, and I didn't know the people that this fellow in France considered heroes. It occurred to me that there was something profoundly wrong with the educational system in Louisiana.

So, I went back home a few months later. And one of the first things I said to my father after "Hello" was "May I borrow your truck?" I drove to Basile, Louisiana, got directions to Dewey Balfa's house, knocked on his door, and said, "Hello. My name is Barry Ancelet. I need to know who you are." He laughed and invited me in, and that's basically how I became involved in folklore and Louisiana French studies.

What I came to understand is that we not only didn't know anything about Dewey Balfa or Nathan Abshire or any of our own performers, we didn't know much about ourselves at all. The eighth-grade Louisiana history textbook had two paragraphs on the Cajuns: one about Longfellow's *Evangeline* and the other about Justin Wilson, neither one of whom has anything to do with who we are, or why we are the way we are. In 1974 I started working with the Smithsonian

Institution on festival projects in Washington and in Louisiana, and I went to Indiana University to study folklore. I came back home in 1977 to the University of Southwestern Louisiana, the place where I had studied French as a foreign language, now to work in the newly created Center for Acadian and Creole Folklore. I wanted to try to get people to understand the importance of our local French culture in the scheme of things.

I quickly understood that we didn't know much about ourselves because we didn't know much about our culture or our past. There was little information available in print. To find out about the culture I would have to try other angles. Folklore opened an important avenue through oral tradition. At Dewey Balfa's insistence I began doing fieldwork on my own, recording stories, songs, and oral histories. Others such as Alan Lomax, Elizabeth Brandon, Harry Oster, and Ralph Rinzler had already recorded substantial collections over the years. I wrote to ask for copies of their tapes, and they generously provided them. They all said that they would have loved to have deposited them somewhere in Louisiana, but there had been no place to leave them. No one had been interested enough locally when they had come through. As copies of these past collections came together in one place, the development of Cajun culture and music became clear. Now we could hear what the music had sounded like from the 1930s through the '40s, '50s, '60s, and '70s, in home recordings as well as on commercial records. The big picture was taking shape.

This was the beginning of the collection project of the Center for Acadian and Creole Folklore. I really didn't mean to create an archive. I was merely trying to understand who we are and where we came from. The collection was turned over to the library in 1980 and is now being catalogued. They didn't know what to do with it at first, and I was too busy collecting and analyzing the material to organize it much. For years, it was essentially my own research bank. I was happy to share it with other scholars and members of the community as they requested, but a lot of careful organizing will be necessary before it is easily accessible to the public.

In addition to acquiring past collections, we initiated an exchange with the researchers who constantly come into south Louisiana for fieldwork. Folklorists, linguists, journalists, and film producers ask the Center to help them find interesting people and places. We began offering to guide them in exchange for a copy of the raw footage of their work. We also keep copies of all student fieldwork projects. It's not a very systematic collection, but it has wide range. I am not a compulsive collector. We don't feel compelled to acquire everything. I appreciate the drive to collect as completely as possible, as in the case of Chris Strachwitz, who has made it his business to gather as many of the commercial recordings of Louisiana Cajun and Creole music as possible. We have certainly drawn on his collection to help us understand the commercial history of Cajun and Creole music. But ours is an incidental collection. Our only goal has been to provide a broad base of useful information from which to study and especially to activate the culture. Our collecting philosophy stresses the recycling function, and our collection serves as a base for radio and television programs, records and books, festivals, concerts, and storytelling programs.

We don't collect all the time. Maybe we should do more. But, after a few years of intensive fieldwork, I began to think that I was recording everything that went on around me. Most of what happens in French in south Louisiana could be thought of as traditional, if you push the definition. And I noticed that, too often, I was not hearing the event, I was hearing the tapes of it the next day. Pete Gregory, an anthropologist over at Northwestern Louisiana State University in Natchitoches, said that he went through the same thing. An American Indian friend of his told him, "There's something wrong with anthropologists."

"Why?" asked Pete.

His friend asked, "Do you remember what I told you about this custom the last time you were here?"

Pete said, "Yes, I recorded it."

"What can you tell me about it?" he asked.

"Well, I don't know," Pete confessed, "but I've got it on tape."

He said, "Do you see? There's something wrong with anthropologists. You fellows can't remember anything."

I have been tempted lately to pay more attention to what's going on and analyze it. So I record less than I once did. But the purpose of our collection is to help keep the culture alive, not to pickle it. For us, processing the collection cannot stop with cataloguing, indexing, and shelving. It must go on to include digesting the information and disseminating it in forms that are appealing and understandable to local audiences as well as scholars.

I'm reminded of Dewey Balfa's story, when he appeared in the Cultural Conservation area of the Smithsonian Institution's Festival of American Folklife a few years ago. He was invited as an example of cultural self-preservation. About half way through an hour-long set, he walked up to the microphone and said to the crowd, "I've been playing songs for you that are about fifty or sixty years old. Now, I'm going to play you some new songs, songs that my brothers and I composed ourselves recently. And I don't have to turn around to know that the people backstage got nervous when I said that, because we're here to represent cultural conservation, but for me, preserving a culture means preserving its life, not preserving it under glass. So, if we are successful at what we're trying to do, then fifty or sixty years from now, there are going to be some young Cajun musicians who need some songs that are fifty or sixty years old, and I made some up and I'm going to play them for you now." Dewey's new songs sounded just like the old ones, because they were coming from the same place and going through the same process that had produced the old ones. The point is that folklorists can and sometimes should work with the life of a culture instead of only with its artifacts.

But if we do this, we must take into account the possibility of success. If our efforts succeed, the culture will have a life of its own and will want to define itself from within. Cajun culture is doing just that. I wrote in *The Makers of Cajun Music* that "Cajun music has refused to conform to values which would stagnate or change it from the outside. . . . Cajun music continues to be what an unruly lot of Cajun musicians insist on playing every weekend, at house dances and in dance halls, on front porches and on main festival stages."[1] Cajun musicians don't often listen to us folklorists and ethnomusicologists, festival and record producers. They continue to do things their own way. They continue to adapt and reinvent and renegotiate their culture in their own terms.

Collecting and recording are not passive activities. The language problem of young Native Americans that Charlotte Heth has alluded to is a problem for people in south Louisiana too. Young people do not speak French as much as earlier generations. Consequently, learning Cajun music and learning Cajun stories and learning life in Cajun terms are changing very rapidly. Some young musicians sing sounds rather than words. They learn to imitate the sounds, usually from records, but have no idea what they're singing. This is something of a problem in a tradition once based largely on improvizational singing, singing from your heart, singing your feelings. The record industry, of course, played a role in the movement away from the improvisational style by fixing versions on vinyl. On the one hand, we wouldn't know what was sung long ago if they had not recorded and preserved the songs. On the other, many singers began to feel that the versions on record were the right versions and drifted away from improvising new versions each time they performed.

The recycling effort of our folklore program includes records, but we try not to compete with commercial record companies, such as Arhoolie, Rounder, and Swallow, which are actively producing Cajun and Creole music. Instead we try to work with these established labels to release records they might not ordinarily attempt. Recent projects have included an album of live performances from the annual Cajun Music Festival in Lafayette, Louisiana, and a double album from the field recordings made by John and Alan Lomax in the 1930s, making available sounds that might have been otherwise forgotten.

Sneaking these projects into the media, on radio and television, and into public performances, at festivals and concerts, is part of what I call "guerrilla academics": trying to program traditional culture in the mainstream, including into the classroom. Dewey Balfa has long been working in the schools, supplementing the textbooks by telling Cajun and Creole children about their history, culture, and music. But we also try to extend the classroom into the media, onto festival stages, anywhere we can speak to a crowd and tell them about themselves. Some of this effort is actually becoming part of the mainstream. Recent books on Louisiana French culture, such as *The Cajuns: Essays on Their History and Culture*[2] and Ann Savoy's *Cajun Music: A Reflection of a People*[3] are finding their way into the classroom as textbooks. In 1987 Dewey Balfa and Creole fiddler Canray Fontenot, were named Adjunct Professors of Cajun and Creole Music, respectively, at the University of Southwestern Louisiana.

The collection continues to serve as the basis for our efforts. It continues to grow in scope as well as in size. We continue to collect field recordings, past and present. We have added collections of commercial records, photographs, and slides. In addition to fieldwork and raw footage from documentary projects, we have begun to acquire documentaries and feature films, especially those which portray the Cajuns or Creoles of south Louisiana, in order to study the development of ethnic images and stereotypes. This growing and diversifying collection will remain at the service of the people whose culture it documents: to help Cajuns and Creoles understand themselves and their culture.

Part Three

*Issues for the
Future*

Allen Tullos

Life as We Knew It

ike other nostalgias, the notion of Southern folk cultures in transition used to seem simpler, easier to track, cut and dried. If you ever have heard the Red Clay Ramblers introduce their version of the Golden Melody Boys' song "Cabin Home," you will know what I mean. "There are two places in old-time music where the singers of the songs don't want to be," Tommy Thompson or Jim Watson would say. "One place singers don't want to be is home, and the other is away from home. If they are home, they want to get away from home. If they are away from home, they want to be home."[1]

Even in the late-twentieth-century South where plumbers don't make house calls, double-wides travel by night on the Lee Highway, and electronic villages post their city-limits signs by modem, the Ramblers' insight remains a good first principle of cultural transition as it affects songs of the South. Weary pilgrims, restless fools, poor boys a long way from home, rank strangers, friends and loved ones left behind have filled out much of the demographic profile of the South's folk and working-class music, sacred and secular, black and white, young and old, male and female.

Yet things have also been changing. And, as eras change so do the meanings of words such as "home" and "away from home," and even the meanings of "natives," and "strangers," and "loved ones." You can hear the Southern changes of the late twentieth century as easily on major-market country radio stations as anywhere else. "I sang 'Dixie,' as he died," sings Kentucky hillbilly outmigrant Dwight Yokam. "People just walked on by, while I cried."[2] Or, in another current country hit by Kathy Mattea:

> I loved life as we knew it
> I still can't believe we threw it away
> Good-bye, that's all there is to it
> Life as we knew it ended today.[3]

If there is a scent of the post-mortem South in the air it is charred from the bonfire of the self-interested 1980s. You probably won't hear Bobby Field's composition "Is This All There Is?" on your local top-forty country station, but neither should you forget the lyrics: "You walked off the scene when I couldn't make your life like *Southern Living* magazine."⁴

So what has changed in the South and what remains the same? First of all there remains something called the South. This is the South in which, C. Vann Woodward insists, its people—black and white—have a shared, rather unpleasant historical experience distinct in America, the enduring South seemingly without end that sociologist John Shelton Reed continually labors to document in that territory which he describes as lying below the Smith and Wesson Line, the South loosely bound together between the covers of the *Encyclopedia of Southern Culture*. Here, I suggest, it is helpful to think of the South not as a *region* but as a *section* of the United States. A section, like the West, or Northeast, which contains many regions and sub-regions. More about these Southern regions in a moment.

Enclaves of Disparity

The South of the 1980s and '90s has become a place in which several predominantly white enclaves of affluence, such as the suburbs of northern Virginia and northern Atlanta, contain some of the wealthiest households in the nation. History prompts me to call these residents "Subourbons." At the same time in the South, overall conditions for working people, and for the poor, continue to be the worst of any section of the nation. Today there are more poor people in the South (some twelve million) and a larger percentage of Southerners living in poverty (about eighteen percent) than a decade ago. Since the mid-1970s we have seen, or have chosen not to see, increasing inequalities of class accompanied by a widespread callousness directed at the unemployed poor, and at those working people who often hold fulltime jobs yet remain in poverty. The gap between the nation's wealthiest and its poorest has never been as large as it is now, nor has so large a portion of this wealth been held by so few people. In the year 1987, forty-four percent of the nation's total income went to the top one-fifth of all U.S. families (up from forty-one

percent in 1973), while only 4.6 percent of the nation's income went
to the bottom one-fifth (down from 5.5 percent in 1973).[5]
    What is true for the nation is truer for the South, which has seen
in the last decade rising poverty rates during a time of declining unemployment. In the historically anti-union South, there are many
jobs worth shoving. In the historically "pro-family" South, poverty
rates for children have soared. The Southern Labor Institute, a Southern Regional Council project that has among its duties the biennial
gathering and analysis of national, state, and local data for the prepa-
ration of its report *The Climate for Workers in the United States*, finds
that the South ranks lowest when compared to other sections of the
country with regard to workers' earnings and income, workplace
conditions, worker protections such as unionization, unemployment
benefits, disability compensation, and overall quality of life.[6]
    One index among several that were considered in the Southern
Labor Institute study—in the "quality of life category"—was infant
mortality. The United States has now fallen to a tie for last place
among twenty industrialized nations in preventing babies from dying
during their first year of life. In this country, eight of the twelve states
with the highest infant mortality rates are Southern—with Alabama
ranked at the bottom. Although a few states stand out as mild exceptions to the rule, Southern states when considered as a section remain the poorest in the nation with regard to median family income.
    If you look at states in which blacks are employed in what have
traditionally been predominantly white-male occupations—better-
paid, higher-skilled, higher-status jobs—there is much that seems
historically and familiarly Southern. At the lower end of the scale,
where fewer than one-quarter of blacks work in the better-paying
occupations, there you find a heavy concentration of Southern states.
In 1987, most states of the South also ranked in the bottom twenty
with regard to the percentage of women employed in occupations
traditionally dominated by white men. And so on.
    If I have so far talked mostly about working people—wage earn-
ers, factory workers, keyboard operators, clerical workers, construction workers, temporaries, labor-pool hands, fast-food workers, jani-
tors, agricultural laborers, farmers—it is because I consider them
and their families to make up a large number of the Southerners who
have become our contemporary "folk."
    Although most of the South's current country songs don't address

themselves directly to the statistics I've mentioned, the facts and figures help shape the context in which the music is made and heard. These days, although I tend to hear only musicians who have major-label contracts, even here the current misery loves company. I've already mentioned Dwight Yokam. Consider such songs as Steve Earle's "Hillbilly Highway," "Someday," or "Nowhere Road." Nancy Griffith's "Trouble in These Fields," with its evocative but ultimately ineffectual solution to the assault on family farming. Lyle Lovett's "This Old Porch." And even Randy Travis's realistic, ol'-boycentered "The Reasons I Cheat."

Despair and Myth

If I were to venture into contemporary Southern black secular music forms, especially rap, about which I know all too little, it would be easy enough to fill a list of songs which carry angry and pointed social complaint. Even in a recent recording of one of the older forms—the talking blues "Mr. President"—North Carolina bluesman Richard "Big Boy" Henry reflects upon the demography of Reagan-Bush trickle-down: homelessness, cuts in assistance to the those most in need, absence of commitment to low-income housing and decent jobs, cuts in education, lack of empathy with people in poverty. "Come live with me a little while," sings Big Boy Henry. "Find out how the situation is here."[7]

On the other hand from this enduringly grim and desperate South, recent years have seen the once-prevalent anxiety over the South's supposed demise replaced by an increasingly more mythical, superficial South of merchandising. Although I could point to numerous projections of this mystique of Southern marketing—in movies, television, and travelogue—the best example remains that of *Southern Living* magazine. Here, advertisements embodying Southern regional "lifestyles" (not "ways of life," which would imply something deeper, less trendy and less easily shucked) cannot always be distinguished from colorful, upbeat articles. Folk and working-class cultures can be prettified into vehicles of purchasable nostalgia. Black faces, when they turn up, tend to appear in non-threatening, comfortable roles as entertainers and athletes. The households of *Southern Living*'s two-million-plus subscribers have a median income of $42,000. No doubt many of these readers have family roots deep in Southern folk cultures. But what *Southern Living* does best is skim and package the entertaining cream that rises above past and present crisis.

Beyond the enduring South of history, and in addition to the mythical South, lie a couple of other Southern changes that need mention. In early autumn of 1988 a film, *Salaam Bombay*, which told of street life in the red-light district of Bombay, India, won a first prize at the Cannes Film Festival. When asked about her next project, the film's director Mira Nair described to a New York *Times* reporter a fiction film that would tell the story of "an Indian family expelled from Uganda by Idi Amin in the 1970s, who now own a motel in the black Bible Belt of the South."[8]

The South (and particular cities and states of the South) is becoming home to significant numbers of such immigrants. Nearly ninety percent of immigrants to the United States between 1983 and 1986 settled in twenty states. Five of these twenty are Southern: Texas, Florida, Virginia, Georgia, and Louisiana. Atlanta, for instance, now has 100,000 Hispanics, 25,000 Koreans, 11,000 Indochinese, and 10,000 Indians. Houston's Hispanic population is over 425,000. Miami—which many never considered as Southern—has 600,000 Hispanics.[9]

The South's history with regard to race relations can hardly encourage the expectation that these newest Southerners will be warmly and quickly embraced. The first Vietnamese resettled along the Texas Gulf Coast met Klan violence and intimidation from anxious Anglo fishing communities. Folklorists and anthropologists will have much to do in interpreting new and existing Southern cultures to each other. With the coming of all these people—including the still-increasing numbers of Yankees and other regional Americans—and the recognition that there are some 190,000 Native Americans living in the contemporary South, Southerners will be "obliged," as Flannery O'Connor anticipated in her short story "The Displaced Person," to "give new thought to a good many things." Not the least of the thoughts prompted by the settling-in of new ethnic immigrants will be those that disclose the unsuspected in the South's old racial arrangements. Black and white Subourbons, for instance, making clear their objections to affirmative-action proposals.

Briefly, a few observations about the continuing emergence of

Figure 14: Our Lady of Guadaloupe Celebration, Cleveland, Mississippi, 1988. *(Photo by Tom Rankin.)*

Figure 15: Recent Vietnamese Immigrants Eating Dinner on a Shrimp Boat They are Building, Biloxi, Mississippi, 1985. *(Photo by Tom Rankin.)*

regions within the South—regions such as the Delta, the Black Belt, Southern Appalachia, the Low Country, the Ozarks, Northern Virginia. These regions are as genuine and persistent, and still emerging, as the South of which they are portions. At the level of day-to-day life, these regions are frequently more significant to the people who live in them than is something called the South. A French Gulf Coast cultural resurgence is well underway in Louisiana, as is an Appalachian consciousness in the Southern Mountains. In the Alabama Black Belt, the legacy of the civil-rights and voting-rights movements has resulted in unprecedented political power for black people, and most recently in cultural projects ranging from the production of a newspaper to a regional folk festival to discussion about a civil-rights history tour along the route of the Selma-to-Montgomery March.

Movements Held Hostage

Yet these emergent regional cultures face familiar troubles. They are not immune from the same sort of celebratory myth making and merchandising which affects Dixie as a whole. Consider what has become of all things "Cajun." French Louisiana is experiencing an intensifying ecological crisis. The disparities of white and black economic resources in the Delta resemble the Third World. And in two of the regions that I have mentioned—the Black Belt and Southern Appalachia—corporate absentee ownership of large tracts of land threatens to hold hostage the movements for regional self-determination.

Finally, there are changes affecting the South's "folk" that only can be briefly noted here. The surge of evangelical fundamentalism is symptomatic of a broader civic and moral retreat and reaction. The fragmentation of traditional Southern emotional, spiritual, and cultural institutions continues helter-skelter. A new synthesis of feminist, democratic socialist, ethnically pluralist, and ecological potentials—has yet to win the day. For now, the emotional landscape is simultaneously alienating and liberating, superficially yet fundamentally altered. Bobbie Ann Mason captures it for a moment in her recent short story "Memphis." Beverly and Jolene, writes Mason,

ate at a Cajun restaurant that night, and later they walked down Beale Street, which had been spruced up and wasn't as scary as it used to be, Beverly thought. The sidewalks were crowded with tourists and policemen. . . . Beverly's parents had stayed married like two dogs locked together in passion, except it wasn't passion. But she and Joe didn't have to do that. Times had changed. Joe could up and move to South Carolina. Beverly and Jolene could hop down to Memphis just for a fun weekend. Who knew what might happen or what anybody would decide to do on any given weekend or at any stage of life?"[10]

Where now was home, and where away from home?

David E. Whisnant

Turning Inward and Outward

*Retrospective and Prospective
Considerations in the Recording of
Vernacular Music in the South*

There have been so many influences, actors, and dynamics in the history of the recording of vernacular music in the South, and the process has by now such a long history, that to attempt to sketch it quickly is a daunting task.[1] From the mid-1920s onward, collectors such as Robert W. Gordon, Guy B. Johnson, Frank C. Brown, Alan Lomax, and others were combing the South and returning with field recordings of both white and black vernacular music.[2] The effort was amplified with the establishment of the Archive of Folk Song in the Library of Congress in 1928, and of the New Deal's Federal Music Project in the mid-1930s.

The commercial recording of Southern vernacular music seems to have preceded such field recordings, however. As early as 1902, the Dinwiddie Colored Quartet went to New York to record "Down on the Old Camp Ground" for Victor, which released it as a "coon shout."[3] The first commercial recordings of what came to be called country music are generally agreed to have been those Eck Robertson and Henry Gilliland made for Victor in 1922. During the subsequent boom years of the late 1920s, an expanding market came to be dominated by such companies as Victor, RCA, and OKeh before the recording industry crashed with the rest.

After World War II, the process was greatly expanded and complicated by the rise of numerous small independent R&B-oriented companies, the later appearance of southern Appalachian and Southwestern-oriented independent producers, and documentary recording projects centered in universities and other public agencies.[4] And over the entire period, tens of thousands of private issues have appeared—fruits of the efforts of aspiring individuals and groups who practiced in garages and living rooms, hired studio space, had a friend take a snapshot for the album cover, and hawked the albums at bluegrass festivals and gospel sings, backcountry and suburban schoolhouses, Cajun clubs, and *cantinas* all over the south.

Those who have done the recording have been moved by the most varied of agendas: desire for financial gain, evangelical fervor, personal passion for a form or idiom (Cajun or bluegrass, honky-tonk or blues, ballads or *corridos*), scholarly interest, public responsibility. Their knowledge of the materials they were recording has ranged from encyclopedic to nearly nil. The impact of their work—on individual performers, on forms and traditions, on audiences—has varied from negligible to epochal.[5]

Luckily, some elements and sectors in this complex history have already been narrated and analyzed in the dedicated work of some persistent and imaginative investigators. In article after article, brochure after brochure, book after book, those scholars and collectors have patiently taught us about some things that have shaped the recording of vernacular music in the South: about how the commercial music industry filtered and selected materials, privileged styles and performers, and created and manipulated markets[6]; about the paradoxical dialectic of cultural opposition and cooptation focused and fueled by Nashville and the Opry[7]; about the folk revival[8]; about the careers of individual performers[9]; about how festivals have done a complex work of cultural excavation, celebration, revitalization and legitimation, showcasing performers and generating audiences—and in the process speaking to the cultural insecurities and anxieties of both.[10]

There are of course other issues and problems that we are aware of but have not yet been able to comprehend.[11] And there are no doubt still others of which we are as yet naively unaware. Thus the opening of the magnificent John Edwards Memorial Collection/ Southern Folklife Collection is a time for both celebration and a deeper and perhaps more critical look at the history of which the collection forms part of the documentary record. What I want in general to suggest here is that the great and creative inward-turning, roots-seeking and home-celebrating enterprise in which so many have been so passionately and creatively engaged for so long must now begin to turn outward and comprehend the links, analogues, and resonances the enterprise has with others elsewhere engaged in their own inward-turnings. As I tried to review the bits of the story which I know, it occurred to me that one might usefully reflect upon a half-dozen or so perhaps not completely obvious factors which have been important in shaping this history: about the costs and benefits of an overarching posture of defensiveness; about the subregional organization of the South; about what for lack of a better term I will call the ambient ethos; about some individuals and institutions; about some powerful canons; about some cultural brokers and the authenticating and legitimizing networks that developed among them; and finally about what again for lack of a better term I will refer to as a political-cultural dialectic.

Defensiveness

Given that the South has been the object of cultural stigmatization at least since Byrd's *History of the Dividing Line* (1729), it should come as no surprise to anyone that the recording of vernacular music in the South has been characterized by an overarching posture of defensiveness.[12] Indeed "South" comes close to being a universally stigmatizing metaphor. South connotes physical laziness, moral laxity and torpor, lack of intellectual capacity, institutional underdevelopment, cultural parochialism, and retrograde religion, to name but a few of the usual connotations. The universality of such attitudes accounts at least partly for the condescension the northern Virginia suburbs express toward their commonwealth brethren in the coalfields of southwest Virginia, for Mencken's snide essay "The Sahara of the Bozart," and for the United States' virtually unrelieved cultural arrogance with respect to its Latin American "backyard."[13] Whether there is a similar dynamic between North and South Dakota I don't know, but it would not surprise me. Certainly Antonio Gramsci was aware of the one between northern Italy and his native Sardinia.

Hence to undertake the work of cultural documentation (to say nothing of advocacy) in any South at any time is inevitably to encounter oneself in a defensive, oppositional posture.[14] And such a posture is a mixed bag. On the one hand it can and does free and focus energy, sharpen sensitivities, and heighten assertiveness and self-

168 *David E. Whisnant*

awareness. But on the other hand—as Frantz Fanon argued in his classic analysis of the problems of cultural resistance and decolonization—it can also dull self-criticism, cloud objectivity, and lead to an uncritical romanticizing of tradition.[15]

Some of that dulling and clouding is in evidence—to take a fairly obvious example—in the two decades of scholarship on country music we have thus far accumulated. That scholarship has been more attentive to the positive achievements within the idiom (which are real and undeniable) than to its dark and persistent underside of opportunism, anti-intellectualism, sexism, racism, and jingoism.[16]

Subregionalization

If we in our particular South have encountered the pitfalls risked by all those who find themselves in defensive postures, as surely we have in some instances, we have at the same time been fortunate to work in a South cut up into small enough subregions to keep us reasonably well grounded in gritty local data which we know better than most of the totalizing stigmatizers.

In view of how nearly universally references to "*the* South" have been employed in a variety of analytical literatures (e.g., literary criticism, sociology, political science), it is surprising how little actual analytical utility the notion has. We all know that there are in fact a number of Souths south of the Mason-Dixon line (and even a not inconsiderable number of small transplanted ones north of it), each with its peculiar topography, soils and crops, business and industrial base, ethnic, racial and religious composition, foods and house types, dialect, music and stories: delta and uplands, coastal (both Atlantic and Gulf), piedmont, mountain, border and interior.[17]

We also know that this subregional diversity is reflected in recorded music and its associated dance forms, where the evidence is as abundant as it is on the land itself: Appalachian ballads and border *corridos*; mining, textile and cowboy songs; blues, breakdowns and Cajun waltzes; string band and *conjunto*; square dance and clog, two-step, polka and *ranchera*.

But is it also possible that the subregional organization of the South has shaped our perceptions of and approach to the very task of recording itself, as well as provided us with diverse materials in which to interest ourselves? How different would have been the dynamics of the recording enterprise had the South not been subregionalized in such a way? How have those subregional distinctions (and their corollary loyalties and specificities of comprehension) organized energies within the documentary and commercial recording of vernacular music?

In the first place, those who have sought out and recorded this music have not been animated by some homogeneous musical South, but by the local wonders of Delta and piedmont bluesmen,[18] border *conjuntos,*[19] coalfields banjo pickers and gospel singers,[20] and Cajun accordion players.[21] Although they have overlapped interregionally and interracially in some areas (notably in blues and gospel), those enthusiasms have been so self-contained that they have developed their own independent networks of scholars and collectors, and their own archives and record producers.

Despite the relatively hermetic character of these enterprises, however, juxtaposition of subregional traditions (Cajun versus Southwestern fiddling, say—not to mention more fine-grained local differences such as those between coalfields and non-coalfields repertories and styles within the Appalachian region) has nevertheless helped to tune ears more sharply to stylistic nuances than they might have been otherwise. Or to put it more simply, someone who has listened carefully to two distinct musical idioms is perhaps more likely to comprehend and appreciate the special characteristics of each than is someone who has heard only one.

Similarly, instead of a single center for radio broadcasting and recording, which might have had a homogenizing effect, multiple subregional ones emerged in Atlanta, Charlotte, Wheeling, Shreveport, Ville Platte, Austin, and elsewhere, each to some degree loyal to local performers, styles, and audiences.[22] Loyal local buyers, in turn, engendered creative competition in the radio and record market. Taken together, the two dynamics have modulated to some degree the homogenizing tendencies of the larger (pan-Southern and national) media enterprise.

Hence a paradox: while mainstream media characteristically (though not invariably) continue to stigmatize "the South"—Mencken's "Sahara of the Bozart"—with a string of totalizing epithets (hillbillies, rednecks, crackers, white trash, and all the rest)—the internally generated documentary records of its culture (literary, musical, material) show above all its rich subregional, local, racial, and ethnic diversity.[23] Our enterprise has therefore above all been complexly comparative rather than totalizing, and that has been theoretically, methodologically, and practically enriching. Thus at the outset we should remind ourselves that the enterprise that produced that record grew up within and was shaped by the familiar characteristics and dynamics of cultural pluralism: of tension and flux, of differentially permeable boundaries, of cross-fertilization and syncretism, and of competition for legitimacy.

Ambient Ethos

If the recording enterprise—both non-commercial and commercial—has developed within a subregionalized and multicultural South characterized by scores of local enthusiasms, it has also consistently proved more hospitable to dealing with certain diversities and syncretisms than with others. This is so partly because it has been shaped in profound ways by what for convenience I will call the ambient ethos: that familiar pan-Southern (it is in fact pan-U.S., but that is another argument) amalgam of racism, sexism, jingoism, anti-intellectualism, and political conservatism. While the music itself was as we all know being shaped by the complex diversities of race, gender, class, and ideology, the recording enterprise has come to acknowledge and deal openly with the resulting divergences only reluctantly and decades late.

It is by now a commonplace in the literature that a kind of musical apartheid partitioned "race" records in the early commercial market; that DeFord Bailey was treated shabbily by the Opry; that instead of the passionate and hard-edged early R&B and rockabilly tunes, most deejays favored the effete Fabianized covers; that city councils passed ordinances against "race-mixing" music and smashed stacks of "nigger music" records (a practice, I am constrained to note, which was by no means confined to the South).

Similarly, sexism—or more broadly, the skewings of gender-linked perspectives—has been a more important shaping factor than one could even begin to acknowledge in these few pages. Although one might quibble over percentages, cite counterexamples, or divine reassuring emerging trends, the fundamental historical fact and contemporary reality is incontrovertible: the great bulk of the documentary record of vernacular music in the South which we have and are continuing to assemble (whether one speaks of documentary or of commercial discs that have come to have documentary value) is a record shaped in still mostly unexamined ways by the vision and the culture of men. In turn, that vision continues to guide (although to a somewhat lesser extent) the interpretative analysis that accompanies the enterprise.

A multitude of consequences flow from that fact, of course. For example, even some of the more glaring and pervasive manifestations of overt sexism in the music (such as those in bluegrass, an idiom which I hazard to say may have received somewhat more than due attention by record companies small and large) have yet to be attended to seriously. Robert Oermann and Mary Bufwak have done exemplary analysis of some aspects of the problem, but much more remains.[24]

We need to understand, for example, how and with what consequences it happened that from a situation at the turn of the century in which women singers, informants, teachers, and collectors held such central positions in the music in much of the South, we have moved gradually to one in which it has long been and still is overwhelmingly under the control of male academics, record company owners and executives, producers, performers, deejays, and critics (the early appearance of "girl singers" and the later proliferation of female country music stars to the contrary notwithstanding).

To compound the problem, political conservatism (particularly in the form of a preference for depoliticized materials and a corollary disinterest in political themes and repertories) has also shaped the documentation of vernacular music in the South for a hundred and twenty-five years at least: from the Port Royal experiment through the industrial and settlement schools in the lowlands and the mountains, to the majority of the academic folksong collectors,[25] to festival organizers such as Bascom Lamar Lunsford,[26] Annabel Morris Buchanan and John Powell,[27] to the commercial industry and Nashville.

This apolitical orientation has existed and continues to exist to such an extent, it seems to me, that were a vital artistic and political movement analogous to Latin America's *nueva canción* to arise in the South, the records would have to be issued by companies outside the South (like Redwood or Paredon or Arhoolie) because most of those inside (at least in the Southeast) would neither be disposed to deal with it nor have much experience upon which to base a strategy for doing so.[28]

Such an orientation has long been a serious problem, and it will be an even greater one if certain current social and political trends continue, as no doubt they will. We are likely to see more Jesse Helms and Newt Gingrich-style reactionary politics, more rollbacks and cutbacks in social programs, and more panicked immigration from countries south of the border whose politics and institutions United States policy has helped turn in reactionary directions.[29] Some of the music people have been and are going to be singing amongst themselves—Appalachian coal miners, black prisoners, populist farmers, Mexican agricultural workers, piedmont mill hands—has reflected and will continue to reflect those dynamics, but such music has thus far figured to a rather paltry extent in the commercially-issued record.[30] It remains to be seen whether the pattern will continue.

But to pass quickly on, I turn from the more generalized ambient factors to the roles of certain individuals and institutions.

Individuals, Institutions, Brokers, and Networks

At least the documentary wing of the recording enterprise (if not the commercial one) has also been shaped by some powerful canons: initially, of course, by Child and by the Anglo-piety of Sharp (for all the latter's virtues, which were many).[31] And by the influential publications of the Lomaxes, Frank C. Brown, Reed Smith, Vance Randolph, and others too numerous to mention.[32] And later on—in a bit of historical irony—by what in some ways became for small independent record companies the canon of commercially recorded old-time and country music of the 1920s and 30s, much of which had been rejected as not of canonical quality by most (though thankfully not all) of the earlier canon-formers.

If one reads a bit in the lives not only of these individuals but also of many others who have played important roles in the formation of canons (published or recorded), one soon discovers that such individuals functioned not only as filters at a certain local point, but also as culture brokers within a much larger context. Moreover, many of them eventually became linked into what were in effect some powerful authenticating and legitimizing networks.

By brokers I mean those energetic, active, frequently passionate individuals—ballad collectors, articulate and entrepreneurial traditional musicians (e.g., Bradley Kincaid), academics, A&R men, owners of small record companies, festival promoters, folk-revival musicians, and public-agency personnel who for a variety of personal, cultural, and sometimes political reasons involved themselves in the recording enterprise as links between the musicians and their actual or potential markets. Sometimes they merely transmitted, but much of the time they reshaped, and always they interpreted in some manner. And in the process they impacted substantially upon both performer and audience.

As examples one thinks immediately of A&R man Ralph Peer's work with scores of Southeastern musicians (pre-eminently, of course, with the Carter Family and Jimmie Rodgers); of Ralph Rinzler's work with Doc Watson, Bill Monroe, and others; of Archie Green's with Sara Ogan Gunning and the music of miners, millworkers and other occupational groups[33]; of D. K. Wilgus and Kenneth Goldstein[34]; of Mike Seeger[35] and Chris Strachwitz; of string bands like the New Lost City Ramblers, Hollow Rock and Fuzzy Mountain String Bands, and the Red Clay Ramblers[36]; of Barry Ancelet and the Cajuns[37]; and more recently of Joe Wilson and his National Council for the Traditional Arts tour groups.

In some ways more important than these individual brokers themselves were the authenticating and legitimizing networks that functioned among them. The individuals I have named come from the recent past, but such brokers have been active since the late nineteenth century, and the networks formed that early as well. In the pre-1920s period (some of whose dynamics were to help shape the emerging commercial recording industry), the links were already numerous and formatively important: between Olive Dame Campbell, the other settlement school women, the Council of the Southern Mountains, and Cecil Sharp; between John Campbell and the Russell Sage Foundation[38]; between Katherine Pettit of Hindman Settlement School and George Lyman Kittredge[39]; between the settlement schools and Berea College[40]; between such schools, the Seven Sisters Colleges, and collector-performers such as Loraine Wyman, Howard Brockway, and Josephine McGill who translated selected parts of Southern mountain music for New York concert audiences.[41] Later, other links developed among the major festival promoters of the thirties (Lunsford, Knott, Thomas, and Buchanan) and between those promoters and the media[42]; between Allen Eaton and the Sage Foundation; between Eaton, Doris Ulmann, John Jacob Niles, and an elite coterie in New York; and—perennially—between Richard Chase and whoever got taken with him or taken in by him.[43]

Of all the brokering networks that formed up through the end of the 1930s, the one made up of New Deal documentarians is perhaps the only one that has received the analytical attention it deserves.[44] In the post-World War II period, one thinks of still other networks that formed around the early country music disk collectors such as Green, Hoeptner, Pinson, John Edwards, and others; around Ralph Rinzler's work at the Smithsonian since the mid-sixties; around the graduate folklore programs; around small record producers such as County, Rounder, and Arhoolie; and more recently around the public folklife programs.[45]

Indeed, one way to understand the history of the recording of music in the South would be to look at these networks (or constellations, to shift the metaphor slightly) and their interactions: the settlement school constellation, the New Deal constellation, the folk revival constellation, the Festival of American Folklife constellation, the JEMF constellation, the Appalachian Film Workshop constellation, the Nashville constellation, the public-sector folklore constellation, and so on.

One need merely follow one or two of the relatively well-known lines of interaction to realize how important both the brokers and the networks have been in selecting, defining, privileging, and disseminating certain images and understandings of the musical culture of the South: from the Russell Sage Foundation to the grant that took John C. and Olive Dame Campbell to the Southern mountains,[46] from Mrs. Campbell to Sharp, from Sharp to some New Deal documentarians who took recording machines and went looking for his informants, from the New Deal archives to the young Seegers and Rinzlers who listened to the disks and in the one case formed the New Lost City Ramblers[47] and in the other established the American Folklife Festival, and from the folk revival and the festival on the mall to the younger scholars like Robert Cantwell and Neil Rosenberg,[48] the small record companies and the still younger state folklorists who cut their musical teeth listening not to cylinders or old 78s or Library of Congress documentary recordings, but to LPs from Folk-Legacy and Rounder and County.

Tracing such a line also suggests immediately that paralleling the brokers and the networks has been array of institutions which have shaped the sound-recording endeavor in a variety of ways: in addition to festivals and the commercial recording industry, which I have already mentioned and with which most of us are at least somewhat familiar, one thinks of universities and government.

The curve of governmental involvement shows a burst of activity in the late twenties and thirties with the opening of the Archive of Folk Song in 1928[49] and the New Deal documentation programs, then a virtual hiatus until the mid-60s, and a rising curve since with the Festival of American Folklife (1967 ff.), the Folk Arts Program of the National Endowment for the Arts, the American Folklife Preservation Act and the American Folklife Center it established in the Library of Congress,[50] and now the folklife programs in virtually every state.

The work each agency has done has varied in perspective and quality, but the calculus of activity has had the undeniable effect of raising respect for the intrinsic worth of vernacular music, sharpening attention to recording and archiving it carefully, and developing models for presenting it intelligently to the public. The impact of the Library of Congress LPs alone, for example, has been far greater than one might have expected in view of the modest resources that have ever been committed to making them.[51]

Although so far as I know no one has yet analyzed systematically the historical role of Southern colleges and universities in the recording or collecting of vernacular music, we know that academic involvement has been sporadic and scattered at best, but very influential when it has occurred. That involvement has arisen, it would appear, more out of the enthusiasms and energies of single animated individuals (Frank C. Brown at Duke, Daniel Patterson at the University of North Carolina, Archie Green at Texas, William Ferris at Memphis and Mississippi, Roddy Moore at Ferrum, Charles Wolfe at Middle Tennessee) than out of any institutional commitment or policy as such. Indeed one must reluctantly conclude—despite the sustained work of such selfless individuals—that until relatively recently colleges and universities in the South have on the whole been remiss in their cultural and political responsibility in this regard. That the

John Edwards collection went first to UCLA because no institution in the South had the vision to accept it (or was willing to run the cultural risk of doing so) is a sad commentary upon the level of political-cultural awareness and commitment of those institutions.

With regard to the role of government and universities in the recording enterprise, one must also think more largely about what might be called the policy context in which the enterprise occurred. That is to say, one needs to comprehend not only the detailed impacts of certain specific policies and programs, but also the import of either the mere absence or presence of public policy as a fact in itself.

To be more specific: the bulk of the entire enterprise of recording vernacular music in the South has occurred in the virtual absence of sustained, reliable, substantial public funding and institutional support.[52] On the negative side, that has meant that the endeavor has never been as systematic, continuous, broadly and coherently conceived, rational, or sustained as it might have been had our cultural policy and institutions been created as early, developed as comprehensively, funded as well or operated as equitably as they should have been. Hence much of the collecting and issuing of the music has been sporadic, localized, discontinuous, entrepreneurial, serendipitous, and sometimes idiosyncratic. Much has undeniably been overlooked, lost, or misinterpreted in the process.

But there is a positive side as well. Can you imagine (to take an intriguing hypothetical example) how a state or federally sponsored and university- or museum-administered disk collecting or record-issuing project in the late 1950s might have responded to a grant proposal from a carpenter in San Francisco, an aerospace engineer at Cape Canaveral, a young old-time picker and conscientious objector working as a hospital orderly in Baltimore, an idealistic young bureaucrat in a public tramway system in Australia, an undergraduate at Antioch College, an industrial research chemist, a California high school teacher, a printer in a lithography plant in San José? Lacking conventional credentials—and hence credibility in the system—these individuals (a.k.a., Archie Green, Eugene Earle, Mike Seeger, John Edwards, Neil Rosenberg, Norm Cohen, Chris Strachwitz, and Bob Pinson, all of whom have done seminal work on vernacular music in the South) and many others would no doubt have found access to the funding trough blocked (though no doubt in an irreproachably "rational" and gentlemanly fashion).

I am tempted to compose a hypothetical letter of rejection from agency X or university Y to one of these people. It would explain criteria and outline procedures, refer discreetly to the applicant's lack of appropriate training, note the absence of previously published work, question the lack of a well-defined theoretical base and methodological approach, beg off by citing the large number of qualified applicants, and wish well. The rhetorical possibilities are indeed tantalizing, but perhaps my point is already sufficiently clear: that if the circumstances offered by the policy context have been less than ideal in some respects, within them many energetic, passionate, and committed individuals have been forced to make up in resourcefulness, imagination, and creativity what they lacked in institutional legitimacy, support, and encouragement.

And yet those very dynamics have had their down side as well. The enterprise has suffered in some respects from the perhaps too random entrepreneurial vitality that has characterized it. For example we have not yet created or sustained very well amongst ourselves a level of critical dialogue that would allow us to question sufficiently our still limited paradigms and rhetorical modes. Consequently we have remained too content with first-level documentation of detail, with a rather indulgent musical hero-worship, with a hesitancy about close reading of the social texts that parallel the stylistic ones, with a necessary but still in some ways obfuscatory defensiveness and defiant celebration.

Hence in general it seems to me that our lacks have been and are great with respect to fine-grained analysis, and that our responses to such few examples of it as have come our way (as in Cantwell's recent book on bluegrass) are sometimes less than fully comprehending.[53] Conversely, we have been too content with books and liner notes that track down the last lost session man or unissued take, but ask fewer probing questions about either than are begging to be asked.

Political-Cultural Dialectic

Finally, I return for a moment to the larger political-cultural dialectic I alluded to briefly at the beginning in my reference to Fanon. In the largest frame, the tens of thousands of phonograph records now housed on the fourth floor of Wilson Library at the University of North Carolina and in a (fortunately growing) number of other repositories are the residue of an intensely contested discourse both within the many Souths, and between them and adjacent contexts and systems over questions of stigmatization and delegitimation *vs.* legitimation and revitalization; of cultural assimilation and acculturation *vs.* cultural survival and organic transformation; of the utility of contending world views and value systems; of the progressive and regressive roles of culture in broader social and political transformation.

Thus while it seems to me vital that we continue to explore and document those details of musical history that have so fascinated us, it seems even more vital that we face and understand the structural foundations and implications of the multi-stranded dialectic.

We all know, for example, that the recording industry shied away from the threatening cultural politics of early rockabilly and turned toward the Pat Boones and Fabians on the one hand, and toward politically safe bluegrass on the other. But what difference have those choices made in the developing internal cultural politics of the South? What have they had to do with where we find ourselves positioned—intellectually, culturally, politically?

As young white Southerners and middle-class urbanites from the Northeast were freed by the civil rights movement to identify with the South without the old guilt and stigma, for example, the majority of them who turned (at first tentatively) to vernacular music gravitated to the more depoliticized strands of it (to Southern mountain fiddling, to bluegrass, to Cajun).[54] Many of them have at length ended up as scholars, teachers, performers on the revival circuit, public-sector folklorists, and record producers—and hence inevitably as the most recent brokers and canon formers and re-formers. And although a few have moved to more politically informed analyses and focuses for work, a preference for the conservative, reactionary or apolitical streams of Southern vernacular music remains much in evidence. To the extent that it continues to do so, it will undoubtedly have a partly regressive impact on the unfolding politics of culture in the South.

This is unfortunate, because in addition to those acts of resistance which inhere merely in the defiant preference for a delegitimated style or form (James Scott has called such preferences or actions "everyday forms of resistance"),[55] there has always been a strong and

vital current of *conscious and articulated* resistance, protest, coun-
terhegemonic opposition (call it what you will) in the vernacular
music of the South: among populist farmers and tenant farmers'
groups; among coal miners and textile workers and their blacklung
and brownlung associations[56]; among black civil rights groups;
among communities opposing population removal by such agencies
as the National Park Service, the Tennessee Valley Authority, the
Corps of Engineers, the military and others. And we need that current
and the perspectives, vocabulary, and strategies it suggests, now
more than ever.

We need it in the first instance to help us rethink and restrategize
about the internal development of the South. But we need it even
more to help us place ourselves within and link ourselves to the
promising reconceptualizations of our common global dilemma—
cultural, economic, political, environmental—that literally lie all
about us: amongst the Amazon Indians,[57] amongst the Quiché high-
landers of Guatemala,[58] amongst the Kurds and Afghanistanis,
amongst South African blacks and Estonians, amongst newly liber-
ated eastern Europeans. Indeed amongst all the enclaved, marginalized, menaced subject peoples of the world.[59] The South needs *un
movimiento de la nueva canción* which so far it ain't had, ain't got,
and shows precious little promise of developing, despite the fact that
the makings of one lie all about.

This lack is both paradoxical and tragic, because as C. Vann
Woodward patiently explained thirty-five years ago, the historical
experience of the American South has been to know poverty,
defeat, submission, and humiliation, to "learn the taste left in the
mouth by the swallowing of one's own words," to endure military
defeat and occupation—in sum, to live through some quite un-
American experience with limits, frustration, and failure. While
that historical experience placed the South in an "eccentric
position" within the nation, Woodward noted, it linked it to and
gave it an opportunity to comprehend the common experience
of the majority of the world's people.[60]

What this leads me to observe is that we have for decades been
doing a work (and in many respects doing it very well) the larger
significance and potential of which we have not yet fully grasped: it
is the work of cultural resistance against those central forces of all

mass cultures which aim (or *function*, whether they consciously aim or not) to contain, to divide and shame, to push beyond the margin and into the ghetto, to homogenize and delegitimize, to render politically sterile and inert.

That we did not grasp that significance earlier has been one of the profoundest shaping influences upon the work we have been doing; that we may yet come to understand it is the brightest hope within it. To the extent that we are able to grasp it we will turn inward with fresh and sharpened critical insight, and outward into new alliances, networks, and cultural-political coalitions.

As we turn inward we will begin to admit that although it is in some senses an act of cultural defiance and resistance to sing, play, or record *any* song from any alternative, marginalized, delegitimized tradition, no matter how sexist, racist, or politically reactionary the song may be, it is not defiant and resistant *enough*. And as we turn outward we will discover affinities of perspective and posture both compellingly interesting and important in themselves, and pregnant with possibilities for broadened and deepened understanding of the music that sustains us and moves us.

Much has been done, but a vast amount remains to do, and a great deal of reconceptualization faces us. The earliest generation of documentarians who ventured into the then almost completely unmapped terrain of Southern vernacular music brought us riches undreamt of, and clarified for us some elemental facts and patterns which continue to shape our own explorations. Thus the great Skillet Lickers and Georgia Wildcats fiddler Clayton McMichen, responding to Fred Hoeptner's and Bob Pinson's questions concerning some of the influences upon his own early recording, responded with blunt clarity: ". . . we played them [Skillet-Licker tunes] like that 'cause they paid us to play it like that."[61] Such a response at least reminds us not to lose sight of the fact that what we are trying to understand has at some levels been shaped by such factors as the relatively familiar behaviors of poor folks who come in from the country (either literally or metaphorically) to sell the little that they have at the stalls of the sharp-eyed hustlers in a gaudy buyer's market.

But McMichen's response also raises more questions than it answers, and if we are to move conceptually and politically as we must in the years ahead, we must attune ourselves to questions which it scarcely occurred to anyone to ask in those early days when young Australian public-transit worker John Edwards began corresponding with hillbilly and country music disk collectors from the other side of the world.

Archie Green

Afterword
"Our Music": Exit Ahead

Southern *vernacular* music's students travel the uncertain lane between academic ballad scholarship (slow) and popular-culture hype (fast). We know the hazards of lane weaving; we keep eyes open for exit signs. During the early 1970s, Guy Clark from Monahans, Texas, found himself a frequent freeway flyer in Los Angeles. His anxiety about escaping the steel/concrete spiderweb with his life intact spilled over into "L. A. Freeway," nominally a nostalgic song about returning to verdant coves and rural fields, if not to cattle corrals and oil-field drilling platforms. I hear Clark's lament also as an appropriate metaphor for companions who probe the secrets hidden within American folk music in all its mutant forms—regional, ethnic, sacred, commercial.

Together, students collect records, compile discographies, interview performers, stage concerts, plan festivals, write articles, gather in meetings, and publish reports. In reading our word-processed findings, armed with cassette tape or colored slide, we travel over imaginative freeways—ribbons of tape, road markers in the shape of CD disks. Particular exit signs read: Cambridge Square, Tin Pan Alley, Music City, Motown, Bourbon Street, Austin, L. A.

Harvard ballad sage Francis James Child helped form the American Folklore Society in 1888. A half-century later, a few of his successors in their respective quarters turned to hillbilly and race records as documentary tools. Bertrand Bronson valued Buell Kazee's "Lady Gay"; Charles Seeger enjoyed Dock Boggs's "Pretty Polly." From twin perspectives of English literature and formal musicology, teachers marveled at Leadbelly's copious songbag: "Old Hannah," "Gallis Pole," "Grey Goose," "Midnight Special." Bronson and Seeger served as representative pioneers who welcomed commercial recordings into the academy and the public archive.

Robert Winslow Gordon, Alan Lomax, D. K. Wilgus, Peter Tamony, Bill Malone, Dick Spottswood, Chris Strachwitz, and their peers also jumped boundaries in their use of sound recordings. Some worked in university offices; others, in governmental agencies; still others, at home. All expanded appreciation of American music, forever linking folksong to the phonograph and its descendants.

During the 1930s, a number of jazz collectors in Ivy League colleges hunted used records, swapped finds, prepared auction lists, and edited mimeographed journals. Such discographical endeavor did not take hold immediately in the parallel fields of old-time or country music. Not until the eve of World War Two did a few fans issue locally printed magazines reporting the geographic extension of Appalachian and Western music.

Prior to such amateur efforts, trade journals such as *Talking Machine World* or *Radio Digest* served the publicity needs of those recording companies which sold vernacular and foreign-language disks. Two benchmark dates call attention to research in old-time and country music. In January 1951 Joe Nicholas (Palmer, Michigan) and Freeman Kitchens (Drake, Kentucky) issued their first *Disc Collector*, the "Official Organ of the National Hillbilly Record Collectors' Exchange." In January 1978 the Country Music Foundation upgraded its previous modest *Journal of Country Music*. The new attractive *JCM* marked Nashville's tentative steps into cultural criticism and interpretive analysis.

As a participant in the Sounds of the South Conference at the University of North Carolina, April 6–8, 1989, I took pleasure in the various papers gathered by Dan Patterson for this monograph. These separate offerings do not require an overarching view, a singular angle of vision. Conference planners did not hold guests to an agreed agenda, a guiding line. Audience members expected all contributors to articulate their separate assumptions and to define their exegetic strategies.

This monograph marks a coming of age in vernacular studies— a sharing of plural perspectives, a willingness to leave Guy Clark's burden behind ("If I could just get off this freeway alive"). Technically, our Chapel Hill gathering celebrated the transcontinental passage of disks and related ephemera from UCLA to UNC. Having corresponded with John Edwards during the 1950s, I know the subsequent long journey of his precious collection.

Literally, some disks had been mailed to Edwards in Sydney, Australia, by Dorsey Dixon from the Carolina Piedmont. After John's death (Christmas Eve, 1960), his mother mailed Dixon's records and many others to Eugene Earle, then in New Jersey. Upon chartering the John Edwards Memorial Foundation, Earle transported the entire collection to UCLA. A quarter century later, he helped pack the disks for their final voyage to the Wilson Library at Chapel Hill.

Eugene Earle, Ed Kahn, Norm Cohen, Fred Hoeptner, Bob Pinson, Ken Griffis, and John Hartford can supplement the JEMF narrative. With the move of the physical collection to North Carolina we altered "Foundation" to "Forum" in our name. In part, our adventure is one of stamina needed to pack and unpack records. More importantly, our story treats the decoding of messages locked into record grooves. Norm Cohen has made a needed start on JEMF history; together, we can extend it to treat large issues inherent in American responses to vernacular culture.

JEMF activists followed no single road in discerning our nation's "ambient ethos," to use David Whisnant's striking term. Aware of internal philosophic differences, we joined in affection for Southern music, and out of a desire to overcome its neglect in the academy and exploitation in commercial marts. Decades ago, Bob Pinson struggled to find a rubric that might encompass musics variously labeled *mountain, cowboy, country, western swing, bluegrass, Cajun, sacred, gospel, jazz, race, blues, soul, downhome, backroads, ethnic, folk.* Lumping these together, he resorted to the shorthand tag "Our Music." I recycle his naming device for this Conference wrap-up commentary.

Readers of our monograph will also find useful the final issue of the *JEMF Quarterly* (Fall/Winter 1985; mailed in January 1991). Paul and Patricia Wells saw it through production, using it to announce their forthcoming journal, *American Vernacular Music.* The last *JEMF Quarterly* combined retrospective accounts of organizational history with four new case-study articles: an Ozark stringband; Charles Nabell, an obscure Western performer; "The Mormon Cowboy"; "Wreck on the Highway."

Listeners who know Roy Acuff's "Wreck" as a lachrymose classic will be challenged by Tony Hilfer's treatment of the song. Previously,

I have alluded to Dorsey Dixon as a pen pal of John Edwards. Here, I credit Dixon as composer of "Wreck on the Highway" and urge readers to pursue Hilfer's eschatological commentary: "If the basic gist of ["Wreck"] were recast to some pre-automotive form of accident, rewritten in Middle English and claimed as a new manuscript discovery from the fourteenth century, it would be read as the brilliantly inventive play on biblical texts and Christian meanings that it is."

Hilfer's analogic assertion tying centuries together enhances appreciation of hillbilly music. Further, listeners gain strength upon hearing a Tar Heel textile millhand's song in full complexity. "Wreck on the Highway" and "L. A. Freeway" can be joined by their moral appeal. I link them also as road signs assisting travelers into Southern vernacular music's territory.

Dorsey Dixon and Guy Clark helped mark my journey from San Francisco to Chapel Hill and home again. Other readers will select their favorite artists—Bob Wills, Willie Nelson, Dolly Parton, Billie Holiday, Clifton Chenier, Michael Doucet, Aretha Franklin, Lydia Mendoza. Lists of exemplary performers stretch endlessly; their songs become mile posts in personal growth, and building blocks in the articulation of reality.

Thirty years have elapsed since John Edwards's death in Paramatta. We speculate whether he would have recognized current exit signs on the musical highway he entered in schoolboy years. We ask whether he would be happy entirely with the key words appropriate in today's analysis of his beloved "Golden Age" disks: *deconstruction, politics of culture, gender, class, community.*

In the two years between our Conference sessions and the completion of Dan Patterson's editorial work on this collective report, we have witnessed Black Beret commandos battering Lithuania's television station, and Kurdish children in high mountain snow. What vernacular songs emboldened Vilnius's defenders? What traditional tales cheered Kurdistan's youngsters? American GI's carried sounds from Nashville and Memphis to Iraq. Will Merle Haggard—forever on tour, tireless in performance—find the freeway or airport arrow to Dohuk?

Such rhetorical queries, posed and unanswered, return us to tasks in building archives of disks, tapes, notes, graphics, and clippings. John Edwards, working in Sydney's Transport Department, poured his entire earnings into serious collecting. We continue his quest in supporting the Southern Folklife Collection at the University of North Carolina.

John, in teen years, could hear the Carter Family on the radio and purchase the Family's disks in Sydney shops. However, he found nothing in any Australian library about Sarah, Maybelle, or A. P. Carter. With many letters and select contributions to collector's magazines, Edwards helped generate a critical body of literature on old-time music. Folklorists and archivists at Chapel Hill extend his mission.

A citation from *The New York Review of Books* (March 30, 1989) illustrates the present-day breadth in country-music research. Literary critic Roger Shattuck opened a review of V. S. Naipaul's *A Turn in the South* with a powerful image:

All day, mechanics and construction workers across America keep a radio twanging next to the socket wrenches or hooked on to bare studs. All night, the ghost army of workers and cleaners who service the offices and classroom buildings in our towns fill the corridors with the same music from their portable sets. To travel in this land today you need not only wheels but also a radio tuned Country. . . . Our *samizdat* is wide open, electronic, and commercially successful. Its wailing or driving rhythms ride on slide guitars and nasal voices. Behind the broken loves and honky-tonk lives celebrated in the lyrics, it doesn't take long to find bedrock.

I submit Professor Shattuck's views as enlarging those of John Edwards and his pen pals who memorialized him at UCLA in an archive/research/outreach center. Shattuck, of course, pointed beyond documentary and preservational skills to questions about the nature of country music's populism and protest. Many scholars have selected jazz or spirituals as the only "true" American music, elevating such forms above native or tribal expression. If American essences are defined by popularity rather than nativity, we need look to country and rock as bedrock musics.

Even the most disciplined student holds clashing norms in judgment—number of listeners, critics' aesthetic codes, community mores, tradition's chains, innovating currents. Those who demystify vernacular music have yet to define clearly the uncertain bounds between their arena and that of Dylan, Springsteen, and Madonna. What freeway carried Madonna Louise Ciccone, "The Bad Goddaughter," from Bay City, Michigan, to Manhattan and Cannes?

Such questions spin faster than answers. No clear markers divide folk, vernacular, and popular music. Clearly, we shall pursue this demon through many mazes. I circle back to Dorsey Dixon, who spliced folk and hillbilly yarn, and to Guy Clark, who helped fuse country and rock idioms.

In mind's eye, I see Dorsey's loom in a red brick Rockingham mill adjacent to old Highway One, and Guy's stained kitchen table in a run-down Hollywood apartment. An actual car wreck lifted a linthead's mind away from everyday work. "L. A. Freeway" tumbled out of a musician's consciousness following an after-work interminable drive home. How many songs flowed out of shuttle and loom or windshield wipers; how many composers reached for a paper scrap or a dashboard envelop to pen a ballad in factory aisle or under street light?

Imaginatively, we are on the road again, following a giant truck that carries John Edwards's records from Westwood to Chapel Hill. The exit signs blur: Indio, Albuquerque, Amarillo, Tulsa, Little Rock, Memphis, Knoxville, Charlotte. How many miles to Little Rock? Can anyone go back to Tulsa? Who did you say it was, brother? Did you hear anybody pray?

In opening this Conference report, Dan Patterson paid homage to discographers and documentarians outside the academy—those working "with the zeal of persons 'called.'" John Edwards had been "called." Bob Pinson, coining the term "Our Music," voiced the inner conviction, the felt connection of a flock gathered in a sacred circle. "Our Music"'s partisans, without formal creed, continue to work with zeal. We pack and transport records, we ponder on their messages.

John Edwards's records at last are home in Carolina—the journey has been long and not without peril. Our Sounds of the South Conference participants are home from Alabama to Alaska. Artifacts, texts, and tapes continue to pour into the Southern Folklife Collection. In accessioning treasures, we seek paths between fast and slow freeway lanes. We switch radio bands, straining for the elusive song, the heavenly melody, the final word. One eye searches the white line; the other, EXIT AHEAD.

Notes

Notes

Introduction

1. Jillian Steiner Sandrock, formerly program officer of the Skaggs Foundation, is currently working to fill the void left by its closing; she is raising an endowment for a new Fund for Folk Culture specifically dedicated to the support of folklife projects.

2. This material has been released on the LP "Down around Bowmantown: Portrait of a Music Community in Northeast Tennessee" (Johnson City: Center for Appalachian Studies and Services, East Tennessee State University, 1990), with an extensive booklet by Stafford and Richard Blaustein.

3. Shortly after the Conference the Smithsonian inaugurated its Folkways Smithsonian Recordings Series.

Evaluating Our Work and Ourselves

1. *Birmingham Quartet Anthology: Jefferson County, Alabama (1926–1953)* (Clanka Lanka Records 144,001/2).

2. *Birmingham Quartet Scrapbook: A Quartet Reunion in Jefferson Country, Birmingham City Auditorium, October 12, 1980*, 20 pp.

3. *Birmingham Boys: Jubilee Gospel Quartets from Jefferson County, Alabama*. Notes by Ray Funk, Brenda McCallum, and Horace Boyer (Alabama Traditions Records 101).

Country Music and the Academy

1. D. K. Wilgus, "A Catalogue of American Folksongs on Commercial Records," M.A. thesis (Columbus: Ohio State University, 1947).

2. Mrs. Jimmie (Carrie) Rodgers, *My Husband, Jimmie Rodgers* (Nashville: Ernest Tubb Publications, n.d.); George D. Hay, *A Story of the Grand Ole Opry* (Copyright by George D. Hay, 1953).

3. Mike Seeger and John Cohen, eds., *The New Lost City Ramblers Song Book* (New York: Oak Publications, 1964).

4. Alan Lomax, "Bluegrass Background: Folk Music with Overdrive," *Esquire Magazine*, 52 (Oct. 1959): 108.

5. D. K. Wilgus, ed., "Hillbilly Issue," *Journal of American Folklore* 78 (1965): 195–288.

6. Harry Smith, ed., *Anthology of American Folk Music*, 3 vols., Folkways Records FA2951-FA2953.

7. Thomas D. Clark, *The Rampaging Frontier: Manners and Humors of Pioneering Days in the South and the Middle West* (Indianapolis and New York: Bobbs-Merrill, 1939) and *The Kentucky* (New York: Rinehart & Co., 1942), p. 127.

8. *I'll Take My Stand: The South and the Agrarian Tradition*, by Twelve Southerners (New York and London: Harper, 1930), p. 233.

9. Frank Owsley, *Plain Folk of the Old South* (Baton Rouge: Louisiana State University Press, 1982). Originally published in 1949.

10. Bill C. Malone, *Country Music, U.S.A.: A Fifty-Year History* (Austin: University of Texas Press for the American Folklore Society, 1968), p. 45.

11. Lawrence Levine, *Black Culture and Black Consciousness: Afro-American Folk Thought from Slavery to Freedom* (New York: Oxford University Press, 1977).

12. Jack Temple Kirby, *Media-Made Dixie: The South in the American Imagination* (Baton Rouge: Louisiana State University Press, 1978; rev. ed., 1986).

13. J. Wayne Flynt, *Dixie's Forgotten People: The South's Poor Whites* (Bloomington: Indiana University Press, 1979) and *Poor But Proud: Alabama's Poor Whites* (Tuscaloosa: University of Alabama Press, 1989).

14. Grady McWhiney, *Cracker Culture: Celtic Folkways in the Culture of an American Region* (Tuscaloosa: University of Alabama Press, 1988).

15. David Whisnant, *All That Is Native and Fine: The Politics of Culture in an American Region* (Chapel Hill: University of North Carolina Press, 1983).

16. Jacquelyn D. Hall, et al., *Like a Family: The Making of a Southern Cotton Mill World* (Chapel Hill: University of North Carolina Press, 1987).

17. James N. Gregory, *American Exodus: The Dust Bowl Migration and Okie Culture in California* (New York: Oxford University Press, 1989).

18. Such scholars as Peter Narvaez and Neil Rosenberg have discussed the important country music tradition in Canada, but the most published student of non-Southern country music is Simon J. Bronner. For example, see his *Old-Time Music Makers of New York State* (Syracuse: Syracuse University Press, 1987).

19. I have explored the relationship between the South and American music in *Southern Music/American Music* (Lexington: University Press of Kentucky, 1979).

20. Bill Ivey, review of *Country Music, USA* (rev. ed., 1985) in *The Journal of Country Music* 11 (1986): 91–93.

Overseas Blues

1. Iain Laing, *The Background of the Blues* (London: Workers' Music Association, 1943), p. 30.

2. Charles Delaunay, *Hot Discography*, 1940 ed. corrected and reprinted (New York: Commodore Record Co., 1943).

3. Albert McCarthy, *The PL Yearbook of Jazz* (London: Editions Poetry London, 1946), pp. 72–107.

4. Yannick Bruynoghe, *Big Bill Blues; William Broonzy's Story As Told to Yannick Bruynoghe* (London: Cassell, 1957).

5. Paul Oliver, *Blues Off the Record: Thirty Years of Blues Commentary* (Tunbridge Wells, Kent: Baton Press; New York: Hippocrene Books, 1984).
6. Paul Oliver, *Blues Fell This Morning: The Meaning of the Blues* (London: Cassell, 1960).
7. Paul Oliver, *Blues Fell This Morning: Meaning in the Blues* (Cambridge and New York: Cambridge University Press, 1990).
8. These appeared originally in *Jazz Hot* (Paris) in 1959, and in an English translation by Ian McLean in *Jazz Journal* (London), June and July issues of 1960.
9. Albert McCarthy, Dave Carey, and Ralph Venables, *Jazz Directory*, 7 vols. (London: Cassell, 1949–1957).
10. Jørgen Grunnet Jepsen, *Jazz Records 1942–1962* (Copenhagen: Nordisk Tidsskrift, 1963–1970).
11. Walter Bruyninckx, *Fifty Years of Recorded Jazz 1917–1967* (Mechelen, Belgium: author, 1968).
12. Brian A. L. Rust, *Jazz Records, 1897–1942*, 2 vols. (London: Storyville, 1970).
13. Robert M. W. Dixon and John Godrich, *Blues and Gospel Records 1902–1942* (n.p., 1963; London: Storyville, 1969).
14. Max E. Vreede, *Paramount 12000–13000 Series* (London: Storyville, 1971).
15. Mike Leadbitter and Neil Slaven, *Blues Records 1949–1966* (London: Hanover Books; New York: Oak Publications, 1968).
16. Mike Leadbitter and Neil Slaven, *Blues Records, 1949–1970, Volume One A–K: A Selective Discography* (London: Record Information Services, 1987).
17. Paul Oliver, *Conversation with the Blues* (London: Cassell; New York: Horizon, 1965).
18. Paul Oliver, *Screening the Blues: Aspects of the Blues Tradition* (London: Cassell, 1968).
19. Paul Oliver, *The Story of the Blues* (London: Barrie and Rockliff; Philadelphia: Chilton, 1969).
20. Paul Oliver, *Savannah Syncopators: African Retentions in the Blues* (London: Studio Vista; New York: Stein and Day, 1970).
21. Bengt Olsson, *Memphis Blues and Jug Bands* (London: Studio Vista; New York: Stein and Day, 1970).
22. Karl Gert Zur Heide, *Deep South Piano: The Story of Little Brother Montgomery* (London: Studio Vista; New York: Stein and Day, 1970).
23. Bruce Bastin, *Crying for the Carolines* (London: Studio Vista; New York: Stein and Day, 1971).
24. Derrick Stewart-Baxter, *Ma Rainey and the Classic Blues Singers* (London: Studio Vista; New York: Stein and Day, 1970).
25. Robert M. W. Dixon and John Godrich, *Recording the Blues* (London: Studio Vista; New York: Stein and Day, 1970).
26. Bob Groom, *The Blues Revival* (London: Studio Vista; New York: Stein and Day, 1970).
27. Tony Russell, *Blacks, Whites and Blues* (London: Studio Vista; New York: Stein and Day, 1970).
28. Mike Rowe, *Chicago Breakdown* (London: Eddison Press, 1973).

194 *Notes*

29. John Broven, *Walking to New Orleans: The Story of New Orleans Rhythm and Blues* (Bexhill-on-Sea: Blues Unlimited, 1974).

30. John Broven, *South to Louisiana: The Music of the Cajun Bayous* (Gretna, Louisiana: Pelican, 1983).

31. Charlie Gillett, *The Sound of the City: The Rise of Rock and Roll* (New York: Outerbridge and Dienstfrey, 1970).

32. Charlie Gillett, *Making Tracks: Atlantic Records and the Growth of a Multi-Billion-Dollar Industry* (New York: E. P. Dutton, 1974).

33. Giles Oakley, *The Devil's Music: A History of the Blues* (London: British Broadcasting Corporation; New York: Taplinger, 1976).

34. Richard Middleton, *Pop Music and the Blues: A Study of the Relationship and Its Significance* (London: Gollancz, 1972).

35. Michael Haralambos, *Right On: From Blues to Soul in Black America* (London: Eddison, 1974; New York: Drake, 1975).

36. A. M. Dauer, *Blues aus 100 Jahren: 43 Beispiele zur Typologie der vokalen Bluesformen* (Frankfurt-am-Main: Fischer Taschenbuch, 1983).

37. David Hatch and Stephen Millward, *From Blues to Rock: An Analytical History of Pop Music* (Manchester, U.K., and Wolfeboro, U.S.A.: Manchester University Press, 1987).

38. Jean-Claude Arnaudon, *Dictionnaire du Blues* (Paris: Filipacchi, 1977).

39. Karel Bogaert, *Blues Lexicon. Blues, Cajun, Boogie Woogie, Gospel* (Antwerp: Standaard, 1972).

40. Gérard Herzhaft, *Encyclopédie du Blues: Etude Bio-Discographique d'une Musique Populaire Négro-Américaine* (Lyons: Fédérop, 1979).

41. Bruce Bastin, *Red River Blues: The Blues Tradition in the Southeast* (Urbana: The University of Illinois Press, 1986).

42. Paul Oliver, *Songsters and Saints: Vocal Traditions on Race Records* (Cambridge and New York: Cambridge University Press, 1984).

43. *The New Grove Dictionary of Music and Musicians*, ed. Stanley Sadie (London: Macmillan, 1980).

44. *The New Grove Gospel, Blues and Jazz: With Spirituals and Ragtime* (London: Macmillan; New York: Norton, 1986).

45. Paul Oliver, ed., *The Blackwell Guide to Blues Records* (Oxford and New York: Blackwell Reference, 1989).

46. Bruce Bastin took a master's degree in folklore at the University of North Carolina in Chapel Hill in 1973, writing a master's thesis on "The Emergence of a Blues Tradition in the Southeastern States," but he had already by that time published *Crying for the Carolines*, many articles, and blues recordings, and done extensive fieldwork on the blues.

Looking for Henry Reed

This is a much-revised version of an illustrated talk presented at the Sounds of the South Conference. I would like to thank Archie Green for introducing me to folklore studies, Lisa Feldman for giving me the Hollow Rock String Band album, and Blanton and Ann for living through the Fuzzy Mountain days with me.

1. *The Hollow Rock String Band: Traditional Dance Tunes*, Kanawha

Records 311, with Alan Jabbour (fiddle), Bert Levy (mandolin), Bobbie Thompson (guitar), and Tommy Thompson (banjo). A subsequent album was *The Hollow Rock String Band*, Rounder Records 0024, with Alan Jabbour (fiddle), Tommy Thompson (banjo, guitar), and Jim Watson (guitar, mandolin, autoharp).

2. Old Time String Band Project, Elektra Records 7292.

3. Alan Lomax, "Folk Song Style," *American Anthropologist* 61 (1959): 929–38.

4. Kanawha Records 311, jacket notes.

5. Recordings by the group are *The Fuzzy Mountain String Band*, Rounder Records 0010, with Malcolm Owen (fiddle), Vickie Owen (dulcimer), Blanton Owen (banjo), Eric Olson (banjo), Bobbie Thompson (guitar), and Bill Hicks (fiddle), and *Summer Oaks & Porch: The Fuzzy Mountain String Band*, Rounder Records 0035, with Bill Hicks (fiddle), Malcolm Owen (fiddle), Sharon Poss (guitar), Vickie Owen (dulcimer), Blanton Owen (banjo, fiddle), Eric Olson (banjo), and Tom Carter (fiddle, banjo, mandolin, guitar). Another of these groups that was to record prolifically was The Red Clay Ramblers, beginning with *The Red Clay Ramblers with Fiddlin' Al McCanless*, Folkways Records FTS 31039, with Bill Hicks (fiddle, guitar), Al McCanless (fiddle), Tommy Thompson (banjo, guitar), Jim Watson (banjo, guitar), Mike Craver (piano), Tom Carter (banjo), and Laurel Urton (washtub bass).

Research Approaches to Black Gospel Quartets

1. See Marion Franklin, *The Relationship of Black Preaching to Gospel Music* (Ph.D. diss., Madison, N.J.: Drew University, 1982).

2. See Ray Allen, *Singing in the Spirit: An Ethnography of Gospel Performance in New York City's African American Church Community*, (Ph.D. diss., Philadelphia: University of Pennsylvania, 1987), and Glenn D. Hinson, *When the Words Roll and the Fire Flows: Spirit, Style and Experience in African-American Gospel Performance*, (Ph.D. diss., Philadelphia: University of Pennsylvania. 1989).

3. Doug Seroff gives information on the early cylinder recordings of quartets as well as the Dinwiddies themselves in "Polk Miller and the Old South," *78 Quarterly*, No. 3 (1988), pp. 27–41.

4. The pre-war discography has also been greatly helped by the recent publication of Kip Lornell, *Virginia's Blues, Gospel, & Country Records, 1902–1943: An Annotated Discography* (Lexington: University Press of Kentucky, 1989), with its detailed annotations and photos for the many quartets from the Tidewater area.

5. Ray Funk, liner notes to *Atlanta Gospel*, Gospel Heritage HT 312 (1987).

6. My wife has long ago given up considering it a hobby and considers it somewhere between an obsession and a destructive addiction.

7. Doug Seroff, "On the Battlefield: Gospel Quartets in Jefferson County, Alabama," in *Repercussions*, ed. Geoffrey Haydon and Dennis Marks (London: Century Publishing, 1985); Doug Seroff, notes to *The Birmingham*

Quartet Anthology (Clanka Lanka Records LP 144,000/001); Doug Seroff, notes to program booklet for *The Birmingham Quartet Reunion 1980.*
8. See Bess Lomax Hawes' account of this event in this volume.
9. Doug Seroff, program for the Gospel Arts Day Nashville, 1988.
10. Kip Lornell, *"Happy in the Service of the Lord": Afro-American Gospel Quartets in Memphis* (Urbana: University of Illinois Press, 1988); Kip Lornell, notes to *Happy in the Service of the Lord: Memphis Gospel Quartet Heritage—The 1980s* (High Water LP 1002); Doug Seroff, notes to *Bless My Bones: Memphis Gospel Radio—The Fifties* (Rounder LP 2063).
11. Lynn Abbott, *The Soproco Spiritual Singers: A New Orleans Quartet Family Tree* (Jean Lafite National Historical Park, 1983); Lynn Abbott, notes to *New Orleans Gospel Quartets 1947–1956* (Gospel Heritage HT 306); Lynn Abbott, notes to *Religious Recordings from New Orleans 1924–1931* (504 Records, forthcoming). Lynn Abbott has almost completed a book-length manuscript on the history of New Orleans gospel.
12. Ray Allen, op. cit., and notes to *New York Grassroots Gospel: The Sacred Black Quartet Tradition* (Global Village GVM 206).
13. The Blue Ridge Institute at Ferrum College, Ferrum, Virginia, is completing record albums that trace the gospel quartet heritage of both communities.
14. Jacqueline Djedje, "Gospel Music in the Los Angeles Black Community: An Historical Overview," *Black Music Research Journal* 9 (1):35–79 (1989).
15. See Michael Licht, *D. C. Gospel Groups 1989*, Folk Arts Program, D.C. Commission on the Arts and Humanities.
16. Ray Funk, "The Imperial Quintet," *Blues and Rhythm—The Gospel Truth*, No. 9 (1985): 4–5.
17. A recent issue of *Downbeat* magazine reports the starting of the Jazz, Blues, and Gospel Hall of Fame in Chicago in conjunction with the Chicago Public Library; presumably an archive will be developed along with that facility. Meanwhile, the Center for Popular Culture at Middle Tennessee State University is developing a research collection that includes gospel music. The Tulane Jazz Archive has also expanded its efforts to build a gospel collection. The Southern Folklife Collection at the University of North Carolina is also in the process of building a black gospel collection of note.
18. See Peter Grendysa and Ray Funk, "The Southernaires," *Goldmine*, June 21, 1985, pp. 16, 24.
19. A revised and updated version is now available from Limelight Editions, 1985.
20. See Laurraine Goreau, *Just Mahalia, Baby: The Mahalia Jackson Story* (Waco, Texas: Word Books, 1975); Mahalia Jackson with Evan McLeod Wylie, *Movin' On Up* (New York: Hawthorn, 1966); Jean G. Cornell, *Mahalia Jackson: Queen of Gospel Song* (New York: Garrard, 1974). Mahalia Jackson is also the focus of a forthcoming special issue of *Rejoice* and a biography for teen readers by Charles Wolfe.
21. Viv Broughton, *Black Gospel: An Illustrated History of the Gospel Sound* (Poole, Dorset: Blandford Press, 1985).

22. Ray Allen, op. cit.; S. Carroll Buchanan, *A Critical Analysis of Style in Four Black Jubilee Quartets in the United States* (New York: New York University: 1987); Joyce Jackson, *The Performing Black Sacred Quartet: An Expression of Cultural Values and Aesthetics* (Bloomington: Indiana University, 1988); Glenn D. Hinson, op. cit.; Kip Lornell, op. cit.

23. Kip Lornel, op. cit.

24. The best mail-order source for black gospel reissues and books is Down Home Music, 10341 San Pablo Avenue, El Cerrito, CA 94530. It issues regular newsletters as well as a blues and gospel catalog.

25. For example, the photo of the Dixieaires on the back cover of *Dixieaires, Let Me Fly* (Gospel Heritage HT 317) is the only known photograph of the group and came from a clipping from the Baltimore *Afro-American*.

26. This does not disregard the fact that Tony Heilbut's seminal book in the field, *The Gospel Sound*, was first published back in 1971. However, for the next decade in-depth research or writing in this field was left almost entirely to him.

27. The author remains happy to correspond with other collectors and researchers and to share his knowledge of the wealth of this vital heritage. Feel free to write him at P.O.Box 72387, Fairbanks, AK 99707. He'll do his best to respond and loves to trade tapes, photos, videos, and information.

The John Edwards Memorial Foundation

Portions of the paper also appeared in Norm Cohen's essay "JEMF and the *Quarterly*: Memories of a Shy and Retiring Editor" in the final issue of the *JEMFQ* 21 (Fall-Winter 1985): 91–96.

1. UNC, Southern Folklife Collection, John Edwards Papers, 20000, Series 3.3, Folder 97.

2. Irene Edwards, "John Edwards: How a Schoolboy Interest in American Folk and Hillbilly Music Became a Lifelong Dedication," *Ralph Stanley International Fan Club Journal* 3, issue 1 (1968?): 18.

3. UNC, Southern Folklife Collection, John Edwards Papers, 20000, Series 1.2, Folder 75: Letter, John Edwards to David Crisp, May 12, 1958, p. [1]. Part of the letter was reprinted by Jazzer Smith in "The Long Journey Home: The Hitherto Untold Story of a Remarkable Man Called John Edwards" in Jazzer Smith, ed., *The Australian Book of Country Music* (Gordon, N. S. W.: Berghouse Floyd Tuckey, 1984), pp. 60–71; subsequently reprinted in *JEMFQ* 21 (Fall-Winter 1985): 86–88.

4. Buell Kazee, *Ralph Stanley International Fan Club Journal* 3, issue 1 (1968?): 34.

5. Vocational Guidance Bureau Report, 10 May 1948 (xerox copy provided by Irene Edwards).

6. *John Edwards Memorial Foundation Newsletter* 1 (October 1965): 1.

7. The final installment of this series appeared in the final issue of the *JEMF Quarterly*, 21 (Fall/Winter 1985): 99–115.

8. "JEMF Initiates Record Reissue Series," *JEMF Quarterly*, 3 (September 1967): 10.
9. "From the Editor," *JEMF Quarterly*, 5 (Spring 1969): 1.
10. *JEMF Quarterly*, 7 (Spring 1971): 3–4.

The Southern Folklife Collection: The Era of Surprise

1. Arthur Palmer Hudson, *Folksongs of Mississippi and Their Background* (Chapel Hill: University of North Carolina Press, 1936).
2. Arthur Palmer Hudson, "An Attala Boyhood," *Journal of Mississippi History* 4 (April 1942): 59–75; (July 1942): 127–55.
3. See "Guy B. Johnson's Sea Island Cylinders Recovered" in *Sounds of the South Conference Update*, No. 2 (July 1990), p. 3.

The Center for Acadian and Creole Folklore

1. Barry Jean Ancelet, *The Makers of Cajun Music/Musiciens cadiens et créoles* (Austin: University of Texas Press, 1984).
2. Glenn Conrad, *The Cajuns: Essays on Their History and Culture* (Lafayette: University of Southwestern Louisiana Center for Louisiana Studies, 1978).
3. Ann Savoy, *Cajun Music: A Reflection of a People* (Eunice: Bluebird Press, 1985).

Life as We Knew It

1. Red Clay Ramblers, "Cabin Home" on *Chuckin' the Friz* (Chicago: Flying Fish Records, 1979).
2. Dwight Yokam, "I Sang Dixie" on *Just Lookin' for a Hit* (Reprise Records, CD 9–25989–2).
3. Kathy Mattea, "Life As We Knew It" on *Untasted Honey* (Mercury Records, CD 422–832 793–2 Q1).
4. R. S. Field, D. Roberts, "Is This All There Is" on Webb Wilber and the Beatnecks, *It Came from Nashville* (Nashville: Racket Records, 1986).
5. Martin Tolchin, "Richest Got Richer and Poorest Poorer from 1979 to 1987," New York *Times*, 23 March 1989, p. A1.
6. Southern Labor Institute, *The Climate for Workers in the United States, 1988* (Atlanta: Southern Regional Council, 1988).
7. For a transcription of the song, see Tom Rankin, "Blues for Mr. President," *Southern Changes*, August–September 1984, pp. 12–13. The song itself appears on the 45-rpm disc Audio Arts 007 (Audio Arts Recording, Rt. 1, Box 59, Hwy 43 N, Greenville, NC 27834).
8. Caryn James, "Mira Nair Combines Cultures to Create a Film on India," New York *Times*, 17 October 1988, p. 17.
9. James P. Allen and Eugene J. Turner, "New Immigrants," *American Demographics*, September 1988, p. 26.
10. Bobbie Ann Mason, "Memphis," in *Love Life* (New York: Harper and Row, 1989), pp. 226, 232.

Turning Inward and Outward

1. Although the conference at which this paper was originally presented was on "the South," it focused primarily upon the Southeast, which is my principal concern here. Unfortunately, my lack of expertise has also forced me to omit native American music.

2. For some of Gordon's recordings see Neil V. Rosenberg and Debora Kodish (eds.), Archive of Folk Song L–68: *Folk Songs of America: The Robert Winslow Gordon Collection, 1922–1932* (Washington, D.C.: Library of Congress, 1978). I have not intended to make this a bibliographic or discographic essay; I have tried merely to include a few suggestive items for those who may be unfamiliar with the literature and pertinent recordings. Those wishing fuller citations should begin by consulting Bill C. Malone's bibliographical-discographical essays in *Country Music U.S.A.* (rev. ed., Austin: University of Texas Press, 1985), pp. 417–509.

3. The recording is available on Vol. I of Richard Spottswood's *Folk Music in America* series issued by the Library of Congress: *Religious Music: Congregational and Ceremonial* (Washington, D. C.: Library of Congress, 1976).

4. A good short discussion of the independents' challenge to the major companies from the mid-1950s onward may be found in Charlie Gillett, *The Sound of the City: The Rise of Rock and Roll* (1970; rev. ed., New York: Pantheon Books, 1983). An extraordinary sequence on a small Tex-Mex oriented independent production company in the Southwest appears in the Chris Strachwitz-Les Blank film *Chulas Fronteras* (1976).

5. Among influential recordings one thinks immediately of Harry Smith's 1952 *American Folk Music* anthology (Folkways FA 2951–53); the early commercial albums of Bill Monroe, the Balfa Brothers and Doc Watson produced by Ralph Rinzler; Harry Oster's early Cajun albums on Folklyric; Sun Records' earliest rockabilly issues; some of Moe Asch's Folkways albums; the John Edwards Memorial Foundation's Blue Sky Boys and Carter Family reissues and the *Minstrels and Tunesmiths* album edited by Norm Cohen; and Victor's Vintage series edited by Brad McKuen in the 1960s.

6. Representative discussions of some of these dynamics may be found in Nick Tosches, *Country: The Biggest Music in America* (New York: Dell Publishing Co., 1970); Colin Escott and Martin Hawkins, *Sun Records: The Brief History of the Legendary Recording Label* (New York: Quick Fox, 1980); and of course in Malone, *Country Music U.S.A.*, esp. pp. 31–76 and 245–268.

7. See for example Paul Hemphill, *The Nashville Sound: Bright Lights and Country Music* (New York: Simon and Schuster, 1970) and Malone, *Country Music U.S.A.*, pp. 245–68. Numerous discussions of the Grand Ole Opry have appeared, from those popular ones by Hay (1953) and McDaniel and Seligman (1952) to more scholarly recent treatments by Charles Wolfe (1973). See especially Richard A. Peterson and Paul Di Maggio, "The Early Opry: Its Hillbilly Image in Fact and Fancy," *Journal of Country Music* 4 (Summer 1973): 39–51.

8. See R. Serge Denisoff, *Great Day Coming: Folk Music and the*

American Left (Urbana: University of Illinois Press, 1971) and Malone, *Country Music U.S.A.*, pp. 278–83, 485.

9. See Charles K. Wolfe (ed.), *Truth Is Stranger Than Publicity: Alton Delmore's Autobiography* (Nashville: Country Music Foundation Press, 1977); Peter Guralnick, *Lost Highway: Journeys and Arrivals of American Musicians* (Boston: D. R. Godine, 1979); R. Serge Denisoff, *Waylon: A Biography* (Knoxville: University of Tennessee Press, 1983); Louis M. Jones and Charles K. Wolfe, *Everybody's Grandpa: Fifty Years Behind the Mike* (Knoxville: University of Tennessee Press, 1984); and a series of biographies in the University of Illinois Press' Music in American Life series: Nolan Porterfield, *Jimmie Rodgers: The Life and Times of America's Blue Yodeler* (1979), Charles R. Townsend, *San Antonio Rose: The Life and Music of Bob Wills* (1976), Bill C. Malone and Judith McCulloh (eds.), *Stars of Country Music: Uncle Dave Macon to Johnny Rodriguez* (1975), and Roger M. Williams, *Sing a Sad Song: The Life of Hank Williams* (1981).

10. See David E. Whisnant, *All That Is Native and Fine: The Politics of Culture in An American Region* (Chapel Hill: University of North Carolina Press, 1983), pp. 181–251, and (ed.), *Folk Festival Issues: Report from a Seminar* (Los Angeles: John Edwards Memorial Foundation, 1979).

11. One of the most searching and analytically sophisticated treatments of country music (specifically of bluegrass) currently available is Robert Cantwell's *Bluegrass Breakdown: The Making of the Old Southern Sound* (Urbana: University of Illinois Press, 1984).

12. One of the more thoughtful and searching considerations of the negative and positive aspects of this stigmatization is of course C. Vann Woodward's *The Burden of Southern History* (rev. ed., Baton Rouge: Louisiana State University Press, 1968), but of course analyses of it stretch back through W. J. Cash's *The Mind of the South* (New York: A. A. Knopf, 1941) and thence into the nineteenth century.

13. Among the many treatments of this cultural dynamic, George Black's *The Good Neighbor: How the United States Wrote the History of Central America and the Caribbean* (New York: Pantheon Books, 1988) is one of the most graphic. The cultural-political nexus over a century and a half period is evident by comparing such works as Robert W. Johannsen's *To the Halls of the Montezumas: The Mexican War in the American Imagination* (New York: Oxford University Press, 1985) and Stephen C. Schlesinger and Stephen Kinzer's *Bitter Fruit: The Untold Story of the American Coup in Guatemala* (Garden City: Doubleday, 1982).

14. I am aware that the hierarchy is not invariably north/south. The pattern of a stigmatized South is nevertheless very frequently encountered.

15. Frantz Fanon, "The Pitfalls of National Consciousness" in *The Wretched of the Earth* (New York: Grove Press, 1963), pp. 148–205.

16. Some jingoistic elements have been scrutinized in Charles Wolfe, "Nuclear Country: The Atomic Bomb in Country Music," *Journal of Country Music* 7 (January, 1978): 4–21, and in Malone's brief sketch of World War II songs in *Country Music U.S.A.*, pp. 194–96.

17. Among the transplanted northern Souths I would include at least Cincinnati's Over-the-Rhine area, Chicago's Uptown, and western Washington's Snohomish County. Although there are enough pan-Southern cultural

affinities and similarities to allow certain generalizations (see for example John Shelton Reed, *The Enduring South: Subcultural Persistence in Mass Society* (Chapel Hill: University of North Carolina Press, 1986) and *One South: An Ethnic Approach to Regional Culture* (Baton Rouge: Louisiana State University Press, 1982)), the multiple and pronounced subregional differences encountered in the South have been the subject of much research and documentation. On the Appalachian South, see for example Henry D. Shapiro, *Appalachia on Our Mind: The Southern Mountains and Mountaineers in the American Consciousness, 1870–1920* (Chapel Hill: University of North Carolina Press, 1978); and David E. Whisnant, *Modernizing the Mountaineer: People, Power, and Planning in Appalachia* (Boone: Appalachian Consortium Press, 1980), Chapter 1, and *All That Is Native and Fine*. On the Cajun area of southwest Louisiana, see William Faulkner Rushton, *The Cajuns: From Acadia to Louisiana* (New York: Farrar, Straus and Giroux, 1979), Barry Jean Ancelet, *The Makers of Cajun Music* (Austin: University of Texas Press, 1984), and Nicholas Spitzer (ed.), *Louisiana Folklife: A Guide to the State* (Baton Rouge: Louisiana Folklife Program, 1985). On the southwest, see Larry Willoughby, *Texas Rhythm, Texas Rhyme: A Pictorial History of Texas Music* (Austin: Texas Monthly Press, 1984) and Jan Reid, *The Improbable Rise of Redneck Rock* (New York: Da Capo Press, 1974). On the offshore islands of South Carolina and Georgia see Charles W. Joyner, *Down By the Riverside: A South Carolina Slave Community* (Urbana: University of Illinois Press, 1984). Recent and ongoing demographic developments have made the southern quarter of Florida ever more heavily Hispanic and therefore culturally distinct.

18. Among the important treatments are Jeff Todd Titon, *Early Downhome Blues: A Musical and Cultural Analysis* (Urbana: University of Illinois Press, 1977) and Bruce Bastin, *Crying for the Carolines* (London: Studio Vista, 1971) and *Red River Blues: The Blues Tradition in the Southeast* (Urbana: University of Illinois Press, 1986).

19. *Conjuntos* are examined in detail in Manuel Peña, *The Texas-Mexican Conjunto: History of A Working-Class Music* (Austin: University of Texas Press, 1985). See also Américo Paredes, *With His Pistol in His Hand: A Border Ballad and Its Hero* (Austin: University of Texas Press, 1958). The splendid work of Chris Strachwitz's Arhoolie records with music of the southwest and of Mexico is especially noteworthy in this regard.

20. Barry O'Connell's "Dock Boggs, Musician and Coal Miner," *Appalachian Journal* 11 (Autumn-Winter 1983–84): 44–57, is an excellent analysis.

21. Harry Oster's early field recording of Cajun musicians and his subsequent fledgling but influential Folklyric label were key factors in bringing wider and more serious attention to Cajun music. Early Folklyric albums are now available through Arhoolie.

22. Ivan Tribe's discussion of West Virginia performers and the media in *Mountaineer Jamboree: Country Music in West Virginia* (Lexington: University Press of Kentucky, 1984) is suggestive.

23. To delineate such differences was an aim of the recent *Encyclopedia of Southern Culture*, edited by Charles Reagan Wilson and William Ferris (Chapel Hill: University of North Carolina Press, 1989).

24. Fortunately, the matter of attitudes toward women in country music

is receiving more attention of late. See for example Mary A. Bufwack, "The Feminist Sensibility in Post-War Country Music," *Southern Quarterly*, no. 22 (Spring 1984): 135–44; Robert K. Oermann and Mary A. Bufwack, "Rockabilly Women," *Journal of Country Music* 8, no. 1 (1979): 65–94, and "Patsy Montana and the Development of the Cowgirl Image," *Journal of Country Music* 8, no. 3 (1981): 18–32; and Robert Oermann, "Mother, Sister, Sweetheart, Pal: Women in Old-Time Country Music," *Southern Quarterly* 22 (Spring 1984): 125–34.

25. For example, Henry M. Belden and Arthur Palmer Hudson's volume 3 of the *Frank C. Brown Collection of North Carolina Folklore* (Durham: Duke University, 1952) contains 110 blackface and minstrel songs, 150 religious songs, but only 37 "martial, political and patriotic songs," almost all of which are from the Revolutionary and Civil War periods. There are 53 "work songs," but the majority are about corn huskings. One (213) is about the abuses of share-cropping, and one ("The Heathen Chinee," 233) is a protest against the hiring of Chinese labor. There are no cotton mill or other industrial songs.

26. On Lunsford, see Bill Finger, "Bascom Lamar Lunsford: The Limits of a Folk Hero," *Southern Exposure* 2 (Spring 1974): 27–37; David E. Whisnant, "Finding the Way Between the Old and the New: The Mountain Dance and Folk Festival and Bascom Lamar Lunsford's Work as a Citizen," *Appalachian Journal* 7 (Autumn–Winter 1979–80): 135–54; and Loyal Jones, *Minstrel of the Appalachians: The Story of Bascom Lamar Lunsford* (Boone, N.C.: Appalachian Consortium Press, 1984).

27. See Whisnant, *All That Is Native and Fine*, pp. 181–252 on the White Top Folk Festival organized by Buchanan and Powell. Powell was a long-time political reactionary and racist organizer by the time he came to the festival.

28. *Nueva canción* (the New Song movement) originated in Argentina and Chile with such performers as Victor Jara in the late 1950s and early 1960s. It utilized traditional musical idioms as a base for compositions on political themes—particularly grass-roots opposition to dictatorships. See Nancy Morris, "Canto porque es necesario cantar: The New Song Movement in Chile, 1973–1983," *Latin American Research Review* 21, no. 2 (1986): 117–36.

29. Two accessible summary treatments of these dynamics may be found in Walter LaFeber, *Inevitable Revolutions: The United States in Central America* (rev. ed., New York: W. W. Norton, 1984) and Black, *The Good Neighbor*.

30. Rounder Records has been a noteworthy counterexample, although its output has not been great in this sector. Most outstanding have been its Hazel Dickens issues, which include *Hard Hitting Songs for Hard Hit People* (0126), *Hazel Dickens and Alice Gerrard* (0054), *Hazel and Alice* (0027), and *They'll Never Keep Us Down* (4012). Rounder also issued *Sarah Ogan Gunning: The Silver Dagger* (0051), *Nimrod Workman: Mother Jones' Will* (0076), *Aunt Molly Jackson* (1002), *Negro Songs of Protest* (4004; from Lawrence Gellert's 1933–37 field recordings), *Come All You Coal Miners* (4005), and *They'll Never Keep Us Down: Women's Coal Mining Songs*

(4012). Chris Strachwitz's Arhoolie includes the splendid *The Mexican Revolution/La revolución mexicana* (Folklyric 9041/44), and Appalshop's June Appal label has issued Mike Kline and Rich Kirby's anthology of antistripmining songs, *They Can't Put It Back* (JA–0012) and Ron Short's *Cities of Gold* (JA–039). Important also are several albums produced by Archie Green during the past two decades: e.g., *Babies in the Mill* (Testament T–3301), *Hard Times* (Rounder 4007), and the two-record *Work's Many Voices* (JEMF 110–11).

31. For discussions of early twentieth-century British collector Cecil Sharp's work in the Southern mountains, see Shapiro, *Appalachia On Our Mind*, pp. 252–59, and Whisnant, *All That Is Native and Fine*, pp. 113–27.

32. See Henry M. Belden, Arthur Palmer Hudson and Jan Philip Schinhan (eds.), *The Frank C. Brown Collection of North Carolina Folklore* (Durham: Duke University Press, 1952–62), vols. 2–5; Alan Lomax, *The Folk Songs of North America* (New York: Doubleday, 1960); Vance Randolph, *Ozark Folksongs* (4 vols., Columbia: State Historical Society of Missouri, 1946–50) and similar collections.

33. See Archie Green, *Only a Miner: Studies in Recorded Coal-Mining Songs* (Urbana: University of Illinois Press, 1972), his long-running series on commercial music graphics in the *John Edwards Memorial Foundation Quarterly*, and his numerous edited documentary and commercial re-issue albums.

34. D. K. Wilgus's M.A. thesis, "A Catalog of American Folksongs on Commercial Records" (Ohio State University 1947) was a pioneer work on recorded country music. Kenneth Goldstein produced early documentary albums of both traditional and revival performers (e.g., *Bowling Green* by the Kossoy sisters and Erik Darling [Tradition TLP–1018]).

35. Seeger's work since the late 1950s as collector, record producer, performer and promoter of second careers for traditional performers (such as Dock Boggs) from the early days of commercially recorded music has been marked by great insight and responsibility. On his work with Dock Boggs, see Barry O'Connell's essay cited in note 20; on similar work with Hazel Dickens, see Richard Straw's interview in *Appalachian Journal* 13 (Summer 1986): 410–424. His most recent work has been with southern Appalachian traditional dance. See his *Talking Feet: Solo Southern Dance: Buck, Flatfoot and Tap* (El Cerrito: Flower Films, 1989).

36. On the New Lost City Ramblers see John Cohen and Mike Seeger (eds.), *The New Lost City Ramblers Song Book* (New York: Oak Publications, 1964). On Fuzzy Mountain see *The Fuzzy Mountain String Band* (Rounder 0010) and *Summer Oaks and Porch* (Rounder 0035). On Hollow Rock see *The Hollow Rock String Band: Traditional Dance Tunes* (Kanawha 311). On the Red Clay Ramblers see *The Red Clay Ramblers with Fiddlin' Al McCanless* (Folkways FTS 31039).

37. See Barry Jean Ancelet, *The Makers of Cajun Music* (Austin: University of Texas Press, 1984).

38. See Henry Shapiro's perceptive discussion of Campbell, the Russell Sage Foundation, and the Foundation's Southern Highland Division in *Appalachia On Our Mind, passim.*

39. See G. L. Kittredge, "Ballads and Rhymes from Kentucky," *Journal of American Folklore* 20 (1907): 251–77. The ballads had been collected by Katherine Pettit from Hindman Settlement School student Josiah Combs, whose 1925 University of Paris dissertation was later edited and published by D. K. Wilgus as *Folk-Songs of the Southern United States* (Austin: University of Texas Press, 1967).

40. See Shapiro's excellent analysis of Berea in *Appalachia on Our Mind*, pp. 113–132.

41. See Whisnant, *All That Is Native and Fine*, pp. 54–56, 96, 118, 183.

42. On Lunsford and Buchanan see notes 26 and 27 above. On Thomas see Archie Green's wide-ranging discussion of Thomas' work with fiddler Jilson Setters [James William Day] in *Only a Miner*, pp. 175–86. On Sarah Gertrude Knott and the National Folk Festival see Green, "The NFFA, That's Who," *National Folk Festival* [program book] (Vienna, Va.: Wolf Trap Farm Park, 1975).

43. On Chase, see Whisnant, *All That Is Native and Fine*, pp. 202–09, 235, 254, 313. Chase's versions of traditional tales have appeared in several volumes, of which *The Jack Tales* (Boston: Houghton Mifflin, 1943) is representative.

44. See for example Jannelle Warren-Findley, "Musicians and Mountaineers: The Resettlement Administration's Music Program in Appalachia, 1935–37," *Appalachian Journal* 7 (Autumn-Winter 1979–80): 105–23.

45. For discussion of some aspects of the city, state and regional folklife programs, see Burt Feintuch (ed.), *The Conservation of Culture: Folklorists and the Public Sector* (Lexington: University Press of Kentucky, 1988).

46. See John C. Campbell, *The Southern Highlander and His Homeland* (1921; rpt., Lexington: University Press of Kentucky, 1969).

47. See introductory essays and headnotes to Cohen and Seeger (eds.), *The New Lost City Ramblers Song Book* for confirmation of these connections and influences.

48. See Cantwell, *Bluegrass Breakdown* and Neil Rosenberg, *Bluegrass: A History* (Urbana: University of Illinois Press, 1985).

49. On the archive see Archie Green, "Commercial Music Graphics, 31: The Archive of American Folk-Song," *JEMF Quarterly* 10 (Winter 1974): 157–64 and Debora G. Kodish, *Good Friends and Bad Enemies: Robert Winslow Gordon and the Study of American Folksong* (Urbana: University of Illinois Press, 1986).

50. On the Act and the Center, see Archie Green, "P.L. 94–201—A View from the Lobby: A Report to the American Folklore Society," in Feintuch (ed.), *The Conservation of Culture*, pp. 269–81.

51. The earliest of the Library of Congress discs appeared in 1941–42. The series eventually embraced black work songs, Anglo-American ballads and songs, sea chanteys, religious music, and native American music. Noteworthy early albums were George Korson's *Songs and Ballads of the Anthracite Miners* (L 16) and Charles Seeger's later *Versions and Variants of "Barbara Allen"* (L 54), which used mostly Southern performers. Carl Fleischhauer and Alan Jabbour's *The Hammons Family: A Study of a West Virginia Family's Traditions* (L 65–66) was especially meticulously done.

52. Dick Netzer's *The Subsidized Muse: Public Support for the Arts in the United States* (New York: Cambridge University Press, 1978), reveals (mostly inadvertently) some of the biases against vernacular culture in public cultural policy, as do Kevin V. Mulcahy and C. Richard Swaim (eds.) in *Public Policy and the Arts* (Boulder: Westview Press, 1982). Karl E. Meyer's *The Art Museum: Power, Money, and Ethics* (New York: Morrow, 1979) addresses more directly the matter of cultural equity.

53. See for example Joseph Wilson's review of Cantwell's *Bluegrass Breakdown* in *Journal of Country Music* 1 (1985): 49–50.

54. There were a few exceptions, such as Michael Kline, who grounded himself in the social-political struggles in the Appalachian region in the mid-1960s (e.g., anti-stripmining, welfare rights, blacklung) and centered his music making in them. On the VISTA and Appalachian Volunteer programs of the late 1960s in Appalachia), see David E. Whisnant, "The Folk Hero in Appalachian Struggle History," *New South* 28 (Fall 1973): 30–47 and *Modernizing the Mountaineer*, pp. 92–125. For one native Appalachian singer's thoughtful recollection of encountering the stigma, see Hazel Dickens, "As Country As I Could Sing," in Jim Axelrod (ed.), *Growin' Up Country* (Clintwood, Va.: Appalachian Movement Press, 1973), pp. 239–48.

55. James C. Scott, *Weapons of the Weak: Everyday Forms of Peasant Resistance* (New Haven: Yale University Press, 1985).

56. See for example Guy and Candie Carawan (eds.), *Voices From the Mountains* (New York: Knopf, 1975), which focuses on music emerging from the Appalachian coalfields from the early 1960s onward. Green's *Only a Miner* carries the analysis backward to the Coal Creek wars of the 1890s.

57. See *Cultural Survival Quarterly* 13, no. 1 (1989)—a special issue on the cultural costs of "economic development" in the Amazon basin.

58. For a splendid narrative by a member of the Quiché community caught in a destructive dynamic of political repression, military violence, and cultural genocide, see Elizabeth Burgos (ed.), *I, Rigoberta Menchú: An Indian Woman in Guatemala* (London: Verso, 1984). See also *Cultural Survival Quarterly* 13, no. 3 (1989)—a special issue on problems of cultural survival in Central America and the Caribbean.

59. See Julian Burger, *Report From the Frontier: The State of the World's Indigenous Peoples* (London and Atlantic Highlands, New Jersey: Zed Books, 1987).

60. C. Vann Woodward, *The Burden of Southern History* (New York: Vintage, 1961).

61. Norm Cohen, "Clayton McMichen: His Life and Music," *John Edwards Memorial Foundation Quarterly* 11 (Autumn 1975): 122.

Contributors and Conference Speakers

Billy Altman may have been the first undergraduate in America to major in popular music (B.A., SUNY-Buffalo, 1973). Since then he has become a respected music critic, writing reviews and articles for *Rolling Stone*, *Esquire*, *Country Music Magazine*, and the *Village Voice*. He currently teaches a course on the history of popular music at the School of Visual Arts in New York City. He is the Executive Producer of the new RCA Heritage Series, which reissues compact discs of early country, blues, gospel, and other traditional music originally recorded on the RCA label.

Barry Ancelet (M.A., Indiana University; Ph.D., Université de Provence) is associate professor of French and Francophone Studies and Director of the Folklore Program at the University of Southwestern Louisiana. He has authored the book *Makers of Cajun Music* and produced a reissue of Cajun music recorded by Alan Lomax in the 1930s. He directs the annual Festival de Musique Acadienne and is host of the weekly live radio program "Rendez-vous des Cajuns."

Guy Carawan (M.A., University of California at Los Angeles) has had a notable career as folk-revival performer, field collector, and editor of song collections and recordings. In 1963 he organized the Sea Island Singers on Johns Island, South Carolina. The Folkways album *Been in the Storm So Long* and the book *Ain't You Got a Right to the Tree of Life* came from the work he and his wife Candie did with these singers. Committed activists, they also edited *We Shall Overcome: Songs of the Freedom Movement* and have served for many years at the Highlander Folk School.

Thomas Carter (Ph.D., Indiana University) teaches in the Graduate School of Architecture at the University of Utah. While working on his M.A. in Folklore at UNC-Chapel Hill, he performed on the second of the Fuzzy Mountain String Band's two albums. His fieldwork in the Meadows of Dan area of Virginia produced an extensive collection of music and oral history recordings that are now part of the Southern Folklife Collection. It also provided material for both volumes of "The Old Originals," issued on Rounder Records and for two other albums. He has recently co-authored the monograph *The Grouse Creek Cultural Survey*, published by the American Folklife Center at the Library of Congress.

Michael T. Casey (M.A., University of North Carolina at Chapel Hill) is Sound and Image Librarian in the Manuscripts Department of the Academic Affairs Library at UNC-Chapel Hill. He is responsible for developing and implementing procedures to preserve and access the Southern Folklife Collection's sound recordings and supportive materials. Casey has directed a series of folklife programs at the ArtsCenter in Carrboro and served as the Executive Director of the Piedmont Council of Traditional Music. His master's thesis in Folklore was a study of traditional flute playing in County Galway, Ireland.

Norm Cohen (Ph.D., University of California-Berkeley) is senior scientist with Aerospace Corporation at El Segundo, California, and one of the foremost authorities on early country music and the railroad in American folksong. His book *Long Steel Rail* was honored with the Chicago Folklore Prize, the ASCAP Deems Taylor Award, and the American Folklore Society's Botkin Prize. He was a leading officer of the John Edwards Memorial Foundation/Forum, editing the *JEMF Quarterly* from 1966 until 1988 and serving as its Executive Secretary from 1969 to the present.

Cecelia Conway (Ph.D., University of North Carolina-Chapel Hill) is Assistant Professor of English at Appalachian State University. A revision of her doctoral dissertation "The Afro-American Tradition of the Folk Banjo" is forthcoming from the University of Tennessee Press. She has collaborated on documentary films on folk music, including "Dink, Pre-Blues Musician" and "Sprout Wings and Fly," the latter (co-produced with Alice Gerrard and Les Blank for Flower Films) on the North Carolina fiddler Tommy Jarrell. She has organized festivals and concerts of traditional artists and edited radio programs of folk music. Dr. Conway was closely associated with the Chapel Hill string-band revival of the 1970s.

Eugene Earle is co-founder and President of the John Edwards Memorial Foundation/Forum and was instrumental in the transfer of the John Edwards Memorial Collection to UNC-Chapel Hill. He corresponded extensively with the late John Edwards, after whose death in 1950 Earle was given control of Edwards's massive collection. Mr. Earle has on his own gathered one of the nation's largest collections of vintage country and western, blues, and Hawaiian records.

Dave Freeman (B.A., Columbia University) owns and operates County and Rebel Records, County Sales, and Record Depot Distributors—primary outlets for contemporary and reissue old-time and bluegrass recordings. A pioneer in the reissue of this music, he has collected early recordings since 1955. His collection includes approximately 4,500 78-rpm discs from the period 1922–1955, 2,000 45-rpm discs, several thousand LPs, and 800 songbooks.

Ray Funk (J.D., University of California-Berkeley) has devoted the past decade to actively researching black vocal harmony music, especially gospel quartets. He has written articles for numerous publications and liner notes for over thirty albums, including the acclaimed Folklyric recordings "A Cappella Gospel Singing" and "The Golden Age of Gospel Singing" and a series of releases on Bruce Bastin's Heritage label. He is also a consulting editor for the new gospel quarterly *Rejoice*. In addition, he writes record reviews and produces a weekly show on traditional music for Alaska Public Radio. Mr. Funk is an assistant attorney general for the state of Alaska and specializes in tort defense.

Alice Gerrard is editor of *The Old-Time Herald* and a founding member of the Blue Ridge Music Association in Galax, Virginia, where she lived for nearly a decade. An outstanding musician and songwriter, she has recorded several albums with Hazel Dickens. She has documented numerous traditional musicians throughout Southwest Virginia and in North Carolina, and with Andy Cahan she co-produced recordings of Galax fiddler Luther Davis and brother-sister musicians Roscoe and Leona Parrish. Along with Les Blank and Cece Conway, she produced "Sprout Wings and Fly," a documentary film on old-time fiddler Tommy Jarrell.

Archie Green (Ph.D. University of Pennsylvania) is a folklorist and author of *Only a Miner: Studies in Recorded Coal Mining Songs* and editor of many folksong recordings, including the Carolina textile-song collection "Babies in the Mill." A long-time member of the United Brotherhood of Carpenters and Joiners of America, Dr. Green is an authority on labor lore, folk music in art, and public-sector folklore. He has taught at the University of Illinois and the University of Texas, and he played a leading role in the creation of the American Folklife Center at the Library of Congress. He has established an Occupational Folklife Studies Endowment Fund at UNC-Chapel Hill, and has donated over 2,000 recordings and documents to the University's Southern Folklife Collection and a collection of labor songsters and other books to its Rare Book Collection. Green has recently completed a book he has named *Wobblies, Pile Butts, & Other Heroes: Laborlore Explorations.*

Bess Lomax Hawes has a distinguished record as Director of the Folk Arts Program of the National Endowment for the Arts, where she has labored since 1977 to foster folk arts and those who work on behalf of them all over the United States. Daughter of John A. Lomax and sister of Alan, she comes from a family that pioneered many directions in the study of American folksong. In addition to her contributions to public-sector folklore, she produced the film "Pizza, Pizza, Daddy-O" and with singer Bessie Jones co-authored the book *Step It Down: Afro-American Children's Songs.*

Charlotte Heth (Ph.D., University of California at Los Angeles) is a member of the Cherokee Nation of Oklahoma and a specialist in Native American music and dance. She served as Director of the American Indian Studies Center at UCLA, and is author and editor of numerous articles, books, records, and videotapes on Native-American music. She has also served as Visiting Professor of Music and Director of the American Indian Program at Cornell University.

George M. Holt is Director of the Folklife Section of the North Carolina Arts Council. The Office of Folklife Programs which he established in the North Carolina Department of Cultural Resources in 1977 was one of the first state folklife programs and is one of the most respected. He has produced and directed many festivals and documentary projects and administers a variety of folk arts grant programs. In 1985, he directed *The Charlotte Country Music Story*, a tribute to musicians who made recordings and radio broadcasts in Charlotte in the 1930s and '40s.

William Ivey (M.A., Indiana University) has served since 1971 as Director of the Country Music Foundation. He wrote and produced the PBS television program "In The Hank Williams Tradition" and was a contributor to the volume *Stars of Country Music*. Ivey has twice served as chair of folk arts panels at the National Endowment for the Arts and has held numerous offices in the National Academy of Recording Arts and Sciences.

Alan Jabbour (Ph.D., Duke University) is Director of the American Folklife Center at the Library of Congress, a position he has held since it was created by Congress in 1976. He served as Head of the Archive of Folksong at the Library of Congress from 1969 through 1974 and became the first Director of the Folk Arts Program at the National Endowment for the Arts the following year. Dr. Jabbour has recorded traditional musicians throughout the Southeast and has produced several influential recordings of old-time music, including the "American Fiddle Tunes" and "The Hammons Family" albums for the Library of Congress. While a graduate student at Duke in the 1960s, he played fiddle with the Hollow Rock String Band, a group that inspired the Chapel Hill/Durham string-band revival.

Dorothy Sara Lee (Ph.D., Indiana University) is Associate Director of the Archives of Traditional Music at Indiana University. She is the former Director of the Federal Cylinder Project sponsored by the American Folklife Center of the Library of Congress, and has done fieldwork on Cijian traditional music and Native American music. Recently she served on a panel to select recordings for the American Folklife Center's *American Folk Music and Folklore Recordings 1987: A Selected List*.

Bertram Levy an original member of the Hollow Rock String Band, currently practices medicine on the west coast. He is an outstanding player of the five-string banjo, mandolin, and concertina and has been twice nominated for the *Frets Magazine* banjo-player-of-the-year award. In 1977 he founded the annual Festival of American Fiddle Tunes in Port Townsend, Washington. Dr. Levy has recorded two albums as a solo artist, "Sageflower Suite" (Centram) and "That Old Gut Feeling" (Flying Fish).

Helen Lewis (Ph.D., University of Kentucky) serves on the staff of Highlander Research and Education Center. She has written extensively on

Appalachian issues and was project director on the film "Long Journey Home." She is editor of the book *Colonialism in Modern America: The Appalachian Case* (The Appalachian Consortium, 1978). Dr. Lewis is currently working on a community research project in Ivanhoe, Virginia, cosponsored by Highlander and Glenway Research Center.

Guy Logsdon (Ed.D., University of Oklahoma) is the former Director of Libraries at the University of Tulsa and a leading authority on the traditional arts and culture of the American West and his native Oklahoma. He has collected a vast amount of information, including thousands of recordings and publications, on the American cowboy, western swing music, Woody Guthrie, and the folklore of the Southwest. Dr. Logsdon's talents are wide-ranging, and he is sought after as a teacher, writer, speaker, consultant, and producer of documentaries.

Alan Lomax is the dean of American field collectors of traditional music and a provocative and innovative student of song style. With his father, John A. Lomax, he performed pioneering field collecting and organizational work for the Library of Congress. He was responsible for introducing Huddie Ledbetter ("Leadbelly"), Aunt Molly Jackson, Vera Hall, and dozens of other major traditional artists to the American public and had a major impact on the folk-music revival in the United States and also in Great Britain, where he collected folksong after World War II. He edited the influential series *Folk Music of the World* for Columbia Records. His wide experience as a field collector provoked his interest in comparative study of song style, which culminated in *Folksong Style and Culture* and in his efforts on behalf of cultural equity for unprivileged artistic traditions. His recent work has focused on an automated data-retrieval system for folksong style, entitled "The Global Jukebox," and five hour-length folksong documentary films in his series *American Patchwork*.

Worth Long is a folklorist and community organizer highly regarded for his efforts to document and present the traditional music of African Americans. He has served as field research specialist for the Smithsonian Institution and has helped to develop numerous cultural organizations and festivals throughout the South. He was instrumental in the creation of the photographic exhibit "Folk Roots: Images of Mississippi Black Folklife," the first exhibition to be curated by African-Americans at the Mississippi State Historical Museum. His film credits include "The Land Where the Blues Began," with Alan Lomax, and "Mississippi Delta Blues." He is currently researching African-American folk traditions along the eastern seaboard.

Bill C. Malone (Ph.D., University of Texas) is a professor in the Department of History at Tulane University. He is one of America's foremost authorities on the history of country music. His books *Southern Music American Music*, *Stars of Country Music* (co-edited with Judith McCulloh) and *Country Music U.S.A.* are the standard texts in the field.

Paul Oliver, an English architectural historian and Fellow of the University of Exeter, Oxford Polytechnic, and Royal Anthropological Institute, is a leading authority on blues and other forms of African-American music. He is the author of nine pioneering books on the subject, including *Blues Fell This Morning*, *The Story of the Blues*, and *Songsters and Saints*. Mr. Oliver received the Sony Award for the BBC series "Before the Blues," the Grand Prix du Disque for the album series "Story of the Blues," and the Katherine Briggs Folklore Award by the American Folklore Society for the revised edition of *Blues Fell This Morning*. He edited the "Blues Series," published by Studio Vista and Stein and Day, and has edited and written liner notes for numerous albums.

Dale Olsen (Ph.D., University of California-Los Angeles) is a professor in the School of Music at Florida State University in Tallahassee. An authority on the traditional musics of Latin America, he is currently President of the Southeastern/Caribbean Chapter of the Society for Ethnomusicology, and a past president of the Florida Folklore Society. His many publications include *The Musical Classification of Native South American Shamanistic Curing Songs*.

Jay Orr (M.L.S., University of North Carolina-Chapel Hill) currently writes about contemporary music in Nashville, Tennessee, and formerly served there as Head of Technical Services at the Country Music Foundation and Media Center. He has worked to promote the recognition of rockabilly music and its traditional roots. He has written book and record reviews for numerous publications and liner notes for reissues of classic country and rockabilly performers, including the recent Country Music Foundation release "Get Hot or Go Home: Vintage Rockabilly from RCA, 1956–1959." He also served as a fieldworker for the Smithsonian's 1986 Festival of American Folklife program on the Memphis rockabilly cummunity.

Blanton Owen (M.A., Indiana University) has served as Folk Arts Coordinator for the Nevada State Council on the Arts. Active in folklife studies since 1970, he has documented folk arts throughout the Southeast and Nevada. He has written liner notes for the old-time music recordings "Clawhammer Banjo, Vol. 3," "Virginia Traditions: Ballads from British Tradition," and the influential "Old Originals, Vol. 2." An outstanding clawhammer banjo player, he performs in two albums as a member of the Fuzzy Mountain String Band. He also toured extensively with fiddler Tommy Jarrell, with whom he appears in the documentary film "Sprout Wings and Fly."

Daniel Patterson (Ph.D., UNC-Chapel Hill) is Kenan Professor of English and former Chair of the Curriculum in Folklore. His books include *Diversities of Gifts: Field Studies in Southern Religion* (co-authored with James Peacock and Ruel Tyson), *Arts in Earnest: North Carolina Folklife* (co-authored with Charles G. Zug, III), and *The Shaker Spiritual*, which received an ASCAP Deems Taylor Award. Patterson has been a co-producer of award-winning documentary films including "A Singing Stream: A Black Family Chronicle" and "Being a Joines." He was a recipient of the Brown-Hudson Folklore Award from the North Carolina Folklore Society.

Barry Poss is the owner and President of the Sugar Hill record label. Specializing in traditional country and progressive bluegrass music, Sugar Hill's nearly 1000 releases have garnered widespread critical acclaim and captured two Grammy Awards. Mr. Poss first became interested in Southern string-band music while a graduate student in sociology at Duke University. He mastered "clawhammer" banjo, played in many of the local revival string bands, and eventually left academia to work with County Records before he founded Sugar Hill in 1978.

Ralph Rinzler is the Smithsonian Institution's Assistant Secretary for Public Service and the Founding Director of its Office of Folklife Programs. For over thirty years he has helped gain widespread recognition of traditional music of the South—through his role as Director of Field Research Programs for the Newport Folk Foundation in the mid-1960s and as Founding Director of the Smithsonian's annual Festival of American Folklife in 1967. He has worked with bluegrass pioneer Bill Monroe and brilliant North Carolina guitarist Doc Watson and been a major force in the revival of Cajun music and culture. He edited influential recordings, including "Old Time Music at Clarence Ashley's" and "Louisiana Cajun Music from the Southwest Prairie."

Anthony Seeger (Ph.D., University of Chicago) was formerly Professor of Anthropology and Director of the Archives of Traditional Music at Indiana University. He currently serves as Curator of the Folkways Archive and Director of Folkways Records for the Smithsonian Institution. He has taught ethnomusicology at the Brazilian Conservatory of Music and served as Chair of the Department of Anthroplogy of the National Museum in Rio De Janeiro, Brazil.

Mike Seeger is an accomplished musician who has devoted his life to documenting, performing, and presenting Southern folk music. Both as a solo artist and a member of the New Lost City Ramblers, he has done as much as any person to introduce audiences to authentic styles of traditional music from the region. He has mastered several instruments and learned a vast repertory of songs and tunes. Over the years Seeger has recorded and presented many important Southern musicians, including Elizabeth Cotten, Dock Boggs, and Tommy Jarrell. He has recently produced a documentary video on Southern dance styles and a reissue of recordings by the great Texas fiddler Eck Robertson.

Tim J. Stafford (M.A., East Tennessee State University) holds the post of Research Associate in the Center for Appalachian Studies and Services. He also a professional musician, playing guitar with Alison Krauss and Union

Station. With Richard Blaustein he produced the album *Down around Bowmantown,* issued from the Center for Appalachian Studies and Services.

Allen Tullos (Ph.D., Yale University) teaches American Studies at Emory University and has for many years edited *Southern Changes,* a bi-monthly journal of social analysis, for the Southern Regional Council. He received his M.A. in Folklore at UNC-Chapel Hill, writing a thesis on Tommie Bass, an herbal healer from the hills of Alabama. He served as co-producer of the folklife documentary films "Born for Hard Luck," "Being a Joines," and "A Singing Stream." The University of North Carolina Press in 1989 published his book *The Habits of Industry: White Culture and Industrialization in the Carolina Piedmont,* which won the Charles S. Sydnor Award of the Southern Historical Association.

Walter C. West (M.S.W. and M.A.T., University of North Carolina at Chapel Hill) is Head of the Technical Services Section of the Southern Historical Collection, Manuscripts Department, of the UNC Academic Affairs Library. He is active in the Society of American Archivists and holds posts in the organization.

David E. Whisnant (Ph.D., Duke University) is Professor of English and serves in the American Studies, Latin American Studies, and Folklore curricula at the University of North Carolina at Chapel Hill. His book *All That Is Native and Fine: The Politics of Culture in an American Region* (1984) was nominated for the Pulitzer Prize, and was awarded the Elsie Clews Parsons Prize by the American Folklore Society. He was co-founder in 1974 of the North Carolina Folklife Institute and has served as a board member of several organizations and agencies, including the Highlander Research and Education Center and the National Council for the Traditional Arts. Dr. Whisnant wrote the notes for a reissue of recordings by the Blue Sky Boys for the John Edwards Memorial Foundation.

Charles Reagan Wilson (Ph.D., University of Texas at Austin) is on the staff of The Center for the Study of Southern Culture at the University of Mississippi, where he teaches history and Southern Studies. He is co-author of the massive *Encyclopedia of Southern Culture,* and his other distinguished books include *Baptised in the Blood: The Religion of the Lost Cause* and *Religion In the South.*

Index

Adams, Ramon, 11
Agrarians, 49
Alderman, Tony, 26
Almanac Singers, 25
Altman, Billy: career of, 207; on RCA
  Heritage Series, 17–18
American Folklife Center: in American
  Memory Project, 17; Federal Cylin-
  der Project of, 16–17; field proj-
  ects of, 16
American Memory Project, 17
Ancelet, Barry: career of, 2, 148–50,
  207; and Cajun Music Festival, 153;
  and Center for Acadian and Creole
  Folklore, 150–51; fieldwork by,
  150; recordings issued by, 153
Appalachian music: and country music,
  47–48, 51; self- documentation in,
  9–10
Appalshop, Inc., 9
Apollo Theatre, 98
Archives. *See* Collections, public

Balfa, Dewey: on cultural conservation
  and innovation, 152; as teacher,
  149–50, 153
Bastin, Bruce, 65, 130, 194
Beaver, Lloyd, 11–12
Benford, Mac, 7, 25
Biddleville Quintet, 104–105
Birmingham Quartet Reunion: album,
  97; evaluation of, 33–38; Fairfield
  Four at, 108; as stimulus to Ray
  Funk, 94
Blaustein, Richard, 25, 83
Blues: discography of, 60, 63–65, 70;
  expatriate singers, 66; field trips to
  the United States, 62–63, 65; magazines about, 63, 69; performers'
  aspirations, 6; photographic exhibition, 66–67; recordings issued in
  Europe, 59, 66, 70–71; research,
  analytical and historical, 60, 66–70;
  research, influence of jazz interest

on, 58–61, 64–65; research, moti-
  vations for, 3–4, 59, 71–72; teach-
  ing of, 72; tours in Europe, 58,
  61–62, 65–66, 69
Boggs, Ralph Steele, 138
Broonzy, Big Bill, 61
Bruton, Hoyle, 129
Bussard, Joe, 11, 12

Cajun music: changes in, 152; documentation of, 150–51, 153; Ralph
  Rinzler's programing of, 6
Carawan, Guy and Candie: career of,
  207; on decline of praise houses,
  20–21; Alan Lomax on, 6
Carter, Thomas: career: 24, 73–75, 130,
  207; on motivations of revival musicians, 83–88; on phases of folk-
  music revival, 74, 79–81, 88
Casey, Michael T., 133, 136, 208
Cavaliers, The, 21
Center for Acadian and Creole Folklore, 150–51, 153–54
Chapel Hill/Durham String Band movement: field collecting stimulated
  by, 79, 85–86, 88; history of, 23–
  24, 74–88; motivations of participants, 81–86; participants' subsequent careers, 24
Clark, Guy, 183
Cohen, Norm: career, 208; and the
  JEMF, 119–125; and the Southern
  Folklife Collection, 130
Collections, public: at African-American
  institutions, 103–4; at the Center
  for Acadian and Creole Folklife,
  150–51; at the Country Music
  Foundation, 14–15; at the Library
  of Congress, 16–17, 94, 103; at the
  Smithsonian Institution, 15–16,
  104–105; at the Southern Folklife
  Collection, 138; dissatifaction of
  users with, 13; gospel music in,
  103–4; problems of, 13; outreach

music, 103; library resources on, 103–6; newspaper sources on, 98–100; photographs of, 97–98; record company files, 106; regional centers of, 33, 35–37, 97; reissues of, 35, 94, 97; research networks, 99; studies of, 107
Grants. *See* Funding
Green, Archie: career of, 209; "Commercial Music Graphics," 119; influence of, xiv, 48, 117–19, 121, 130–31 ; and John Edwards, 117, 185; and the John Edwards Memorial Foundation, 117–19, 121–23, 125; and the Southern Folklife Collection, 130–31, 138
Gregory, Pete, 151
Griffis, Ken, 121, 123, 125

Hanchett, Tom, 91, 97, 104
Hand, Wayland, 117, 121
Hartman, Pete, 24
Hawes, Bess Lomax: career of, 7, 25, 209; on the Birmingham Quartet Reunion, 33–38; on difficulties of early fieldwork, 4; on evaluation of presentations, 37–39; on funding priorities, 7; on Library of Congress concert, 39–40
Henry, Richard "Big Boy," 160
Heth, Charlotte: career of, 209–10; on Native American musicians, 8; on self-documentation by Native Americans, 9–10; on sensitive issues in Native American music, 8, 10
Hicks, Bill, 24, 85
Highwoods String Band, 88
Hilfer, Tony, 185–86
"Hillbilly Issue," *Journal of American Folklore*, 46
Hinson, Glenn D., 131
Hoeptner, Fred, 117, 180
Hollow Rock String Band: contributions of, 79–81; influence of, 74, 77–81, 88; parties, 24, 84; personnel, 80
Holt, George M.: career, 24, 210; as string-band musician, 85
Horton, Laurel M., 130
Hudson, Arthur Palmer, 127–29

Irwin, Ken: on Rounder Records and sales, 19; on collaboration of pro-

ducers with mail-order distributors, 20
Ivey, Bill: career of, 210; on changes affecting work with vernacular music, 22; on the Country Music Foundation, 14–15; on grant support for documentation, 7; on membership in the National Academy of Recording Arts and Sciences, 20

Jabbour, Alan: career of, 24, 210; on collecting tunes from Henry Reed, 79; and the Hollow Rock String Band, 80–81, 83; and instrumental style, 80; on projects of the American Folklife Center and the Library of Congress, 16–17; on the spread of tunes collected, 24–25; on the string-band revival, 24–25
Jaffe, Allen, 6–7
Jarrell, Tommy, 25–26, 73, 82–83
John Edwards Memorial Foundation: collection at Chapel Hill, 130, 133; collection at the University of California at Los Angeles, 118–21; founding of, 118, 185; fund-raising for, 118–21; *The JEMF Quarterly*, 122–25, 133, 185; legacy of, 125–26; newsletter of, 118–19, 122; record Reissue Series of, 119–20; renamed Forum, 185; Reprint Series, 121; Special Series, 121
Johnson, Guy B., 129
Joplin, Janis, 46

Kahn, Ed, 48, 117–19, 125
Kazee, Buell, 116
Kennedy, Philip, 129
Klatzko, Bernie, 12
Kuykendall, Pete, 25

Ladysmith Black Mambazo, 36, 108
Lee, Dorothy Sara: career of, 210; on archival problems, 13–14; recommendations to collectors and donors, 14
Legal issues: for archives, 22
Levy, Bertram: career, 24, 210; as string-band musician, 80, 83
Lewis, Helen: career, 210–11; on self-documentation in Appalachia, 9–10
Library of Congress: American Memory Project, 17; Archive of American

Library of Congress Cataloging-in-Publication Data

*Conference on Collecting and Collections of Southern Traditional Music :
(1989: Chapel Hill, N.C.)
Sounds of the South : a report and selected papers from a Conference
on the Collecting and Collections of southern Traditional Music held in
Chapel Hill, April 6–8, 1989, to celebrate the opening of the Southern
Folklife Collection with the John Edwards Memorial Collection in the
Manuscripts Department of the Academic Affairs Library, University
of North Carolina / edited by Daniel W. Patterson.
p. cm.—(Occasional papers / Southern Folklife Collection ; no. 1)
Sponsored by the Folklife Section of the North Carolina Arts Council and
the University of North Carolina Academic Affairs Library and Curricu-
lum in Folklore.
Includes bibliographical references and index.
1. Folk music—Southern States—History and Criticism—Congresses. 2.
Popular Music—Southern States—History and criticism—congresses. I.
Patterson, Daniel W. (Daniel Watkins) II. University of North Carolina at
Chapel Hill. Southern Folklife Collection. III. North Carolina Arts Council.
Folklife Section. IV. University of North Carolina at Chapel Hill. Library.
V. University of North Carolina at Chapel Hill. Library. V. University of
North Carolina at Chapel Hill. Curriculum in Folklore. VI. Title. Vii.
Series: Occasional papers (University of North Carolina at Chapel Hill.
Southern Folklife Collection) : no. 1.
ML3544.5.C66 1989   781.62'00975'075—dc20   91-30427*

ISBN 0-8223-1343-X